Teen Television

Teen Television

Essays on Programming and Fandom

Edited by SHARON MARIE ROSS
and LOUISA ELLEN STEIN

McFarland & Company, Inc., Publishers
Jefferson, North Carolina, and London

LIBRARY OF CONGRESS CATALOGUING-IN-PUBLICATION DATA

Teen television : essays on programming and fandom / edited by
Sharon Marie Ross and Louisa Ellen Stein.
     p.   cm.
Includes bibliographical references and index.

ISBN 978-0-7864-3589-0
softcover : 50# alkaline paper ∞

    1. Television programs for youth—United States.   2. Television
and teenagers—United States.   I. Ross, Sharon Marie.   II. Stein,
Louisa Ellen.
PN1992.8.Y68T44   2008
302.23'450835—dc22   2008002818

British Library cataloguing data are available

On the cover: from top, Kristen Bell as Veronica Mars in *Veronica
Mars*, 2005-2006 (UPN/Photofest); Teen watching TV ©2008 Shut-
terstock; Alexa Vega as Vanessa in *Odd Girl Out*, 2005 (Lifetime/
Photofest)

Manufactured in the United States of America

McFarland & Company, Inc., Publishers
  Box 611, Jefferson, North Carolina 28640
  www.mcfarlandpub.com

For Tom and Ben, who have more or less willingly watched hours upon hours of teen television—and even proclaimed to enjoy it.

Contents

PREFACE 1

INTRODUCTION: WATCHING TEEN TV 3

◆ **Part I—The Industrial Context of Teen TV** 27

1. *TV Teen Club*: Teen TV as Safe Harbor
   Jeff Martin 27

2. Teen Television and the WB Television Network
   Valerie Wee 43

3. Defining Teen Culture: The N Network
   Sharon Marie Ross 61

4. Rocking Prime Time: Gender, the WB, and Teen Culture
   Ben Aslinger 78

◆ **Part II—Teens on TV** 93

5. "Normal is the watchword": Exiling Cultural Anxieties
   and Redefining Desire from the Margins
   Caralyn Bolte 93

6. Riding the Third Wave: The Multiple Feminisms of
   Gilmore Girls
   Francesca Gamber 114

7. "That girl of yours—she's pretty hardboiled, huh?":
   Detecting Feminism in *Veronica Mars*
   Andrea Braithwaite 132

8. The Portrait of an Artist as a Young Fan: Consumption
and Queer Inspiration in *Six Feet Under*
Barbara Brickman 150

9. "They stole me": *The O.C.*, Masculinity, and the
Strategies of Teen TV
Sue Turnbull. 170

◆ **Part III—Cultures of Reception** 185

10. Fashion Sleuths and Aerie Girls: *Veronica Mars'* Fan
Forums and Network Strategies of Fan Address
Jennifer Gillan 185

11. The Adventures of a Repressed Farm Boy and the
Billionaire Who Loves Him: Queer Spectatorship in
Smallville Fandom
Melanie E.S. Kohnen. 207

12. Pushing at the Margins: Teenage Angst in Teen TV and
Audience Response
Louisa Ellen Stein 224

CONTRIBUTORS 245
INDEX 249

Preface

Teen TV—be it on the now defunct WB and UPN, or the newly evolving CW or the N—offers a crucial space for the negotiation of political, social, and cultural issues. The images and narratives of adolescence found in Teen TV are relevant to a wide range of viewers. From *The Many Loves of Dobie Gillis* to *Buffy* and *Veronica Mars*, television featuring the lives and experiences of teens not only touch on coming of age issues, but also on questions of self, identity, gender, race, and community. Teens and older viewers, male and female, engage with these representations—at times sporadically and at times as dedicated fans who use these programs as a touchstone for their own senses of self and society.

This collection of essays looks closely at the diverse industrial contexts, representations, and forms of engagement that make up the world of Teen TV. The title of our introduction, "Watching Teen TV," references not only the images of teens that fill our screens each day and night, but also the scholarly import of studying this realm of cultural production and reception. Because of Teen TV's seeming newness and link with consumerist culture, academia has not studied these programs consistently. Teen TV offers a rich yet overlooked resource for understanding the dynamics of our contemporary popular culture, and for understanding the complexities of popular culture's history. Vital cultural narratives and cultural shifts play out in the spaces of Teen TV programming and reception. The concept for this book evolved from the editors' and contributors' conviction that Teen TV programs call for close academic as well as popular attention. Thus, drawing from a breadth of methodological approaches, this book offers close case studies and larger industrial and cultural frameworks for studying the complex arena of Teen TV. It is our hope that this book opens the door to further investigation of the ever-evolving, rich cultural world of televised adolescence.

We would like to thank our contributors, whose enthusiasm and dedication has been evident from the beginning of this process to its end. We'd also like to thank our family and friends for their support and patience throughout: Tom Skapes, husband, best friend, and always willing to lend an ear or read a page. Ben Stein, husband, best friend, and supporter through everything. Amanda Lotz, who inspired us and always made it seem possible to tackle a big project, offering words of advice at just the right time. Sara Livingston, who always asked how the project was going and let Sharon barge into her office to talk things through, both book and non-book related. Michael Niederman, who provided practical and conceptual support, allowing Sharon to be stressed out for over a year. Kristina Busse, true friend, indispensable editor, and priceless colleague. Melanie E.S. Kohnen, whose support, wisdom, fierce editing skills, and positive outlook have kept Louisa sane through this and many other projects. Tim Shary, whose passion about teen film may be partially to blame for the direction Louisa's research has taken. And finally, from Louisa, a special thanks to Evelyn, Juree, Natalie, and Sandra—on whatever coast (or in whatever country), you are the best friends and supporters anyone could have. And from Sharon, a special thanks to Susan, Kelly, Liz, Beau, Annette, and Helcha—you have done a great job keeping Sharon young at heart and willing to try new things, from TV shows to book projects. Our deepest appreciation to everyone.

Introduction:
Watching Teen TV

Multiple Meanings and Understandings of Teen TV as Genre

In the world of TV stories ... A popular cheerleader discovers that her destiny is to protect the innocents of the world from vampires. A social outcast befriends the troubled boy from the wrong side of the tracks. An innocent teen girl turns private eye when her best friend is murdered. A Korean teenager hides her extensive music collection from her mother under the floorboards of her room. Three alien teens struggle to keep their extraterrestrial identity a secret from their classmates, schoolteachers, and parents.

In the world of TV viewers ... A teen girl writes novels based on her favorite television program and shows her writing to others who share a similar interest. Fashion featured on the prime time programs of teen-oriented networks such as the WB and UPN (now the new CW) graces not only the pages of teen magazines but also (in affordable versions) the bodies of teenagers in high schools across the country. Music with various cultural meanings is featured on "mainstream" teen programming and finds its way onto the mp3 players of teens and adults, via television soundtracks or torrent downloading. A mother and daughter share a weekly ritual as they watch their favorite Teen TV television program. Conservative religious organizations campaign against the possible dangers of the combination of sexuality and fantasy that they see embodied in *Buffy the Vampire Slayer*.

These are but a few of the narratives that run through and surround what we think of as "Teen TV." The first set you may have recognized as elements from a range of Teen TV shows, from *Buffy*, *The O.C.*, and

3

Roswell, to *Veronica Mars* and *Gilmore Girls*—all series that the essays in this volume explore. The second set is no doubt familiar as well, for they are but a few of the pervasive spectator experiences that accompany and discursively define our understandings of Teen TV. Both sets of narratives touch on issues ranging from sexuality, individuality, style, and the self to family, culture, and religion—all elements crucial to (studies of) teen culture in general and Teen TV in particular. This book explores this range of contexts, meanings, and investments that are part of the texts and meta-texts of Teen TV. The emphasis on both text and culture indicates that this book will combine close textual analysis of teen television programs with explorations of production and industrial contexts, and with considerations of cultures of reception.

Our book is not so much concerned with delimiting the category of Teen TV as with understanding its complex manifestations as it intersects with other cultural meanings within various meta-textual arenas. The spectrum of essays in this volume reflects our engagement with a more fluid approach to genre, addressing a wide variety of programs that could be considered "teen" because of content, audience address, programming context, or demographics of reception (or any combination of these elements). The essays approach teen generic discourse from a variety of angles, exploring industrial, historical, social, and audience discourses as well the texts of programs themselves.

We can understand the term "Teen TV" as a generic cultural category in the sense outlined by theorists such as Jason Mittell (2004) and James Naremore (1998). In a significant reconfiguration of the notion of genre and genre studies, Mittell posits genres as constantly shifting, culturally constituted categories, which gather hollow "clusters" of meaning and association (17). Similarly, in his expansive study of film noir, James Naremore considers genre as *idea* rather than category (11). These approaches move past simply determining the generic identity of a specific televisual text to exploring surrounding meta-texts, including producer, network, and audience discourses. Mittell argues usefully for de-centering the televisual text in genre analysis, so that the TV program itself is not privileged as the central site of generic meaning. He suggests instead that we look at genre as something which functions beyond the limits of specific media texts and which is constituted in a range of ways by a range of speakers. If we consider genre as it plays out organically, in industrial and audience discourses as well as in the texts of the programs themselves, we can see that genre discourse does not function only to categorize or name, but also to promote associations, build meanings, and reference related texts (Stein 2005).

In popular discourse, Teen TV is associated as much with its assumed audience (of teens) as with its content. Most public commentary on Teen TV assumes a one-to-one age-content ratio—accepting the premise that teens will watch programming about teens or marketed as "teen." However, content does not necessarily determine actual audience, or, for that matter, even intended audience. While Teen TV may be associated popularly with a teen audience, and while networks and advertisers certainly desire teen viewers as a market, this does not exclude the possibility that Teen TV programs may also address, court, and successfully draw in both pre-teen and older viewers. Indeed, as we have suggested, a wide range of elements beyond audience demographic might associate a given television program with Teen TV. Rob Owen (1999) tracks the trend of adult viewers watching teen television to Generation X (those born between the mid–1960s and the mid–1970s)—the first generation for whom television became the centerpiece of cultural interaction. He notes that as this generation aged, it has continued to invest in Teen TV; and one might note that many of this generation are those who produce and write for current teen programs—certainly an area of study worthy of discussion. Further, as the essay in this volume by Jeff Martin demonstrates, even early teen television programs such as Paul Whiteman's *Teen TV Club* may have presented themselves as directed at a teen audience while in truth they worked to draw in a more varied audience through a specific (and limited) depiction of what it is to be a teenager. The same could be said of the other programs discussed in this volume, from *Gilmore Girls* to *Veronica Mars*.

It is also important to acknowledge that teens and teen themes are represented on television beyond the televisual spaces distinctly named (or overtly branded) as teen. For example, programming on subscription networks such as HBO often features teen characters and teen issues, engaging with ideas of teen culture and teen identity while situating these teen characters within multigenerational family or pseudo-family contexts. *Six Feet Under*, *Queer as Folk*, *Big Love*, and *The Sopranos* are all examples of this type of programming. If we do not restrict our understandings of Teen TV to only the most obvious (the WB and UPN networks, and now the CW), we can see similarities between programs such as *Everwood* and *Gilmore Girls* that intermesh teen and adult storylines, and those "quality" cable television programs which include teens in their broader cast of characters. From this perspective, the difference between *Everwood* and *Six Feet Under* as Teen TV is more in degree of teen focus (and overt teen branding) than in scope or nature.

Thus, we can consider a surprisingly wide range of texts as part of the shifting discursive rubric of Teen TV, from programs nominally about teens but directed at older audiences to programs not defined as teen but featuring teen characters, themes, and concerns. Teen TV can include half-hour-long sitcoms and hour-long melodramas, network television, subscription TV, MTV, and reality TV. While we cannot cover every element of what might be considered Teen TV in this one anthology, we have gathered a selection that we feel demonstrates the diversity of texts and meta-texts referenced by the term "Teen TV."

A central part of this project is to reconsider our preconceptions of what constitutes Teen TV—and to expand our notions of the implications or value of the study of Teen TV. If Teen TV is no longer just for teens, and no longer just about teens—but in some way touches on this crucial category of teen—then the study of Teen TV reveals as much about media culture as a whole as it does about teen culture specifically. We argue that by bringing an interdisciplinary approach to the study of Teen TV, we reveal how nuanced, complex, and culturally significant these television programs are. One of our closing essays, by Melanie E.S. Kohnen, explores how viewers of the teen Superman program *Smallville* read this contemporary teen representation of the all–American Boy Scout queerly. In so doing, Kohnen reveals not only what queer theory has to offer a study of a Teen TV program like *Smallville*, but also how *Smallville*'s reception complicates avenues of queer theory. Bringing together multiple perspectives (not just production, text, and context, but also the varying theoretical disciplinary approaches drawn on by all of these essays) reveals Teen TV's contributions to a wide range of disciplines. This also reveals the extent to which these disciplines might help to widen our perception of the impact of Teen TV in culture and society.

Understandings of "Teens," Understandings of "TV"

Together, the two sets of narratives with which we opened this introduction involve interrelated subjects: the history of television and the cultural category of the teen or adolescent. To explore Teen TV, we must consider what we mean when we say "teen" as well as what cultural associations or logics emerge with the addition of the medium-specific "television." At the same time, we must be aware that perceptions of Teen TV are indeed shaped by cultural and academic conceptions of the medium of television and its position within contemporary popular culture, complete with gender, race, and class associations.

Let's begin with the first ("teen") half of "Teen TV." Notions of Teen TV are bound up with culturally specific ideas about adolescence and what it means to "be" teen. Furthermore, since much of Teen TV is watched by viewers who are not teenagers themselves, the discourses about Teen TV also address ideas of what it means to be a viewer or consumer of Teen TV regardless of age (or rather, despite one's age). To speak of something as "teen" or "teenage" associates it with the liminal category of "adolescence." Adolescence—a period during which bodies begin to exhibit sexual development and adult characteristics (and yet when one has little social power)—is an inherently contradictory, transgressive experience. As a culturally constituted category, adolescence purposefully contains and attempts to fix the experience of crossing from one identity (childhood) into the next (adulthood). The transitional nature of adolescence encompasses not only issues of individual identity but also of community, including an adolescent's place within broader communities and within a community of adolescents (where teen cultures might form). Popular discourse also links perceptions of "teen" with perceptions of consumerism and commercial teen culture. Thus, the "teen" half of Teen TV signifies a culturally transgressive yet commercial, mainstream group— a liminal position, from the academic perspective, to be sure.

The "television" half of the term Teen TV is, of course, medium-specific, and brings with it its own set of associations and expectations. From the condemnation of television as a vast wasteland (a perception that is still surprisingly pervasive) to the popular and academic association of television with female and working-class viewers, TV itself remains marked as a suspect category. While teen film as a cultural category suffers from associations with B movies and mass-pleasing, predictable, cliché-ridden scripts, Teen TV brings with it specific perceptions of TV *overall* as a low brow, deeply commercial medium.

Serial television (within which we could include much of contemporary Teen TV, or at least much of what people think of as Teen TV) is further suspect due to its soap opera heritage, its association with highly engaged yet distracted female viewers, and its distance from more closed, traditional narratives. Soap operas have been denigrated in mainstream culture because of their extreme seriality and slow narrative pacing, not to mention because of their supposed appeal to bon-bon eating, overly-engaged, overly-emotional female viewers (see Baym 2000). While not all of Teen TV is situated clearly within serial television, seriality remains an undeniable aspect of the vast majority of Teen TV. Even an episodic sitcom such as *Saved by the Bell* still incorporates serial arcs as the characters age and face new issues, with adolescence necessarily propelling them along life's trajectory. Indeed, viewers and critics label many Teen TV programs "teen soaps"; as such, much of Teen TV cannot escape the tinge of the stereotypes of soaps and soap viewers. The teen dimensions (and the associated negative perception of youth culture as commercialized and conformist) compound assessments of Teen TV's cultural value, and strengthen perceptions that those engaged with Teen TV programming may be impaired in their ability to distinguish between reality and fiction, or between consumerism and self-expression.

In these ways, cultural conceptions of Teen TV are deeply imbricated in characterizations of the nature of TV audiences and TV spectatorship as well as in notions of adolescence and teen consumer culture. "Teen TV" thus specifically calls up images of consumerist teen culture as filtered through television programs dedicated to selling lip gloss, face wash, and jeans, so that the already commercialized dimensions of teen culture are compounded by our sense of TV as a commercial medium. All of these elements combine to ensure a cultural arena that may be highly desirable from an industrial perspective, but that may be looked down upon by the broader culture and society (and that is also no favorite of the academy). Thus, Teen TV is a complex, culturally weighted category that combines various cultural arenas that have traditionally been framed as problematic via their associations with "low brow" commercial culture.

However, teen television cannot be relegated easily to the realm of low brow culture; Teen TV's association with commercialization and the gendered seriality and emotionality of soap opera always intersects with its engagement of discourses on "quality television," positioning "Teen TV" somewhere between "mainstream" and "elite." Indeed, Teen TV lends itself to cult status, with much of it existing on smaller networks and relying on a core audience to "spread the word" about any given program. Collectively then, Teen TV straddles mainstream and marginal, popularity and quality, and combines traditional episodic narrative programming and the punctuated seriality of soap operas.[1]

The "teen" programs on the WB and UPN also engage with generic mixing, thus further contributing to their liminality as media texts. The generic nature of much Teen TV programming is not easy to pin down in any singular, fixed way, for even as we discuss these programs primarily as Teen TV, they rely on other generic elements substantially, from those found in science fiction to those found in horror and film noir. As is the case with many HBO series, this extensive generic mixing (which elsewhere Stein [2005] has discussed as transgenericism) functions as an aspect of network branding and program differentiation, as well as a draw for multiple niche audiences. In their transgenericism, these programs again venture into the realm of "cult" television. For example, in the many instances in which Teen TV incorporates elements of the romance and fantasy genres (the gothic horror of *Buffy the Vampire Slayer*, the melodramatic science fiction of *Roswell*), Teen TV becomes associated not only with teen culture, but also with other subcultures and subcultural identities, including fantasy fans and soap fans.

It appears then that Teen TV has the potential to raise considerations of marginality on a regular basis. Perhaps because Teen TV probes such a wide range of culturally weighted categorical divides, and also because of its recurring engagement with questions of identity and self-discovery, some of the programs explored here and the meta-texts surrounding them go beyond addressing specific teen issues to negotiate questions about class, race, gender, and sexuality. Programs such as *The O.C.*, *Gilmore Girls*, *Veronica Mars*, and *Buffy the Vampire Slayer* take on issues of gender overtly, and at times issues of race and class.[2] All of these layers of meaning contributed to the design of this book. We believe that such intersections may be fruitful, revealing that the study of Teen TV should be of interest to those invested in a range of subjects, including teen culture, girl culture, gender studies, studies of race and ethnicity, GLBQ studies, audience communities, cult television, and reception studies.

Academic work on teen visual media and the teen genre has predominantly focused on teen film rather than television, with much relevant work also done in the areas of youth culture and youth music. Studies of teen film range from explorations of central teen thematics and exemplary teen films, such as Thomas Doherty's *Teenagers and Teenpics*, to Timothy Shary's *Generation Multiplex*, which is an expansive generic study of everything that could be considered to be teen film from the 1980s through the 1990s.[3] The lack of corresponding academic texts on Teen TV is remarkable. While we can also trace a relevant literature on children's media and children's TV, Teen TV itself remains largely unstudied—the one clear exception being Glyn Davis and Kay Dickinson, eds., *Teen TV: Genre, Consumption and Identity*, which begins to chronicle and contribute to this vital area of study (2004). Roz Kaveney's *Teen Dreams: Reading Teen Film and Television from "Heathers" to "Veronica Mars"* addresses a compact range of post–1980s teen films and the ways in which teen TV relates to these films, moving towards a fuller picture of the complexities the very concept of teen media evokes. Beyond that, numerous essays have been written, but no other full books or collections have been published.[4]

If we throw our net wider, we find another set of books, written by a mix of academic and industry-involved authors for a primarily popular audience. These books focus on specific teen television shows, and are designed primarily to appeal to fans who wish to probe production histories and the recurring themes and cultural impact of their favorite teen programs. Books such as those within the ever-growing literature on *Buffy the Vampire Slayer* approach highly visible Teen TV shows from a variety of disciplinary perspectives, but with an intended audience primarily popular and only secondarily academic.[5]

The presence of this literature suggests another arena of academic study within which this book could be situated: work on cult television. Books such as Sara Gwenllian Jones and Roberta Pearson's *Cult Television* consider *Buffy* within their purview (2004). While programs such as *Dawson's Creek* and *The O.C.* rarely seem to fit the bill for studies of cult TV, one could argue that because of Teen TV's ambiguous cultural and industrial status, the Teen television programs considered in this book could be considered alongside histories and theories of cult television. Correspondingly, Teen TV audiences could be considered in relation to cult TV audiences.

Furthermore, as Valerie Wee's essay in this volume renders especially clear (and as we have already discussed in relation to HBO's teen-inclusive programming), discourses about Teen TV can also be positioned in relation to traditions of quality television. Through a combination of self-referentiality, prolonged seriality, and genre mixing, these programs seek to establish themselves as different from standard televisual fare. While we find work on *Buffy* (always the forerunner) included in books such as *Quality Popular Television*, public and industrial discourse about programs such as *Gilmore Girls*, *My So-Called Life*, *Roswell*, and *Everwood* also draw on concepts of "quality" television and "quality" entertainment.[6]

Other media literatures provide important contexts for this book, and this book contributes to them. For example, examining changing viewing habits over the decades, one can see the increasing importance for teens of other media and technology—from the earliest inclusion of popular music in TV aimed at teens, to the rise in the number of TV sets in the home, to the near inseparability for teens today of the TV, the Internet, and the cell phone. Indeed, we cannot consider contemporary Teen TV without taking into account the multimedia context of its production, exhibition, and reception. A close look at Teen TV and its associated cultures offers a vital perspective for thinking about media convergence; contemporary Teen TV and its related metatexts function as central forums within which new directions in multimedia development and audience address take place. Television, film, music, fashion, video games, and online content all come into play in dynamic ways in Teen TV, arguably paving the way for similar multi-media approaches in the broader media market. Thus, a study of Teen TV that looks not only at the televisual text but at its context, as do many of the essays in this collection, contributes to current strides being made in the study of media convergence by scholars such as Henry Jenkins at the MIT Media Labs (2006). Moreover, much of this work is concerned with the engagement of young adults with (if not their representation in) media, as young people are seen as early adapters of the more extensive possibilities of new modes of media engagement.[7]

While we as scholars applaud those moments in academia when areas of studying culture merge in some of the ways outlined above, it is disheartening that more often than not book-length studies of teens or of media overlook television and its important role in people's lives. There is a significant dearth of work on Teen TV. While we might attribute this absence to the lack of cultural and industrial recognition of Teen TV as a genre until at least the 1980s, as we briefly explain in the following section, history shows us that Teen TV has played a role in the media industries of the U.S. for much longer (and in much deeper ways) than most studies acknowledge.

A Brief History of (Teen) TV

Today more than ever we can see that "Teen TV" made in the United States has become a global phenomenon of epic proportions. Given that the majority of shows featuring or marketed to teenagers have emerged from the U.S., mapping a history of what, precisely, Teen TV has been and is involves considering shifts that have occurred in the television industry within this country. As Thomas Doherty argues in *Teenagers and Teenpics: The Juvenilization of American Movies in the 1950s*, the history of mass media in the United States is always a commercial history (2002). Doherty's book focuses on a period of history in the United States that saw not only a rise in films marketed to teens, but also the solidification of television as the mass medium of choice for entertainment in the American family. Indeed, while Doherty's book focuses on the history of teen film, there is another interrelated media history to tell—that of the role of TV in the broader media experience of American families and, more specifically, the teens who grew up in those families. It is telling that Doherty links the marketing of teen films in the 1950s to the encroachment of television upon the film industry. During this same period, the television industry also sought out teenagers—but in a much more roundabout, unfocused way in comparison to the efforts of the film industry. While Doherty does not offer an explanation as to why, teenagers were viewed as the only remaining reliable market for film in this era—suggesting that from "day one" teens were multi-media consumers, watching television with their families and seeing films with their peers. (Doherty notes that by 1960, eight out of ten homes in the United States had TV sets on for five hours or more daily [19].) In addition, Doherty's picture of one media industry (film) responding to the competition offered by another (television) foreshadows a trend important to the solidification of teen television in later decades. As the Big Three in the television industry faced internal competition in the form of cable and then three additional broadcast networks, overall the industry found an increased value in the teen demographic.

similar to Thailand [handwritten margin note]

The key difference between Doherty's film history and the one we are addressing here, of course, is that the "medium" under siege (the Big Three) ignored teens for some time; instead, it was the newer networks and cable that saw teens as a viable force for competition. ABC, NBC, and CBS struggled to maintain mass audiences while MTV, then FOX, then the WB (and to a degree UPN), and finally the N and the new CW built their networks to significant degrees on appeals to teen viewers. This is not to say that the history of Teen TV does not start until the 1980s— but it is important to note that from a pop culture historical perspective, the 1980s is indeed the decade when critics and TV historians begin to pay the most attention to Teen TV as a potential genre with its own aesthetic components. Thus, it often seems, when researching the history of Teen TV, that shows "for" teens appeared out of thin air in the 1980s.

This is most decidedly not the case. Throughout the history of television in the United States, the domestic sitcom's popularity has rested in part on its steady inclusion of teen characters, and at times the teen characters rose to prominence within the show's narrative. One notable early example of this is *The Adventures of Ozzie and Harriet* (ABC 1952–66), a hit family show that increasingly centered its narratives on the exploits of rising teen music star Ricky Nelson. In fact, the program regularly aired "videos" after episodes, featuring Ricky singing his newest hit. If we define Teen TV today as essentially multi-media in nature (and we are aware that this is one of many, many approaches we can take), it could be that this venerable classic of family sitcoms is actually one of the first full-on teen shows.

This awareness of lineage is key not just for historical purposes, but also for cultural purposes; cultural history evaluates the family sitcom with much more benevolence than has been traditionally accorded to the "Teen show." As Bill Osgerby notes in his examination of the lineage of Teen TV, television has always to some degree seen younger viewers as a unique market (2004). In fact, "the younger and smaller ABC [in the 1950s] developed a strategy of competition in which it courted more specialized markets ... developing a reputation for programming aimed at youth and young families with children" (73). Reaching out to young children and their parents, while clearly an approach linked to later appeals towards teen viewers, is more culturally acceptable to viewers, critics, and industry professionals themselves than is reaching out to teens exclusively. It is perhaps no coincidence that, as Osgerby notes, attempts to exclusively address teens specifically as the primary audience failed more often than not through the 1980s on the Big Three. The notable exceptions are likely key to any attempt to pin down the roots of how we understand Teen TV and its success today. *3 patterns of teen TV*

Several patterns emerge when we consider early teen shows. First and foremost, as we alluded to earlier, the majority of series that featured teen characters through the 1970s co-featured other demographics—notably parents, and also pre-teens in the form of siblings. Thus, most shows with main teen characters did not necessarily privilege those characters' experiences or points of view.[8] Second, those narrative fictional programs that did manage to privilege a teen character's point of view successfully were sitcoms situated within a domestic framework—such as *The Many Loves of Doby Gillis* (CBS 1959–63), *The Patty Duke Show* (ABC 1963–66), and *Gidget* (ABC 1965–66).[9] And third, the programs that most directly sought out teen viewers were, in fact, non-fiction series that emerged from local market successes.

We find this third pattern especially relevant to the project at hand. Aside from the obvious relevance of one of our essays focusing on non-fiction, localized programming (Jeff Martin's "*TV Teen Club*: Teen TV as Safe Harbor"), U.S. culture commonly conceptualizes teen TV as a serialized melodrama or dramedy—a generic classification that discounts the historical lineage of early non-fiction shows such as *American Bandstand* (which aired locally in Philadelphia from 1952 to 1957, then nationally on ABC from 1957 to 1987). Osgerby notes astutely the importance of non-fiction programs to the very survival of early television, as series featuring teen music and teen "issues" provided local stations with inexpensive programming. One of the goals of this anthology is to solidify the connections that exist between such early attempts to appeal to teen viewers, and current trends toward hour-long fiction entertainment programming. While authors such as Miranda Banks (2001) and Rachel Mosley (2001) note that teen serials organically tap into the emotional turmoil of teen experiences, such observations can often obscure historical specificity. We hope that the essays in this anthology collectively paint a nuanced picture of Teen TV, taking into account shifts in historical and industrial contexts (as well as the possibility that other demographic groups not necessarily marked by age identify with similar themes of emotional turmoil).

One need not look all that far back in history to see the importance of non-serial or non-fiction programming to current understandings of Teen TV. In 1981, MTV launched with an explicit goal of capturing the young white male audience with music videos. When Viacom took over in 1986, those "wanting their MTV" expanded to include first white teen girls and then urban teens, as programming on the network expanded correspondingly to include game shows, documentaries, and reality TV series such as *The Real World* (1992–). As Ben Aslinger notes in his essay in this volume, music in particular remains a strong draw for teen viewers along a variety of aesthetic lines. Further, as those familiar with MTV's programming from its earliest days know, the network's ability to sustain links between different media (music, film, advertising, television) established patterns of marketing that remain prominent in American television aimed at teens today.

Almost simultaneously with the growth of MTV, FOX emerged as a fourth network and relatively quickly developed the strategy of reaching out to teens with low-cost programming. Like ABC before it, FOX saw the value in narrowing its primary target market—in this case to white teen viewers (*after* establishing itself among African American viewers via its early 1990s sitcoms and comedy or variety shows). While the Big Three hesitatingly began to develop programs offering teen perspectives in the mid–1980s and into the 1990s (e.g., *Growing Pains* on ABC, 1985–92; *Head of the Class* on ABC, 1986–91; *A Different World* on NBC, 1987–93; *The Fresh Prince of Bel Air* on NBC, 1990–96; *Blossom* on NBC, 1991–95), such series were extensions of earlier strategies to incorporate a teen perspective into the established domestic sitcom genre. (The rare and notable exception here is ABC's failed 1994–95 series *My So-Called Life*, which achieved greater popularity re-purposed on MTV after failing at ABC.) FOX, on the other hand, took risks with its attempts to privilege teen voices—developing shows that (like the Big Three network series just noted) were not necessarily "for" teens, but that (unlike the series just noted) were "not your parents' domestic sitcoms," either. Shows such as *The Simpsons* (1989–) and *Married with Children* (1987–97) established an "attitude" (for lack of a better term) that became prevalent in shows considered to be teen-friendly: a cynical outlook towards life, family, and nation within a narrative framework that privileged media literacy—where media literacy translates to being aware of pop culture trends, past and present.

Valerie Wee discusses this development of the teen genre in her essay on the development of the WB as a teen network, noting how the WB sought to differentiate itself from what many cultural historians had begun referring to as Gen-Xers' media sensibilities. Yet, as we hope this anthology makes clear, every move towards differentiation inevitably

teen. consumerist convergence

links itself to what has come before. The multi-media literacy approach to programming content and marketing solidified in WB teen shows not only has roots in series like *The Simpsons* or in MTV's blend of media, but also takes us back to *Ozzie and Harriet*'s Ricky Nelson and *American Bandstand*'s dancing teens. Further, the WB's appeal to teen viewers cannot be separated from the context of the competition: Both the WB and UPN emerged in 1995 as changes in financial-syndication rules made it necessary for both Warner Brothers and Paramount to ensure there would be distribution venues for their programming. Like "smaller" networks before them (ABC, MTV, FOX), financial concerns drove the trend towards niche marketing. While the WB, "by targeting programming specifically to teens and young adults ... established a focused and successful broadcast network in an era defined by cable television's incursion into the national television broadcast audience" (Clark 2004, 2503), "UPN (like its netlet brethren, the WB) turned to narrowcasting to build an 'urban' audience base—adopting the 'black block' programming strategy first utilized by FOX in the early 1990s" (Runyon 2004, 2416). The WB *could* go after teens because FOX had demonstrated, with the success of shows like *Beverly Hills 90210* (1990–2000) and *Party of Five* (1994–2000), that the melodramatic teen serial could be profitable—and because as the WB and UPN moved in, FOX was seeking to broaden its audience base beyond teens, leaving a gap in market address. This move on FOX's part also meant that UPN *could* go after black viewers because FOX had abandoned that market first as it segued to focusing on white teens and then continuing as it (ironically) sought to reach out further, beyond the teen market.

By the late 1990s, then, WB programming *was* teen programming from a pop culture standpoint. To a degree, this seems due as much to the WB's successful marketing of itself as a teen network as to the content of the programming proper. The WB continued the trend of incorporating teen perspectives into family shows (now hour-longs rather than half-hour domestic sitcoms—though those still existed on WB's Friday evenings). In fact, one of the network's earliest and longest-running hits was the family-friendly *7th Heaven* (1996–), about a minister, his wife, and their seven children (only three of whom were teens at the beginning of the series). The network continued to develop critically acclaimed shows in this mode with *Gilmore Girls* (2000–) and *Everwood* (2002–06), both centering on families with teens living in small towns filled with lead non-teens. Yet, it was in fact teen and young adult-dominated programming that came to represent the network, as Valerie Wee notes. The "break-out" hits were *Buffy the Vampire Slayer* (1997–2001, continuing on UPN 2001–03) and *Dawson's Creek* (1998–2003), series in which the parents were secondary (as had been the case with FOX's *Beverly Hills* and *Party of Five*) and the comedy and media literacy components strong (as had not been the case with *Beverly Hills* and *Party of Five*).

The fact that one network managed to become associated with Teen TV to such a degree is significant on many levels. Beyond a demonstration of marketing prowess, the WB's work to define teen television has had important cultural and social ramifications if one considers (as we do) television to have power in the realm of social and cultural agenda setting. The teen characters and narratives that have come to represent the essence of Teen TV obscure a variety of things. On a perhaps benign level, there is the fact that sitcoms have had a continuous appeal to actual teen viewers; the Teen Choice Awards (1999–), voted on by viewers, have consistently recognized actors from sitcoms as well as sitcoms themselves. It is worth thinking about why, then, Teen TV today is so often associated with the hour-long drama. At a more significant level, issues of race, class, and, to a degree, gender are pushed to the sidelines by a vision of Teen TV that is white and middle class centric. Sharon Marie Ross considers some of these issues in her article in this volume on The N; this digital cable network that seeks today to wear the crown of Teen TV has marketed a vision of teens that is aggressively multicultural. We believe it is significant that this newer network (The N launched in 2002) seems to be offering itself as an antidote to Teen TV as we "know" it—featuring, importantly, a slate of syndicated *sitcoms*, some of which star African American actors (*Moesha, Fresh Prince of Bel Air*). Melodramas on this network also trend towards multicultural casting; the network built itself around the popular Canadian import *Degrassi: The Next Generation*, which features characters from a variety of racial and ethnic groups, as well as a variety of socio-economic groups.

While The N is a small network even in comparison to the WB and UPN, its multicultural agenda is important—and perhaps even more so now that the WB and UPN have merged under the auspices of CBS/Warner Brothers (and perhaps ironically so, given CBS's corporate connection to The N via parent network Nickelodeon). Scholars and industry insiders have been waiting and watching with interest to see the results of this new "niche network devoted to serving only young adult viewers" (Carter, C4). As we mentioned earlier, FOX's turn to teen viewers left UPN an opportunity to become "the" network for African American shows (primarily sitcoms). The WB had also flirted briefly with this niche, but then followed FOX's lead in catering to teens instead. With the merger of WB and UPN, will the black sitcom disappear? If so, what does it mean culturally and socially if the only other competing Teen TV channel lives on digital cable?

Early indications are not heartening. The summer before CW's launch, the new network's website offered a promotional video highlighting the fall 2006 season lineup. While the black sitcom has not disappeared per se, a familiar pattern is evident: four black-cast sitcoms from UPN survived and became clustered (or "ghettoized") onto Sunday evening, along with *America's Next Top Model* (a reality show popular with female teen and young adult viewers and African American viewers in general, featuring contestants from a variety of ethnic backgrounds). Of these Sunday night programs, only one offers the perspective of a teen character—*Everybody Hates Chris* is a family sitcom told from the perspective of young teenager Chris, an African American growing up in the 1980s in the Bedford-Stuyvesant neighborhood of New York. The new "niche network devoted to serving only young adult viewers" appears to be having an identity crisis of two sorts: the Sunday night lineup offers little in the way of young adults, regardless of race; and the remainder of the week consists primarily of teen-focused former WB programs that offer little in the way of racial and ethnic diversity. While Dawn Ostroff (head of programming at CW, formerly head at UPN) has noted publicly that "our goal is to reflect the eighteen-to-thirty-four-year-old audience, 35 percent of which are now minorities and growing every year," the majority of the teens and young adults slated to be on the screen appear to be white (Hontz 2006, 56).

Such concerns are but a small indication of the vast scope in operation when attempting to understand fully the social and cultural (let alone industrial) force of that which we call Teen TV. A sort of butterfly effect kicks in when one begins to examine this area of popular culture; one might begin by studying one TV series, only to find that a full understanding of that show takes one in myriad directions. We are fully aware that this anthology offers an examination of what is but a slice of the Teen TV spectrum. For the most part, the essays in this volume take as their subject Teen TV programs and viewing cultures associated with teen girl and female teen culture. What of the programs that teen boys watch, such as those on the Sci-Fi network? What of the nominally "adult" programs that teens watch, including reality TV programs like *The Bachelorette* and *America's Next Top Model*? Might we also explore the Cartoon Network and teen engagement in anime and anime-influenced television programs?

While on the one hand we might benefit from an expansion of discussions of Teen TV to explore these viewing patterns, this collection focuses on the more (nominally, at least) female-oriented teen TV programs—for several reasons. For one, such programs (female-oriented, serial, hour-long melodramas which feature teen characters and are marketed to teen viewers) have shaped (and continue to shape) the predominant perception of Teen TV at this cultural moment. Secondly, reality

TV, anime, and science fiction programming are all topics covered by other areas of media and cultural studies, partially because they may not be quite as taboo in their overlap of low brow arenas as are the female-oriented "teen soaps."[10] Thus, the essays in this collection dwell predominantly on programs that are a) most commonly thought of as Teen TV in contemporary public discourse, and b) not being considered at length in other academic media studies arenas.

Overview of Book

The first section of our book approaches the topic of Teen TV from an industrial perspective. Essays in this section explore the contexts of production, addressing both the cultural and economic frameworks within which Teen TV has been produced. Jeff Martin's essay on Paul Whiteman's *Teen TV Club* considers the production of a program that features the phrase "Teen TV" in its very title and yet was created and aired decades before the eras one would commonly associate with Teen TV. By opening our book with a close look at the production of *Teen TV Club* (1949–54), we gesture to Teen TV's (pre)history—a history much longer than one might assume, coinciding with the very earliest years of television. As we see through Martin's analysis, early televisual images of teens worked to negotiate the cultural anxieties brought forth by the liminal figure of teen as consumer, cultural participant, and cultural producer. *Teen TV Club* thus exposed the distance between teen and adult cultural positioning, while revealing adult investment in teen identity and activity.[11]

All of this cultural work regarding the teenager was occurring, of course, within a program addressed at both adults and teens. Situating *Teen TV Club* as a televisual iteration or revival of the "teen canteen," Martin demonstrates how Teen TV programs have roots in both teen and mainstream culture. He goes on to reveal how cultural discourses about teens on TV intersect with issues of race, normativity, and cultural change, with TV perceived as a tool to negotiate and diffuse the teen threat together with other more generalized social anxieties. All of these issues are equally relevant today, perhaps most clearly demonstrated in the complex intertwining of address (or lack thereof) to teen and black audiences in the transition from the WB and UPN to the CW.

From Martin's analysis of what we might consider the prehistory of Teen TV, we turn to Valerie Wee's overview of the formation of the first TV network to define itself clearly as "teen." In 1995, Warner Brothers set out to create a niche network directed at a specific, desirable demographic, featuring teen-focused programming. Wee traces the emergence of clear patterns in those prime-time dramas that came to mark this network as the "teen" network, noting the unique vision of adolescence these programs offered. The WB did not represent any and all conceptions of teens. The WB's teens were for the most part alienated, emotional and sympathetic, attempting to make the right choices as they struggled towards adulthood. This WB brand image of Teen TV differed notably from the other contemporaneous teen network—MTV—which featured nihilistic, ironic teens rebelling against rather than striving to become part of adult society. In contrast to MTV, the WB's specific teen branding incorporated elements of so-called "quality" TV, as these programs combined cinematic technique with self-reflexive popular cultural references to create a sense of teen identity both specific and poised toward mainstream (and adult) cultural engagement. Through this intermeshing, as was the case for *Teen TV Club*, the WB strove to draw both teen and adult audiences with its representation of teen characters and issues. Teen television programs appearing on other networks, such as Fox's *The O.C.* and UPN's *Veronica Mars*, then copied this approach.

Sharon Marie Ross' essay on The N pursues these ideas further in its consideration of Nickelodeon's teen-directed narrowcasting network, a network that promotes itself as the site for authentic teen stories. The N raises questions of how producers are envisioning and reaching teen audiences, with a history of blending syndicated teen sitcoms and original dramatic programming. The N emphasizes diversity and a commitment to being cutting edge, and Ross explores what these concepts mean in terms of program development, marketing, and understandings of what is "real" for teens in the New Millennium.

Finally, we close this section with Ben Aslinger's consideration of the role of music in the airing of Teen TV. Teen TV networks and producers have incorporated music into the text of Teen TV to create converged markets, seeing the music marketing potential of the Teen TV audience as a way to secure a less expensive soundtrack with a contemporary cultural cache. At the same time, these programs draw on music to enhance the identificatory power of their teen protagonists. The convergence of image and sound opens up many possibilities for interpretation beyond the most obvious or normative, thus having a significant effect on both TV aesthetics and audience engagement. Aslinger argues that the WB's specific approach to music incorporation (and the resulting expansion of possible meanings or interpretations of the Teen TV texts themselves) sprung from a watershed moment in the history of music on TV, as licensing issues encouraged the WB to offer to "profile" the music of new and upcoming often Indie or alternative musicians. These industrial imperatives resulted in unexpected unions of music and sound, and in so doing, reconfigured expected representations of masculinity, femininity, and youth identity. Thus, Aslinger's essay bridges our opening focus on industrial context with our following focus on the texts of Teen TV.

Of course, we cannot focus on the text of Teen TV without also taking into account the cultures in which these programs are created and circulated. All four essays in the second portion of our book closely analyze the texts of Teen TV to consider how they reflect and at times push further the cultural contexts in which they are created. These essays examine how teen shows touch on crucial social issues such as feminism, class, and gender as articulated through reconfigurations of genre, femininity, masculinity, sexuality, engagement, and fannishness.

Caralyn Bolte argues that Teen TV performs cultural work originally assigned to the novel, interrogating the cultural conflicts of everyday life. Programs such as *Buffy the Vampire Slayer* and *Veronica Mars* feature exiled teen protagonists and thus offer a specific focus on the experience of those who navigate the margins of society. Through close textual analysis, Bolte suggests that these shows give voice to marginalized experience and encourage viewers to engage affectively with the protagonists' experience of liminality. Buffy Summers and Veronica Mars are both able to critique the social world around them precisely because of their exiled social positions. Moreover, Bolte argues that such a focus on marginality in the texts of these programs is facilitated by the marginal positions of the smaller networks on which these programs air, networks that must take risks and reach beyond the mainstream in order to solidify their own niche audiences.

Francesca Gamber turns to *Gilmore Girls* to explore representations of feminism and its possibilities in the contemporary moment. Gamber argues that *Gilmore Girls* posits a vision of multiple feminisms, played out through a multiplicity of characters (the "Girls" of the show's title) and most especially evident in the program's attention to teen Rory's coming of age experiences. In Rory's adolescent experimentation, she tests out the multiple modes of feminism and femininity she encounters both in her personal life and in popular culture. From this perspective, interrelationships between women of different generations become crucial in the revitalization of a third wave feminism, one concerned with making feminism personally meaningful. Thus, Gamber situates *Gilmore Girls* in a specific contemporary moment of feminist discourse.

In her discussion of Veronica Mars as a "Chick Dick," Andrea Braithwaite considers the eponymous TV program as an iteration of the hard-boiled detective novel. *Veronica Mars* re-envisions the hard-boiled private eye as the empowered yet marginal teenage girl protagonist of

Teen TV. Braithwaite thus suggests a different relationship between Teen TV's representation of young women and postfeminism than that described by Francesca Gamber. Braithwaite argues that Veronica's dual position as teenage girl and private eye—combined with the program's double architecture as detective genre and teen genre—enables a critique of the social viability of postfeminism. *Veronica Mars*'s hard-boiled teen narrative exposes a world still structured by social inequalities, most especially revealing the limited choices available to young women.

Veronica's liminal position functions as an allegory for female experience in contemporary society, while at the same time, her appropriation of the private investigator figure (a position both marginalized and empowered) facilitates a critique of the constructed, performative nature of gender, generational and class constraints. Finally, Braithwaite argues that Veronica is not alone in her teen televisual investigative position, but rather that her role is echoed in other teen girl protagonists of Teen TV programs such as *Roswell* and *Buffy the Vampire Slayer*. The young female protagonists in these series might not take on the mantle of the hard-boiled P.I. as Veronica does, but they do investigate and expose the social conditions of their world as they find their way in it.

Barbara Brickman's essay "The Portrait of an Artist as a Young Fan: Consumption and Queer Inspiration in *Six Feet Under*" turns to a program one might less obviously think of as Teen TV and yet which presents a compelling televisual representation of teen experience. Indeed, Brickman argues that the teen character in HBO's *Six Feet Under*, Claire, plays a central role as the embodiment of the program's overall thematic concerns. Brickman reads Claire as queer fan girl, whose investment in female objects, artistically if not sexually, places her in a queer position outside of both homosexuality and heterosexuality. As such, Claire as teen liminal fan artist embodies the program's thematic concerns and perhaps functions as surrogate of the series' creators. Thus, through Brickman's analysis, we see how even in a program not marketed as teen, offered by an adult-oriented network, the figure of the teen and teen generic themes can be central to the program's purpose.

As did Jeff Martin's essay on *Teen TV Club*, Sue Turnbull's essay "'They stole me': *The O.C.*, Masculinity, and the Strategies of Teen TV" questions common assumptions of the "newness" of teen TV. Investigating what we might rush to call "new" representations of teens (and teen boys specifically), Turnbull situates Fox's *The O.C.* in a history which includes iconic film representations of teen boys, such as *Rebel Without a Cause*, the 1950s sitcom *The Many Loves of Dobie Gillis*, then later *Beverly Hills 90210*, *Degrassi Junior High*, and *21 Jump Street*. Turnbull specifically traces the possibilities of "emotional androgyne"—recognizing the figure of the boy who may reflect female desire in not only *The O.C.*'s Seth and Ryan, but also in James Dean/Jim Stark, Dobie Gillis and his best friend Maynard, and Johnny Depp. Finally, Turnbull provocatively suggests that this reconfiguration of our view of teen media representation could lead us to consider the way in which contemporary Teen TV facilitates identifications past gender and generational boundaries.

Our final section explores the cultures of reception (including realms of unofficial production) in which teens and consumers of teen media become authors in their own right. We open with Jennifer Gillian's consideration of discourses of fashion and consumerism in *Veronica Mars*. Gillian explores the embrace by viewers (in many cases viewers older than the characters featured on *Veronica Mars*) of the teen fashions central to the style of *Veronica Mars*. The program's emphasis on fashion and fashionable technological use creates a vision of a teen lifestyle not limited to teens but available to viewers of a range of ages. However, as fans appropriate the material elements they see on screen and incorporate them into their self-representation, they participate in class marking—a dynamic which seems to directly counter *Veronica Mars*'s focus on class difference. However, at the same time, the viewer culture created out of this engagement provides a forum for the discussion of the themes of class and social difference raised by *Veronica Mars*. Finally, Gillian argues that Veronica's outsider status is questionable, as she still maintains connections to the wealthy culture that she has supposedly been forced out of, and that her position in turn echoes that of *Veronica Mars*'s original network home. For like Veronica, UPN may have proclaimed itself an edgy, underdog network, but it was in truth a subsidiary of Viacom and CBS, providing an outlet for Paramount content. *Veronica Mars*'s new network home, the CW, is even less marginal, in terms of industry relations at least, as it brings together CBS and Warner Brothers. Thus, Gillian complicates both the text of *Veronica Mars* and its industrial location, but at the same time considers the subtlety of audience engagement with the issues of class, race, and generation brought out by *Veronica Mars*'s most clearly consumerist dimensions.

Melanie E.S. Kohnen investigates specific instances of cultural engagement with social issues hinted at in the texts of Teen TV, in her exploration of fan discourse surrounding the teen Superman program *Smallville*. Audience engagement with *Smallville* reveals the embrace of a queer (and male) perspective on the part of female fans who self-identify as straight. Fans' interaction on the website Television Without Pity (TWOP) suggests that fans do not consider the nominal heterosexuality of the show's characters as something that is self-evident in *Smallville*'s narrative. Rather, fans perceive that the adolescent Clark Kent and Lex

Luthor's heterosexuality needs to be continually established and repeated, and if it is not, viewers in turn celebrate the very lack of such stabilizing repetition. From the fans' point of view, the characters' heterosexuality is precarious, even questionable. This practice of "seeing queerly" evident in reception of *Smallville* thus constitutes an interesting moment in which pop cultural discourse and queer theory echo one another. One of the central arguments of queer theory puts forth that heterosexuality isn't always already established, but only comes to be through continuous repetitive practices that always fall short of their idealized discursive counterparts.

The extensive discussions on TWOP about characters, storylines, producer intentions, and numerous other topics underline how *Smallville* fans take up an attitude towards heteronormativity that reflects academic discussions on the same subject. Moreover, in addition to questioning presumptions about the division between "critical" and "fan" discourses, this attitude and its theoretical implications challenge long-standing traditions of analyzing queer spectatorship as the nearly exclusive "property" of gay and lesbian viewers. Theorists considering queer spectatorship usually only mention in passing the possibility that "straight" spectators might participate in or develop similar ways of "seeing queerly." Rather than regarding this as a mere oversight, one has to speak of a symptomatic absence that has shaped academic discussions of queer spectatorship. An analysis of fan discourse on TWOP thus not only allows an insight into how viewers negotiate queerness on Teen TV, but also forces a reformulation of previous scholarly engagement with these issues.

Similarly, Louisa Ellen Stein's essay looks at how stories and art created by viewers of teen television both embrace and take further the issues of societal constraint such as class, gender, and sexuality raised with different levels of opacity by the programs themselves. The themes of adolescent limitation featured in programs such as *Smallville*, *Gilmore Girls*, and *Veronica Mars* resonate specifically with the dynamics of fan creativity. Fan authors and artists often focus on issues of constraint and self-expression, reflecting these concerns in both form and content, as they author new texts in the face of various levels of constraint, creating fiction and art within the limitations presented by already existing commercial media, generic and cultural expectations, and the structuring tools of new media. Through a close study of Teen TV fan fiction and fan art, Stein explores how these texts posit adolescence as metaphor for other ranges of social constraint, from the issues of gender raised in *Gilmore Girls*, to race in *Veronica Mars*, to sexuality in *Smallville*.

In the pages ahead, we invite the reader to explore the world of Teen

TV in all of its complexity. We invite the reader also to consider the many ways in which this genre of television has impacted our society and most especially the teens (past, present, and future) who inhabit that society. As important as teenagers are to the ways in which U.S. culture operates, so, too, are the cultural manifestations of those teenagers.

Notes

1. Interestingly, other programs we have mentioned which feature teens in broader contexts are also found in a liminal network arena—subscription television—within which networks strive to present themselves as something other than mainstream TV. This self-professed marginality is perhaps most evident in the case of HBO's efforts at self-definition; HBO has worked to build a network brand via an assertion of quality dependent on the rejection of its very medium (and the associations inherent within) in the omnipresent tagline, "It's Not TV, It's HBO." Yet HBO's programming combines soap-like seriality with other generic cues (including a focus on teen themes and characters) in order to achieve said "quality."

2. Still, as we will address in a following section, as a cultural category of identification, race poses especially important challenges for how popular teen series define "being" teen.

3. For work on teen film see: David Considine (1985), Jon Lewis (1992), Thomas Doherty (2002), and Timothy Shary (2002).

4. These essays include: Beth Braun (2000), Will Brooker (2001), 456–72, and Richard Campbell and Caitlin Campbell (2001).

5. The most prominent collections on *Buffy the Vampire Slayer* include: Rhonda V. Wilcox and David Lavery, eds., *Fighting the Forces: What's at Stake in Buffy the Vampire Slayer* (Lanham, MD: Rowman Littlefield, 2002); Roz Kaveney, ed., *Reading the Vampire Slayer* (London: Tauris Parke Paperbacks, 2003); James B. South, ed., *Buffy the Vampire Slayer and Philosophy* (Chicago: Open Court, 2003); and Glenn Yeffeth, ed., *Seven Seasons of Buffy* (Dallas: BenBella, 2003). In addition, *Slayage: The Online International Journal of Buffy Studies* (http://www.slayage.tv/) is a peer-reviewed online journal that addresses *Buffy* from a wide range of disciplinary perspectives.

6. For related work on quality TV see: Jane Feuer, Pall Kerr, and Tise Vahimagi, eds. (1984), Sue Brower (1992), Mark Jancovich and James Lyon, eds. (2003), and Matt Hills (2004).

7. For work on youth culture and media engagement, both contemporary and historical, see: Nancy Kaplan and Eva Farrell (1994), Henry Jenkins (2004), and Kelly Schrum (1998).

8. In fact, even popular series set in high schools focused on adults rather than teens (for example, *Mister Peepers*, NBC 1952–55 and *Our Miss Brooks*, CBS 1952–56).

9. While *Gidget* was not a success technically (it lasted only one season), it did remarkably well in summer reruns and established the character (played by Sally Field) as a 1960s "all–American girl" icon. This series is also notable because of its roots in a film series from the 1950s (when Sandra Dee played Gidget)—demonstrating again the multi-media roots of TV aimed at or featuring teens.

10. For complementary studies of youth engagement with contemporary media, see: John Tulloch and Henry Jenkins (1995), Heather Gilmour (1999), Yasmin B. Kafai (1999), Kelly Chandler-Olcott and Donna Mahar (2003), Wardrip Fruin and Pat Harrigan, eds. (2004), Tara Kachgal (2004), Susan Murray and Laurie Oullette, eds. (2004), James Newman (2004), and Susan J. Napier (2006).

11. Martin's study highlights many of the central issues which Teen TV must negotiate, and which we will see recur in the discourses surrounding more recent programs such as *Buffy*, *Gilmore Girls*, and *Veronica Mars*. Primarily, the representation of that which is "teen," as produced within a broader industrial context, is often directed at an audience that may include both teens and adults.

References

Banks, Miranda. 2004. "A Boy for All Planets: *Roswell, Smallville* and the Teen Male Melodrama." In *Teen TV: Genre, Consumption and Identity*, ed. Glyn Davis and Kay Dickinson, 17–28. London: BFI.

Baym, Nancy. 2000. *Tune In, Log On: Soaps, Fandom, and Online Community*. Thousand Oaks, CA: Sage Publications.

Braun, Beth. 2000. "*The X-Files* and *Buffy the Vampire Slayer*: The Ambiguity of Evil in Supernatural Representations." *Journal of Popular Film and Television* (Summer): 88–94.

Brooker, Will. 2001. "Living on *Dawson's Creek*: Teen Viewers, Cultural Convergence, and Television Overflow." *International Journal of Cultural Studies* 4: 4 (December): 456–72.

Brower, Sue. 1992. "Fans as Tastemakers: Viewers for Quality Television." In *The Adoring Audience: Fan Culture and Popular Media*, ed. Lisa A. Lewis, 163–84. New York: Routledge.

Campbell, Richard and Caitlin Campbell. 2001. "Demons, Aliens, Teens and Television." *Television Quarterly* 34: 1 (Winter): 56–64.

Carter, Bill. 2006. "With Focus on Youth, 2 Small TV Networks Unite." *New York Times*. January 25, C4.

Chandler-Olcott, Kelly, and Donna Mahar. 2003. "Adolescents' Anime-inspired "Fanfictions": An Exploration of Multiliteracies." *Journal of Adolescent and Adult Literacy* 46: 556–66.

Clark, Lynn Schofield. 2004. "WB Network." In *The Encyclopedia of Television*, 2nd edition, ed. Horace Newcomb, 2503–06. New York: Fitzroy Dearborn.

Considine, David. 1985. *The Cinema of Adolescence*, Jefferson, NC: McFarland.

Davis, Glyn, and Kay Dickinson, eds. 2004. *Teen TV: Genre, Consumption and Identity*. London: BFI.

Doherty, Thomas. 2002. *Teenagers and Teenpics*. Philadelphia: Temple University Press.

Feuer, Jane, Pall Kerr, and Tise Vahimagi, eds. 1984. *MTM: Quality Television*. London: BFI.

Fruin, Wardrip, and Pat Harrigan, eds. 2004. *First Person: New Media as Story, Performance and Game*. Cambridge: MIT Press.

Gilmour, Heather. 1999. "What Girls Want: The Intersections of Leisure and Power in Female Computer Game Play." In *Kids' Media Culture,* ed. Marsha Kinder, 263–92. Durham: Duke University Press.

Gwenllian-Jones, Sara, and Roberta E. Pearson, eds. 2004. *Cult Television*. Minneapolis: Minnesota University Press.

Hills, Matt. 2004. "*Dawson's Creek*: 'Quality Teen TV' and 'Mainstream Cult?'" In *Teen TV: Genre, Consumption And Identity*, eds. Glyn Davis and Kay Dickinson, 54–67. London: BFI.

Hontz, Jenny. 2006. "And Then There Were Five." *Emmy Magazine* XXVIII, no. 3: 152–6.

Jancovich, Mark, and James Lyon, eds. 2003. *Quality Popular Television*. London: BFI.

Jenkins, Henry. 2006. *Convergence Culture: Where Old and New Media Collide*. New York: New York University Press.

———. 2004. "Why Heather Can Write." *Technology Review* February 6, available at http://www.technologyreview.com/Biztech/13473/ (accessed April 15, 2007).

Kachgal, Tara. 2004. "'Look at *The Real World*. There's Always a Gay Teen on There': Sexual Citizenship and Youth-Targeted Reality Television." *Feminist Media Studies* 1, no. 3 (November): 361–64.

Kafai, Yasmin B. 1999. "Video Game Designs by Girls and Boys: Viability and Consistency of Gender Differences. In *From Barbie to Mortal Kombat: Gender and Computer Games*, eds. Justine Cassell and Henry Jenkins, 293–315. Cambridge: MIT Press.

Kaplan, Nancy, and Eva Farrell. 1994. "Weavers of Webs: A Portrait of Young Women on the Net." *Electronic Journal on Virtual Culture* 2, no. 3 (July 26): available at http://www.infomotions.com/serials/aejvc/aejvc-v2n03-kaplan-weavers.txt (accessed April 15, 2007).

Kaveney, Roz, ed. 2003. *Reading the Vampire Slayer*. New York: I.B. Tauris.

_____. 2006. *Teen Dreams: Reading Teen Film and Television From "Heathers" to "Veronica Mars."* New York: I.B. Tauris.

Lewis, Jon. 1992. *The Road to Romance and Ruin.* New York: Routledge.

Mittell, Jason. 2004. *Genre & Television: From Cop Shows to Cartoons in American Culture.* New York: Routledge.

Moseley, Rachel. 2001. "The Teen Series." In *The Television Genre Book*, ed. Glen Creeber, 41–46. London: BFI.

Murray, Susan, and Laurie Oullette, eds. 2004. *Reality TV: Remaking Television Culture.* New York: New York University Press.

Napier, Susan J. 2006. *Anime from Akira to Howl's Moving Castle: Experiencing Contemporary Japanese Animation.* New York: Palgrave Macmillan.

Naremore, James. 1998. *More Than Night: Film Noir in Its Contexts.* Berkeley: University of California Press.

Newman, James. 2004. *Videogames.* New York: Routledge.

Osgerby, Bill. 2004. "'So Who's Got Time for Adults!': Femininity, Consumption and the Development of Teen TV—From *Gidget* to *Buffy*." In *Teen TV: Genre, Consumption and Identity*, eds. Glyn Davis and Kay Dickinson, 71–86. London: BFI.

Owen, Rob. 1999. *Gen X TV: The Brady Bunch to Melrose Place.* Syracuse: Syracuse University Press.

Ross, Sharon. (forthcoming). *Tele-Participation: Understanding TV in the Age of the Internet.* Malden, MA: Blackwell Publishing.

Runyon, Steve. 2004. "UPN Television Network." In *The Encyclopedia of Television*, 2nd edition, ed. Horace Newcomb, 2416–18. New York: Fitzroy Dearborn.

Schrum, Kelly. 1998. "'Teena Means Business': Teenage Girls' Culture and *Seventeen Magazine*, 1944–1950." In *Delinquents and debutantes: Twentieth Century American Girls' Culture*, ed. Sherrie Inness, 134–63. New York: New York University Press.

Shary, Timothy. 2002. *Generation Multiplex: The Image of Youth in Contemporary American Cinema.* Austin: University of Texas Press.

South, James B., ed. 2003. *Buffy the Vampire Slayer and Philosophy.* Chicago: Open Court.

Stein, Louisa Ellen. 2005. "'They Cavort, You Decide': Transgenericism, Queerness, and Fan Interpretation in Teen TV." *Spectator* 25, no.1 (Spring): 11–22.

_____. 2005. "'A Transcending-Genre Kind of Thing': Teen/Fantasy TV and Online Audience Culture." Diss. New York University.

Tulloch, John, and Henry Jenkins. 1995. *Science Fiction Audiences: Watching Doctor Who and Star Trek.* New York: Routledge.

Wilcox, Rhonda V., and David Lavery, eds. 2002. *Fighting the Forces: What's at Stake in Buffy the Vampire Slayer.* Lanham, MD: Rowman Littlefield.

PART I—THE INDUSTRIAL CONTEXT OF TEEN TV

1. *TV Teen Club*: Teen TV as Safe Harbor

Jeff Martin

It seems an unlikely starting point for the culture of teenage television: a parade of young people playing accordions, singing vaudeville tunes, performing acrobatic stunts, competing for cash and prizes such as refrigerators—all presided over by a balding, rotund, middle-aged bandleader given to outdated slang interjections (e.g., "Solid, real solid!") Yet, ABC's *TV Teen Club*, which aired between 1949 and 1954, can be seen as that starting point—albeit one that sent mixed messages about the teens to whom it was supposedly aimed. This paper examines the story behind the creation of the show, which involved an almost mythological tale of one man's efforts to battle juvenile delinquency. That tale assumed that television had the power to create a "virtual space" in which teenagers could congregate in small groups nationwide, under the watchful gaze of parents. I argue that, although the show seemed to be straightforward amateur-hour fare, the ways in which it (and its sponsors) addressed its audience, along with the ways in which it critiqued teenagers' aesthetic judgments, sent mixed messages about its teenage viewers.[1]

"All was not well with adolescents"

The concept of "teenagers" as a social grouping distinct from adults and children had barely entered the American consciousness before the country became aware that teenagers were both troubled and troubling.[2] Alarm bells about juvenile delinquency were sounded almost immediately after

27

America entered the Second World War in late 1941, often fueled by reports of increased juvenile crime in England following the beginning of the war two years earlier (Reckless 1942).

The perception of crisis began to peak in 1943. Ominous statistics were rampant in both popular and professional literature: articles cited increases of as much as 20 percent in American cases of delinquency between 1941 and 1942 (Cook 1943); more than twice as many boys committed to Massachusetts correctional schools in February 1942 over the same month in 1941, and so on (Glueck 1942). This seeming rise in criminal behavior was also linked to bewildering cultural developments. A writer in *The Annals of the American Academy of Political and Social Science* summarized the events that were alarming parents: "The rise in juvenile delinquency, Los Angeles and Detroit riots involving youth, the many evidences of negative behavior by adolescents in the average home, the phenomenon of Frank Sinatra 'bobby sox' fans and Harry James' youthful theater mobs ... convinced the American public that all was not well with adolescents" (Sorenson 1944, 148). In fact, there was conflicting evidence as to whether there truly was a rise in juvenile delinquency. FBI statistics—often cited in popular-magazine articles written by FBI head J. Edgar Hoover—seemed to imply that delinquency was indeed increasing. On the other hand, the federal agency charged with monitoring the welfare of the nation's youth—The Children's Bureau—publicly took a more sanguine view. If the statistics were debatable, public dialogue about the problem was not (see Gilbert 1986).

A particular concern was the lack of supervision brought about by the war: fathers were often in the service, mothers worked outside the home for the first time. The fear was that teenagers, naturally seeking recreation, would end up in unsavory situations and would gravitate to "the local pool room, to a dine and dance honky tonk, or to some other place where they can meet and loaf with their friends" (Solomon 56). Thus a widely recommended solution to the problem of juvenile delinquency was supervised, clean recreation—the organization of activities interesting and pleasurable enough to draw teenagers off the streets and into spaces where they could remain under adults' (presumably unobtrusive) watchful gaze. A practical and cost-effective way of providing this recreation quickly gained popularity: the teen canteen. Teen canteens were supervised, ad hoc recreation centers that evoked the Hollywood and Stage Door Canteens famously serving soldiers in Los Angeles and New York City at the time.

Generally, a local adult organization (e.g., the PTA, a lodge or women's club, or a religious group like the Knights of Columbus) sponsored these teen canteens. Nominally at least, a board of teenagers supervised them, determining activities, organizing dances, etc. *The Journal of Educational Sociology* described the enthusiasm with which said teenagers greeted this idea:

> They have begged for them; petitioned for them; earned them; cleaned, scraped, and painted them; and now they have a large voice in planning their programs and managing them. And so from Oakland to New York and from Fort Lauderdale to Vermont, the teen-age crowds are gathering in their own fun spots, which have been given such typical names as Swing Inn, the Rec, the Dry Dock, the Bar None Corral, the Bee Hive, and the Coop [*Journal of Educational Sociology* 1945, 401].

The canteens ran the gamut from basic to deluxe. A canteen in Fort Worth, Texas, was housed in an elaborate entertainment building left over from the 1936 Texas Centennial exposition (Adams 1945). A more typical operation in Altoona, Pennsylvania, was located in two vacant commercial rooms, supplied with a piano, ping-pong table, and furniture from railroad lounge cars donated by the Pennsylvania Railroad (Schott 1945). Nearly all seem to have offered space for dancing to records, along with an array of organized activities.

Publications aimed at educators and other professionals offered guidance for supervising adults, right down to the specifics of location: canteens should be located "on the main floor or down one flight. For some peculiar reason youth does not like to go upstairs for a hangout, but doesn't mind going downstairs" (Solomon 56). More critically, these articles stressed one point: the need for unobtrusive, but firm, adult guidance. Though the idea of the teenage club was to allow young people to control their own recreation, that control was limited: adult chaperones and supervision were never far away.

The problem of juvenile delinquency, of course, did not end with the war. Indeed, the dawn of the Cold War placed a new emphasis on the need for protecting America's youth from the perils of delinquency. In this fight, however, postwar parents could wield a new weapon: television. The idea that teenagers can be kept from harm by being brought home to watch television is an interesting contrast to contemporary attitudes about younger children. Gomery (2001) notes that during the early days of network television, popular discourse about the relationship between children and television centered on the fear that it would keep them away from healthful pursuits like outdoor play. It was only later in television's development that concerns about program content came to the fore. For children, then, the world outside the home was portrayed as a safe and healthful one, superior to the indoor, televisual world. But for teenagers, that world was potentially dangerous, full of inducements to delinquent behavior that were more dire than mere idleness in front of a television set.

The idea of bringing a teen canteen to television first surfaced in 1946, in a program called, simply, *Teen Canteen*. Telecast by WRGB in Schenectady, New York, the show visited actual canteens in the area—and in the process, it appears to have pioneered a television format that would eventually become famous: teenagers dancing to popular records of the day. According to *Variety*, however, the boys refused to participate, leaving the girls to dance with one another (*Variety* 1946). Two other local shows (in New York City in 1948—produced by the same woman who produced the 1946 Schenectady show—and in San Antonio Texas in 1950) would use the same title for programs featuring a grab bag of teenaged performers and activities (*Variety* 1948, 1950).

In 1949, the underlying idea—if not the title—would be tried on a national scale, with two major additions: first, the presence of a prominent entertainer, and second, the explicit goal of using television to combat juvenile delinquency. That entertainer, Paul Whiteman, became the first in a series of adult figures to mediate between teenagers and the television audience. But allowing teenagers to make their own entertainment would prove to have its limits.

Paul Whiteman, a.k.a. "Pops"

By the late 1940s, bandleader Paul Whiteman had been a well-known figure in the entertainment world for 25 years. His fame centered around two aspects of his persona: his role as the man who "legitimized" jazz music in the 1920s, and his role as a "star-maker"—a discoverer and promoter of young talent. Both of these factors would be key to the development and success of *TV Teen Club*.

Born in 1890, Whiteman first came to prominence in the late 1910s, when he organized a smooth dance band that incorporated aspects of the jazz music being performed by African American artists at the time. Giving white audiences a taste of so-called racial music without requiring contact with the "dangerous" culture of African Americans brought Whiteman immense success. His all-white orchestra sold millions of records at a time when there were only six million phonographs in America, a volume that helped shift the focus of the music industry from the sale of sheet music to the sale of recordings (Jerving 2003). Whiteman's stature was such that his contemporary, the legendary African American arranger Fletcher Henderson, was referred to as "the Paul Whiteman of the race" (Magee 2000). For his part, Whiteman was known as the King of Jazz.[3]

By the late 1940s, Whiteman had also developed a reputation as a man with an eye for young talent, largely due to the number of prominent musicians who had once performed in or with his orchestra. Among the alumni of the Whiteman band were Bing Crosby, Mildred Bailey, the Dorsey Brothers, and Bix Beiderbecke, not to mention names that were prominent in the 1930s and 1940s, though now largely forgotten—Jane Froman, Helen Jepson, and Morton Downey (Alden 1967). Additionally, though it was not necessarily part of his public persona, Whiteman was an early adopter of media technologies: in addition to phonograph records, Whiteman also appeared on radio and in talking pictures early in their development. When television arrived, Whiteman's move into the new medium seemed only logical.

Teen TV's Creation Myth

It was during the late 1940s that Whiteman made his first inroads into television. How that transition came about was widely reported in newspapers and popular magazines in strikingly uniform language. Because primary documentation of how *TV Teen Club* was created did not survive, these secondary sources today provide the bulk of our information about how the show came into being. Taken in sum, they have the feel of a creation myth, in which one man's actions lead not just to a fight against delinquency, but also to the creation of a television genre.

In 1947, Whiteman, who still worked as a bandleader, also held the position of vice-president of music at the ABC radio network. His status as network executive made him a respectable citizen of Hunterdon County, New Jersey; he was a member of the Rotary Club, and involved in local civic groups. As that respectable citizen, he was alarmed by an increasing level of petty crimes being committed by teenagers in the area. When local leaders approached him for help, he offered to set up a program of weekend dances and entertainment to keep these teenagers off the streets (Long 1950).

The first such dance was held on Halloween 1947, in the recreation hall at St. John's Church in Lambertville, New Jersey (Brandon 1948). Initially, the dances featured professional musicians, including Whiteman's band, but Whiteman would later write of his realization that teenagers were perfectly happy to create their own entertainment. The Saturday dances evolved into amateur talent nights—and in them, Whiteman saw potential for public service on a larger scale. He told *The Christian Science Monitor*:

It's my hope ... that every city and town in this country will have a club of this kind. They can be held in church auditoriums, lodge or grange halls, or any other town buildings that have space.... It may seem like a lot of trouble at first to get a thing like this going. But if you're in trouble for good, that's good trouble [*Christian Science Monitor* 1947].

A syndicated columnist summed up Whiteman's goals more bluntly: "He was going to give the kids something better than a marijuana jag on Saturday night. He was going to give them something that would make them stay off the street—not force them into a jail cell" (Robinson 1948).

Sometime in early 1949, Whiteman approached the management of WFIL-TV, ABC's television affiliate in Philadelphia (the major city closest to Lambertville) with the idea of bringing the Saturday night dances to television, thus potentially serving a much wider audience than local Saturday-night activities ever could. WFIL agreed, and on April 2, 1949, *Paul Whiteman's TV Teen Club* went on the air.[4]

When *TV Teen Club* premiered, it was broadcast from an armory in North Philadelphia in what *American Magazine* described as a "bleak neighborhood" (Long 1950, 28). The telecast itself was the centerpiece of an evening's activities described by the television critic for the *Chicago Tribune* as "an outsize ice cream social, dance, and party [besides the hour long video show] which goes on from 6:30 to 11 P.M." (Wolters 1950a).

The show's format was a direct replication of the inexpensive amateur shows that proliferated in early television: *Arthur Godfrey's Talent Scouts, Chance of a Lifetime, Doorway to Fame, Judge for Yourself, Ted Mack and the Original Amateur Hour*, etc. On the air, Whiteman would let teenagers know about weekly auditions in New York and Philadelphia, as well as the days when his scouts would be in cities across the country. During its first three seasons, the show followed a very basic pattern. After some simple opening titles, Whiteman welcomes the teenage audience (both in the studio and at home) and begins announcing the acts. In some extant episodes, he is accompanied by co-host Nancy Lewis, a teenage singer who got her start as a contestant on the show.[5]

In viewing these episodes today, one aspect of the show's presentation of the contestants is immediately striking: in contrast to shows like *American Idol* and its many offspring, and even in contrast to contemporary amateur-hour shows, *TV Teen Club* provides no background narrative for the teenagers. Whiteman gives their ages and hometowns, but beyond that meager information, viewers receive no information that might inspire identification or sympathy. Teens watching the show are given no reference points as to whether these performers are "regular folks," or uniquely talented individuals. In contrast, in a typical episode of *Ted Mack and the Original Amateur Hour*, telecast in 1952, Mack interviews an African American contestant to elicit the information that he is an industrial chemist and World War Two veteran who has always dreamed of a singing career. This American Dream–style narrative, so much a part of today's talent-based programming, is not accorded the ostensible stars of *TV Teen Club*.

Moreover, despite Whiteman's supposedly personal concern for the welfare of young people, his interaction with the teenagers is extremely limited; in fact, it is rare even for him to share the same frame with them during the show's early seasons. Instead, he and Lewis stand behind a podium emblazoned with the sponsor's logo; the camera then cuts to the acts onstage.[6] The performances take place in front of very simple backdrops, evocative of the vaudeville stage. Whiteman leads the audience in applause at the conclusion of each act, and re-announces each youth at the end of the show as each one gives a "reprise" of his or her performance, prior to the final judging by the audience. Reviews of the first-season premiere in 1949 indicate that a panel of teenagers judged the acts. The earliest available episodes, however, feature judging by the audience via an applause meter—in this case, it is labeled "Pops' Talent Meter."

The acts during the first seasons were a varied lot, with little discernable pattern to the type of acts that were performed, or that won. One 1950 episode featured two girls tap-dancing to "Puttin' on the Ritz," a high school band playing ragtime, a boy singing "God's Country," a 17-year-old male athlete doing stunts, a trio (two boys and a girl) playing banjo, guitar, and accordion, and a boy playing a clarinet solo. Other episodes offered equally eclectic bills. Two general observations can be made about the performances themselves, however: first, the choice of material is curious for a teen-focused show. Nearly all the songs performed are more than ten or fifteen years old; contemporary hits that teens might be buying as records aren't here. Instead, young people perform "Who Cares," "Crazy Rhythm," "I Got Rhythm," "Puttin' on the Ritz," "Toot Toot Tootsie," and other hits of the 1920s and 1930s. Second, the show's approach to racial issues is interestingly benign. Though the majority of performers are white, African Americans also appear on the show, performing the same kind of material as white teens; they are treated no differently than white performers. Moreover, cutaways to the show's audience (including a shot that is included in the show's third-season opening title sequence) show that the audience was integrated; black and white teens are watching the show together.

In its inimitable style, *Variety* described the show's premiere episode as "a teenage vaudeo presentation, but one with a new idea—the combating of juve delinquency" and gave it a positive review: "Result is good entertainment plus a good public service gesture" (*Variety* 1949). Within a month of its first broadcast, the program was picked up by the ABC network for live broadcast to the Midwest via coaxial cable, and was distributed beyond the reach of the extant network hookups via kine-scopes shipped to distant affiliates. When nationwide broadcast became possible in November 1951, the show was apparently considered impor-tant enough to ABC that it was one of the network's first to take advan-tage of this technology. *TV Teen Club* would remain in the ABC primetime lineup for five seasons, and press accounts would continue to refer to its role as a tool against juvenile delinquency. Underlying those accounts— and the show itself—were some basic assumptions about the way televi-sion could affect Americans' behavior in its early years.

Teens and the Televisual Space

Though it was designed to combat delinquency, *TV Teen Club* was not trying to overtly influence juvenile behavior, to convince teenagers to act in a certain fashion, or to present explicitly positive role models. Instead, it hoped to draw teenagers, moth-like, off the proverbial street corner and into the family circle.

As Anna McCarthy notes in writing of television in taverns, during the late 1940s and early 1950s, social agencies such as the Salvation Army sought to use television as a lure that would draw men away from taverns and into a "safer" space. McCarthy describes these supposedly vulnerable men as "watchers who were themselves more easily watched" (McCarthy 1995, 39). Indeed, as *TV Teen Club* was going on the air, Whiteman him-self described an identical effect as he discussed his hopes for the new medium's impact on American musical culture. He wrote an article in *Etude* magazine (a publication dedicated to classical music), titled "The New World of Television," saying,

> There is no question that television is keeping thousands and thousands of peo-ple who formerly went out "of an evenin'" at home. Many men saw their televi-sion first at taverns and bars. Now they see the shows at home, and if they are drinking men they do their drinking at home in the family where they are likely to drink far less. It certainly looks as though television might reduce the amount of drinking [Whiteman 1949, 341].

Tavern drinkers and adult men were not the only ones who could be brought under supervision by the lure of television, however. Sheila John Daly, a syndicated columnist writing about teen-age issues, wrote in 1949 of the way in which television could provide diversion for teen-agers while keeping them under adult observation: the "television date."

Citing "part time jobs for boys [being] harder to find and ... the high cost of dating," she noted approvingly that teenagers were staying at home for dates rather than going out. "Parents are silently cheering the TV parties that are currently popular with high schoolers, who gather in groups as large as 30 to watch Milton Berle, sport contests, and variety shows under the watchful eye of doting mamas and papas" (Daly 1949).

With wartime's disruption of home and hearth so pointedly to blame for juvenile delinquency, the use of television to rebuild that hearth is not surprising. Lynn Spigel (2001) cites a 1948 article in *Parents Magazine* that describes how TV could do for the family what radio no longer could: "...With practically every room having a radio, it was not uncommon for all to scatter to enjoy particular programs. With the one television set, our family is brought together as a unit for a while after dinner" (193). These factors only served to strengthen the true purpose of *TV Teen Club*—the creation of a virtual teen canteen, a space in which adults could monitor and control teenage behavior.

However, as Daly's laundry list of genres above shows, these teens were not watching "teen TV" but instead "Milton Berle, sport contests, and variety shows"—programming conceived for adult audiences. That teen-oriented narrowcasting had yet to be developed is not a surprise—with one set in the home, and in many cities only one or two available channels, television networks did not have the luxury of appealing only to a small segment of the audience. Who, then, was really watching *TV Teen Club*?

Specifics about the show's audience are almost impossible to come by. Demographic information about viewers was not yet being collected in detail by the networks. Gomery (2001) uses the term "macrodata" to describe the raw numbers that are available from this period—for example, the total number of households that had televisions. Comparing the relative popularity of one show to another is complicated by the fact that not all shows were carried in all available markets. Since many cities still had only one or two television stations, an ABC show might not receive a truly nationwide airing. In January 1951, for example, *Texaco Star Theater* was carried in sixty cities; *TV Teen Club*, in only thirteen (*Advertising Age* 1951).

Moreover, the ways audiences were measured during this period were not necessarily comparable to those used today. In Chicago, for example, *TV Teen Club* was reported to be number four in the overall television ratings for November 1949, a ranking measured cumulatively across the month, with 45.6 percent of sets in operation tuned to the show during its broadcast. It was also ranked third both in total number of viewers during the month, and in terms of viewers' positive opinions of the show (Wolters 1949).

Beyond these numbers, however, clues as to the show's true audience can found in the programs themselves—particularly, in their advertising. Sponsors changed over the show's five seasons—and moved between products that could legitimately be pitched to teenagers, to products only parents could purchase. The first surviving episodes are sponsored by the Griffin Shoe Polish company, and feature live commercials acted out by youthful performers, aimed at teen consumers. One such spot begins as an apparent production number, as a young man sings, "I've got a date tonight." Eventually, the number segues into a sales pitch as he realizes that his date requires him to take advantage of the sponsor's shoe polish.

For the show's second season, the American Dairy Association picked up its sponsorship, with commercials aimed at teenagers directly. The slogan, "for the lift that lasts, drink milk," was highlighted in a live commercial in which a baseball player, stuck in a slump, came out of it after drinking milk. *Variety* noted, "It has good possibilities for selling the under-20 set on drinking milk in lieu of soda pop" (*Variety* 1950).[7] According to an article in a Syracuse, New York, newspaper, August C. Ragnow, a vice-president of the Association's ad agency, told a group of dairy farmers there, "The milk industry starts out with the youngsters of the nation as 100 percent heavy milk consumers ... then consumption drops about one-half over the span of teen-age years." Ragnow went on to tell his audience that the show highlighted the fact that "it's smart to drink milk, and smart kids drink it" (*Post-Standard* 1950).

The next season, however, found *TV Teen Club* with yet another sponsor, and this time, the language of the live commercials changed completely. This new sponsor was the Nash-Kelvinator Corporation, maker of automobiles and kitchen appliances. In one episode broadcast in November 1951 (announced in the opening titles as "a half-hour of fun and frolic for the whole family") a group of teenage girls start the show with a cheer saluting the sponsor. Wearing "N-K" sweaters, they announce: "There is nothing greater/Than the Nash-Kelvinator/TV Teen Club Show!" The live commercials are aimed squarely at the adult audience, not touting virtues that might be of interest to teens (the cars' speed, for example, or Nash's legendary seats that folded flat to form a bed) but instead, the car's "Airflyte" Construction, which was "strong, safe, rattle-proof." Viewers were advised to "go to your Nash dealer and take a test drive." At the show's climax, the winning performer, a tap-dancing 17-year-old boy from Astoria Queens, is presented with a Kelvinator refrigerator—with no reference to the oddity of such a prize for a teenage boy.

Describing *TV Teen Club* during this third season, syndicated colum-nist John Crosby assumed the role of grumpy parent: "Both the audience and the performers have a whip of a time but I'm not sure anyone at home will. That is, unless you are a collector of young girls who can imi-tate the Andrews Sisters which isn't among my hobbies." His reaction to the advertisements was equally cynical: "This is the first inkling I've had that the automobile and refrigerator people were after the teen age crowd. My allowance never got into that bracket and hasn't to this day" (Crosby 1952). It is the tension Crosby described—is the show serving adults or youth?—that seems to have triggered an overhaul of the show for its final season.

"Really fine talent that is really well schooled"

The most explicit expression of that tension within *TV Teen Club* came on the episode broadcast on May 9, 1953. That week, a special guest appeared to award Whiteman a plaque "for outstanding achieve-ment in bringing about a better understanding of the American way of life." Dr. Kenneth D. Wells, president of the conservative group Freedom's Foundation, told Whiteman:

> You've sort of brought out that wholesome love of God and Country and
> you've brought out that spirit that's America, put the emphasis on the individ-
> ual boy and girl, and Freedom's Foundation wants to extend its greetings
> through it's distinguished awards jury to you ... these are pretty critical times,
> with Communism swaggering around the world, and now's the time to tell the
> story of our fundamental belief in God, and our Constitutional government, and
> the sort of thing you've done so well of emphasizing the individual boy and girl.

Interestingly, in responding, Whiteman avoids the issue of Communism altogether. As he sidesteps the issue of the show's anti–Communist value (an odd choice, considering how potent such an endorsement could have been at the time), Whiteman instead draws attention to one of the per-ils of the teen-judged amateur format: that the teens will not choose the "uplifting" fare that their parents wish they would:

> Well, I don't know how much of that *I've* done.... I do think our show is a little
> different than many shows ... we try to encourage kids that have had a pretty
> good musical education, and I have to admit, they don't always win around
> here, because I think the kids like somebody that'll really hop the buck or play
> loud, but we feel that we should have, one really fine talent that is really well
> schooled.

Though Whiteman makes no more specific reference to how this may be a problem for the show, six months later, when *TV Teen Club* premiered for its final season, its format was entirely new. Rather than the standard stage with curtain, performances now took place on a set evoking a nightclub, complete with tables at which audience members sat. For 1953-54, no more were teenagers judging teenagers, with the potential for grand prizes continually going to acts that "really hop the buck." Instead, judging duties now fell to a panel of celebrities or talent agents who watched the show at home in cities across the country rather than in the studio—ostensibly, to get a clearer sense of the contestants' televisual appeal.[8] The show's climax now came not with the show's applause meter, but with phone calls to the show's set, during which contestants were offered contracts with various agencies.

During the season premiere, which aired on October 3, 1953, the first act is not an amateur talent, but the show's co-host, Nancy Lewis. Whiteman lets her know that he has sent telegrams to "Arthur Godfrey, Bing Crosby, Ed Sullivan, George Jessel, Milton Berle, Eddie Cantor, all just everybody I know, and they're all gonna look and listen in." After Lewis sings and plays the piano, Whiteman ostentatiously announces that she has a phone call from "Mr. Abe Lastvogel, one of the really big biggies at the William Morris Agency." Lastvogel, who can be heard over the telephone, tells Lewis, "I think you gave a great performance ... I think you're very telegenic," and offers to represent her through his agency. The show's next act featured a young pianist who performs Whiteman's theme song, "Rhapsody in Blue," with Whiteman's orchestra. It is a complete performance of the Gershwin concert piece, which in this case runs nearly nine and a half minutes long—almost a third of the program devoted to a single concert work. In this episode, the show eventually declares no "winner"; instead, each teenage performer is rewarded with a contract.[9]

A surviving episode from February 2, 1954, does declare a winner: over a tap-dancing quartet, a tap-dancing duo, a baton twirler, and a very young African American contralto who sings the uplifting ballad "I Believe," the victor is a Juilliard student who plays the cello. By this point, *TV Teen Club* has clearly undergone a complete transformation: from a program designed to create a teen-centric space, with entertainment by and for teens, *TV Teen Club* has evolved into a showcase that privileges "high" culture over "teen" culture.

After TV Teen Club

Aside from guest appearances on such shows as *The Bell Telephone Hour*, and the occasional tribute program, Whiteman's television career withered after the cancellation of *TV Teen Club*. A 1954 Whiteman-hosted (non-teenage) amateur hour show was poorly reviewed and quickly cancelled (Gould 1954). Two different programs (on ABC and NBC) were announced for Whiteman in 1956 but neither made it to air (Adams 1956).

Whiteman did have one close encounter with just the kind of music 1950s parents feared—and suffered an all too common fate. On July 10, 1956, *The New York Times* reported that Jersey City, New Jersey, had refused to allow the use of Roosevelt Stadium for a rock and roll concert featuring Bill Haley and His Comets. The show's promoter and host: Paul Whiteman. According to *The New York Times*, Whiteman's response echoed his role as the man who had made a lady out of jazz three decades earlier: "Mr. Whiteman maintained that the event Friday night was not designed to be a typical rock-and-roll session, the type that could result in a youthful riot. ' It was to be a concert,' he said."

TV Teen Club had a direct descendant in the teenage television arena: the announcer for the show's last two seasons—Dick Clark—began hosting the local teen show *Bandstand* a year after Whiteman's program went off the air. *Bandstand* went national—as *American Bandstand*—in August 1957. Yet, Clark's program differed in fundamental ways from *TV Teen Club*—ways that gave *American Bandstand* a much more narrowly teen-centric focus.

In the same way that *TV Teen Club* was patterned after the popular radio genre of amateur talent contests, *American Bandstand* was an outgrowth of radio disc jockey shows that began to appear in the late 1940s. The music heard on the program was not determined by contestants but by record sales—and with teenagers becoming primary consumers of popular music, teens themselves were shaping the show's content. (It also allowed teenage viewers a form of indirect interaction with the program—buying the records showcased on *Bandstand*.) The show's use of records as its primary source of music also meant that the show's visual focus was, by necessity, on the dancing teenagers themselves—a mass of teens with whom viewers could identify, rather than a small group of exceptional performers.

Clark's persona, moreover, was quite different from that of "Pops" Whiteman. In addition to his relative youth (Clark was 26 years old when he assumed host duties on *Bandstand*; Whiteman was 59 when *TV Teen Club* went on the air), he was an unknown announcer with no established history, as opposed to Whiteman's track record as patriarchal discoverer of young talent. Clark's on-camera approach to teenagers was different as well. Whiteman spent the majority of his on-camera time alone or with only his co-host, rarely even appearing in the same frame with teens, much less interacting with them. Clark, however, regularly moved among the teenagers, sat down with them, asked them their names and schools. Where Whiteman announced his performers from behind a podium (often bearing his name and caricature), Clark frequently announced records while surrounded by his studio audience of dancers, direct surrogates for the home viewer.

A more critical way in which *American Bandstand*—and the multi-tudinous local teen shows that followed it—allowed more specific address to teenagers was its time slot. *TV Teen Club*, by virtue of its position in a prime-time schedule with a very limited number of available channels, *had* to appeal to a broad audience, and based on its ratings and sponsors' discourse, was indeed watched by that broad audience. *American Bandstand*, however, was broadcast in an after-school, pre-dinner timeslot during which teenagers could control the television choices. While Mom was busy and Dad was still at work, television could create a purely teen-centered space.

In the end, *TV Teen Club* has less to say about the specifics of teen culture in the 1950s than about the anxieties that surrounded that culture. Ostensibly aimed at teens, it spent equal time appealing to parents. As it praised its teenage performers, it lamented its audience's musical tastes—and eventually turned away from those tastes in favor of celebrating "uplifting" fare. Yet, during its run, it also provided at least one small glimpse of what was to come. In 1952, in a performance that survives only as a scratchy, homemade audio recording, a teenager named Charlie Gracie took the stage to sing and play the electric guitar, performing a cover of the song, "Rock This Joint." He proceeds to do just that, in rockabilly style. The recording captures audience applause—but not Whiteman's reaction. Gracie won for five straight weeks on *TV Teen Club* and whether Whiteman knew it or not, he had just seen the real future of teenage culture—one far removed from the accordionists and tap dancers his show had championed.[10]

Notes

My thanks to readers Lucas Hilderbrand and Margie Compton for their feedback. Thanks also to Margie for her assistance in viewing *TV Teen Club* at the UGA Libraries Media Archives & Peabody Awards Collection (a treasure trove of child- and teen-related television, especially at the local level) and to J. Fred MacDonald for allowing me access to the episode held by MacDonald & Associates. Thanks also to Charlie Gracie, Jr., for providing the audio recording of his father's performance of the show.

1. At least 18 episodes from the series' four seasons survive, out of a total run of roughly 150. For this essay, I viewed shows at the following institutions: at MacDonald & Associates in Chicago, Illinois, an episode that aired in November 1951; at the University of Georgia, the episode that aired on October 3, 1953, as well as three undated episodes from 1950; at the Museum of Television and Radio in New York City, shows from March

28 and May 9, 1953, and from February 6, 1954. The University of Georgia holds eight more episodes that are currently not viewable due to shrinkage of the 16mm kinescopes. The UCLA Film and Television Archive contains one more episode, broadcast on January 12, 1952.

2. Though the use of the noun "teens" to designate those between the ages of thirteen and nineteen dates to the 17th century, "teenage" (or "teen-age") and "teenager" (or "teen-ager") came into use in the 1930s and 1940s (Oxford English Dictionary, s.v. "Teen," "Teenage," "Teenager," http://dictionary.oed.com/ [accessed March 1, 2007]). A 1942 journal article discussed such short-lived contemporary alternatives as "tweenteeners" and "twixteens" (M.B. 1942).

3. Though he was praised by the mainstream media of the time, Whiteman's reputation has never been high among jazz critics, who tend to portray him as watering down "true" jazz for mass consumption—a usurper who anticipates similar charges laid against white pop stars of the 1950s like Pat Boone.

4. The program's opening titles, and its description in newspaper program listings, varied over the years: sometimes *Paul Whiteman's TV Teen Club*, sometimes simply *TV Teen Club*.

5. Whiteman's original co-host was his daughter Margo. Margo's mother was actress Margaret Livingston, best known as the Woman From the City in F. W. Murnau's *Sunrise*. When the 18-year-old Margo got married in 1950, Lewis, 16, was hired to replace her (Wolters 1950b).

6. Close viewing of the shows tends to indicate that these shows were probably telecast using only two cameras. It is difficult to ascertain the physical layout of the performance space, as there are never any full establishing shots, only isolated views of Whiteman's podium, the performers, and very occasionally, the studio audience.

7. No episodes sponsored by the American Dairy Association appear to have survived. The ADA would eventually go on to sponsor *Shindig*, one of the most popular teen-oriented shows of the mid–1960s.

8. Judges in January 1954 (as announced in an ad for sponsor Tootsie Roll in the *Chicago Daily Tribune* on January 10) included actor Eddie Bracken (watching from Chicago), Dennis James (watching from New York), and Philadelphia city council president James Finnegan (in Philadelphia).

9. *Variety* took a cynical view of the proceedings: "At the end of each stint, the telephone calls ... seemed too pat, even if they were the McCoy ... The 'Goshes!' and Gees!' whipped up for this momentous occasions fell flat" (*Variety*, "Review of *Paul Whiteman TV-Teen [sic] Club*," *Variety*, October 7, 1953).

10. Gracie's prizes: a refrigerator and a record player. (Gracie, Charlie, Jr., e-mail to author, February 26, 2007.)

References

Adams, Jessie Clayton. 1945. "A Texas Teen-Age Center." *Journal of Educational Sociology* 18, no. 7 (March): 402–4.

Adams, Val. 1956a. "News and Notes from the TV-Radio World." *New York Times*, April 8, 13.

_____. 1956b. "Whiteman Series on TV Called Off." *New York Times*, June 12, 71.

Advertising Age. 1951. "Videodex Ratings of All TV Network Shows." February 26, 60.

American Sociological Association. 1945. "Role of the Teen-Age Center. *Journal of Educational Sociology* 18, no. 7 (March): 400–01.

Brandon, Dorothy. 1948. "Whiteman Contributes His Music at Dances of Town's Teenagers." *New York Herald-Tribune*, February 6.

Christian Science Monitor. 1947. "Youth Recreation Centers Launched by 'King of Jazz,'" November 22, 7.

Cook, Katherine M. 1943. "The Schools Speed Up the War on Juvenile Delinquency." *Marriage and Family Living* 5, no. 2 (Spring): 27–29.

Crosby, John. 1952. "Radio and Television." *Portsmouth* (Ohio) *Times*, July 6, 13.

"Dairy Industry Seeks Teen-age Business." 1950. *Post-Standard* (Syracuse, NY), October 11, 11.

Daly, Sheila John. 1949. "TV Opens New Way of Dating for Teen-ager." *Chicago Daily Tribune*, September 11, G8.

Gilbert, James. 1986. *A Cycle of Outrage: America's Reaction to the Juvenile Delinquent in the 1950s.* New York: Oxford University Press.

Glueck, Eleanor T. 1942. "Wartime Delinquency." *Journal of Criminal Law and Criminology* 33, no. 2 (July-August): 119–35.

Gomery, Douglas. 2001. "Finding TV's Pioneering Audiences." *Journal of Popular Film and Television* 29 (Fall): 121–29.

Gould, Jack. 1954. "Television in Review." *New York Times*, July 9, 14.

Jerving, Ryan. 2003. "Jazz Language and Ethnic Novelty." *Modernism/Modernity* 10, no. 2 (April): 239–68.

Long, Jack. 1950. "Pops Has Hundreds of Talented Kids." *American Magazine,* February 28–29.

M.B. "Commercial Jottings." 1942. *American Speech* 17, no. 1 (February): 41.

Magee, Jeffrey. 2000. "Before Louis: When Fletcher Henderson Was the 'Paul Whiteman of the race.'" *American Music* 18, no. 4 (Winter): 391–425.

McCarthy, Anna. 1995. "'The Front Row Is Reserved for Scotch Drinkers': Early Television's Tavern Audience. *Cinema Journal* 34, no. 4 (Summer): 31–49.

Reckless, Walter C. 1942. "The Impact of War on Delinquency, Crime, and Prostitution." *American Journal of Sociology* 48, no. 3 (November): 378–86.

Robinson, Elsie. 1948. "Listen World." *Olean* (New York) *Times-Herald*, February 13, 4.

Schott, Nancy Jane. 1945. "Youth Activities, Incorporated, Altoona, Pa." *Journal of Educational Sociology* 18, no. 7 (March): 404–07.

Solomon, Ben. 1947. *Juvenile Delinquency: Practical Prevention.* Peekskill, N.Y.: Youth Service Inc.

Sorenson, Roy. 1944. "Wartime Recreation for Adolescents." *Annals of the American Academy of Political and Social Science (Special Issue: Adolescents in Wartime)* 236 (November): 145–51.

Spigel, Lynn. 2001. *Welcome to the Dreamhouse: Popular Media and Postwar Suburbs.* Durham: Duke University Press.

Variety. 1946. "Review of *Teen Canteen*," May 8.

_____. 1948. "Review of *Teen Canteen*," July 7.

_____. 1949. "Review of *TV Teen Club*," April 6.

_____. 1950a. "Review of *Teen Canteen*," July 5.

_____. 1950b. "Tele Follow-up Comment." August 30.

_____. 1953. "Review of *Paul Whiteman TV-Teen [sic] Club*," October 7.

Whiteman, Paul. 1949. "The New World of Television. *Etude*, April, 341–42.

Whitman, Alden. 1967. "Paul Whiteman, 'the Jazz King' of the Jazz Age, Is Dead at 77." *New York Times,* December 30, 1.

Wolters, Larry. 1949. "Chicago Rates Star Cavalcade 1st in TV Shows." *Chicago Daily Tribune*, November 18, B16.

_____. 1950a. "Whiteman at 60 Is Having Time of Life with TV." *Chicago Daily Tribune*, November 19, NW14.

_____. 1950b. "The Televiewer." *Chicago Daily Tribune*, February 27, A7.

2. Teen Television and the WB Television Network

Valerie Wee

In the 1999–2000 fall television season, when the WB television network marked its fifth anniversary on the air, it did so as the acknowledged teen-oriented network. In its first five years, the network had evolved from what critics called "a struggling, almost pathetic sixth-placer in the prime-time wars," into a media site engaged actively in creating, mediating and (re-)shaping teen entertainment culture (Bierbaum 1998, 30). The network's success at attracting and servicing the entertainment demands of the teen demographic made it popular with advertisers and consumer corporations who were targeting that demographic.

This essay first considers why the WB television network chose to ignore the traditional mass television audience to focus on targeting a niche teen audience. It examines Time-Warner's decision to enter the broadcast network arena in what was dubbed the post-network, post-broadcast era, and considers the industrial, social, and programming considerations that shaped the WB network's commitment to niche marketing and narrowcasting and the circumstances that motivated the WB to target a teen demographic. Consequently, it discusses the network's evolution from its launch in 1995 to 2000, the year the WB network became a recognized and successful teen network. The second part of this essay traces the various strategies the WB utilized in marshaling the increasingly vital teen market for the network's survival and success. The decision to target the teen demographic resulted in the creation of programs and a format that collectively constituted the WB as a teen-oriented cultural artifact in itself. The characteristics and qualities that

43

marked the WB's teen shows and the ways in which these texts were shaped by the specific industrial, economic, and creative contexts of the period are the key issues considered. This section examines a range of WB teen shows (including *Buffy the Vampire Slayer*, *Dawson's Creek*, and *Roswell*) and pays particular attention to the ways in which these shows borrowed from the tradition of quality television texts. Also considered is how this tradition shaped the WB teen brand, ultimately helping the WB establish itself as the network of choice for the youth/teen audience.

Television in the 1990s

From Network Broadcasting to a Post-Network, Post-Broadcast Era

Any attempt to trace the rise of the WB must begin with an overview of the contemporary television landscape and the numerous changes that have taken place within the industry in the last few decades. During the heyday of network broadcasting, between the 1940s through to the 1960s, "television" consisted of a three-channel universe ruled by three established broadcast networks, NBC, CBS, and ABC. Television meant broadcasting to the widest, most general audience and delivering a mass market to advertisers. The 1970s, however, marked the beginning of numerous changes and developments within the television industry. The advent of cable technology saw the television universe expand from the three available channels to an almost infinite number. This led to the emergence of cable networks that rejected the broadcast, mass-market mandate in preference of narrowcasting to a select, niche market. The subsequent development of alternative entertainment delivery platforms, including video, digital entertainment, and, more recently, web-based television, have resulted in a much more complex, fragmented, and highly competitive television market, marking the broadcast networks' steadily declining dominance over the medium.

After the 1970s, television viewers began turning their attention to these alternative delivery systems and network broadcasters saw their audience numbers decline from 95 percent of the nation-wide television audience in the 1960s to fewer than 50 percent of the audience in the 1990s. These developments highlight the decline of the network broadcasters' supremacy over the medium. Clearly, television in the 1990s could no longer be defined by or restricted to purely conventional broadcasting and network terms. In fact, by the late 1980s and early 1990s, the mainstream and trade press acknowledged these developments and began predicting the demise of traditional broadcasting and of network television, forecasting the rise of a post-network, post-broadcast era.

Yet, in the midst of these events, two different Hollywood studios, Warner Bros. and Paramount, both chose to enter into the business of network television. Undoubtedly, both studios were in part inspired by the success of FOX, the television network launched by Rupert Murdoch and 20th Century–Fox Films in 1986. FOX demonstrated the tremendous economic benefits that could accrue from such a venture.[1] With FOX, Murdoch and 20th Century–Fox profited greatly from controlling the entire process of production, distribution and exhibition in television. As a supplier of programming for the networks, 20th Century–Fox Studios had long been committed to program production. Owning their own network gave the studio control over the distribution of these programs, liberating the studio from its dependence upon the other networks for distributing 20th Century–Fox programming. Furthermore, FOX's exhibition arm, its owned and operated television stations, profited greatly from advertising revenues. As then Fox vice-president of marketing David Johnson points out, "If you can link together production and distribution in the television business, you can face enormous growth..." (quoted in Farber 1987, 33). FOX therefore served as both an inspiration and model for both the WB and Paramount's UPN network.

Having control of a television distribution platform became even more vital with the lifting of the FCC's "financing and syndication" rule ("fin-syn"). This regulation had prohibited broadcast networks from owning and producing their own entertainment programming. In 1991, however, media watchers were predicting that the FCC's "fin-syn" rules would be phased out.[2] In that event, the general consensus was that the four major broadcast networks would begin producing their own prime-time entertainment programs in-house, leaving the studios without a guaranteed means of distribution for their products. As the number one supplier of prime-time programming, animated programming, and first-run, syndicated programs, the stakes became especially high for Warner Bros. Acting in anticipation of this potentially significant upheaval in the studio-network relationship, both Warner Bros. and Paramount decided, in 1992, to create their own networks in order to ensure themselves a distribution platform for their own programs.

LAUNCHING THE WB NETWORK

In the summer of 1992, Warner Bros. embraced the challenge and signed on Jamie Kellner, the man responsible for launching the FOX television network in 1986, as the managing general partner of the WB network. Kellner believed that conventional network practices were no longer viable routes to success for a newly launched television network. He was convinced that the WB needed to deviate from the traditional network commitment to mass marketing and broadcasting. He argued that the future of a network, particularly a fledgling one, lay in the cable-inspired strategies of niche marketing and narrowcasting. Realizing that a new television network could never successfully compete with the established big three networks by broadcasting to a broad, general audience, Kellner steered the WB towards narrowcasting to a select, niche audience. Unlike the three established network powerhouses' long-held commitment to the broadest range of television audiences (the general 18–49 age-group of both sexes), Kellner decided to target a younger, more narrowly defined demographic: 12-to-34-year-olds of both sexes (Mifflin 1998, E). Kellner's strategy was to market the network to a specific segment of viewers and advertisers by committing to shows that would appeal to this core audience.

THE RISE OF THE TEEN MARKET

The WB's decision to target the niche teen demographic serendipitously coincided with a demographic shift that occurred in the mid-nineties, one that paved the way for the renaissance of the teen market and teen popular culture.

Prior to the mid–1990s, the teen market was largely ignored by the entertainment industries that believed that the teen demographic did not have a large enough presence to support strictly "teenaged" entertainment products.[3] According to Peter Zollo (1999), president of Teenage Research Unlimited, the teen population had begun to decline in 1976, "after the last of the baby boomers aged out of their teen years" (19). It was the beginning of sixteen years of continuous decline in teen numbers. The turnaround, however, occurred in the 1990s. Beginning in the mid–1990s, significant numbers of children began entering their teenaged years. This particular generation of teenagers is the offspring of the original baby boomers who were responsible for the emergence of teen culture in the 1950s and 1960s, and their numbers rival those of the original boomers. Labeled the "echo-boom" and "Generation Y," these teenagers represented the largest market to come along since their baby-boomer parents. In 1998, there were "76 million American echo kids [who were] the offspring of 79 million American boomers" (Foot and Stoffman 1998, 2). In addition to strength in numbers, Gen Y also wielded significant economic power, coming of age in a period of booming economic growth in America. In 1998, American teenagers spent in excess of 141 billion dollars (Zollo 1999, 12).

In response, the advertising, marketing, and media industries constructed a youth/teen demographic market that encompasses 12- to 24-year-olds. And advertisers and marketers were increasingly anxious to respond to this niche. Madison Avenue's interest ultimately played a significant role in motivating the development of media channels and vehicles to deliver this valuable audience. If the WB could successfully attract these teens, the network would be in a strategic position to service advertisers eager to reach that demographic. Significantly, although the 12–24 set is a narrow slice of the total television audience, it is generally regarded as the most elusive and hard to reach. As Kellner notes, "From an advertising standpoint, teens are the hardest-to-reach audience on TV. People make their brand decisions at an early life, and follow them for the rest of their life. It's an extremely valuable audience for advertisers and thus a business..." (quoted in Graham 1998, D3). Furthermore, while advertisers had the option of numerous shows by which to reach older viewers, relatively few can be counted upon to draw the under-thirty crowd—NBC's average viewer in 2001 was forty years old and CBS's was fifty-three years old, and few of the established networks were focused on the teen audience, especially during prime-time. It is worth noting, for example, that only 5 percent of NBC's viewers are teenagers. Furthermore, FOX, the only other "teen"-oriented network, had been steadily "aging up" into the general broadcast demographic since the early 1990s.[4] As a result, advertisers are often willing to overpay to reach this prime segment. Courting this niche audience makes even more sense because, as Kellner points out, "our audience ... replenishes itself. Kids move into teens, teens move into 18-to-34's. We're focused on 12-to-34's, but with a big spillover both up and down" (quoted in Mifflin 1998, E1).

It is worth noting that by the 1990s, the notion of "teenage" and the teenage identity had evolved; the term "teen" had less to do with biological age and increasingly more to do with lifestyle and shared cultural tastes and interests. "Teenage" in the late 20th century has achieved a much broader appeal and has come to represent a range of idealized qualities such as vitality, excitement, vigor, promise, and cutting-edge interests. These qualities may be associated with youth but, increasingly, more of society embraces this mindset, regardless of age. In the youth-obsessed culture of American society in the 20th and 21st century, it is no longer how young you are, but how young you think you are, or choose to be, that matters. Consequently, in skewing towards a teen demographic, the WB network was not restricting itself to a demographic defined by actual age. Rather, it was aligning with a broader market that could relate to and embrace a teen lifestyle and, more importantly for advertiser interests, its products.

Establishing the WB Teen Brand

CONSTRUCTING THE WB TEEN

The WB began consolidating its teen-identified brand by launching a number of distinctly teen-targeted television series. In January 1997 the WB premiered *Buffy the Vampire Slayer* (henceforth *Buffy*), a fantasy-horror drama which revolved around a teenage girl who, as the world's one designated "vampire slayer," is forced to battle all manner of evil monsters with the aid of her high-school friends.[5] In the middle of the 1997–98 season, the WB launched *Dawson's Creek*. Revolving around four teenage friends in a Cape Cod–like town, the series explored the angst, relationship crises, and the coming-of-age dilemmas faced by a group of introspective, intelligent, self-aware high schoolers. The show's teen-identity and credibility were further reinforced by its pedigree: it was the creation of Kevin Williamson, the writer of the highly successful teen-pics *Scream* (1996), *Scream II* (1997), *I Know What You Did Last Summer* (1997) and *Scream III* (2000). In 1998–99, the network increased its teen programming and further expanded its schedule with *Roswell*, a series about a group of teenage aliens growing up in the alien-obsessed town of Roswell, New Mexico. The network also purchased *Charmed*, a fantasy drama about three sisters who discover they are witches, and *Felicity*, a series that followed a group of teenage friends as they embarked on their college years.

All of these shows share a range of distinct characteristics: they feature a young and highly attractive ensemble cast and they all trace the experiences of youth and growing up with an appealing blend of intelligence, sensitivity, and knowing sarcasm. In addition, the shows addressed many sensitive and relevant teen and youth issues, such as self-destructive teenage behavior, alcoholism, teenage sex, and sexual identity. Furthermore, these shows' central focus revolved around the relationships and friendships of the key protagonists. These characteristic qualities may be traced to the WB's attempt to distinguish itself from its primary competition for the teen audience, MTV. If the WB hoped to attract a teen audience, it needed to offer programming that would provide an alternative to what was available on the teen-oriented cable network. The WB, therefore, needed to construct a brand identity via programming, publicity, and format that was distinctly different from its stronger and more established competitor.

An examination of the WB's teen identity/brand indicates a distinct deviation from MTV's. Unlike MTV's more irreverent, hedonistic, and anti-establishment teens, the WB's teenagers were significantly more morally idealistic.[6] The WB teens struggled to do the right thing, they loved and supported their siblings and friends, and they respected their parents. The main teenage protagonists in the shows listed above tended to be thoughtful and introspective, serious and responsible, mature and self-aware, while also attractive, intelligent, fun loving, and young. Although the WB's teen characters often made mistakes, they invariably learned from them. They faced numerous social, personal, emotional, and sexual crises but continually struggled to do the right and responsible thing. They suffered teenage angst but also knew how to have fun and enjoy their youth. These teen constructions lay distinctly outside the urban edginess of MTV. It was also noteworthy that the "WB teen" tended to exist in a white, affluent, and suburban context that was in distinct contrast to the multi-racial, urban "MTV teen."[7]

Of course, going this more conservative route was more appropriate for a mainstream "broadcast" network rather than a cable network.[8] Unlike MTV, the WB did not enjoy the leeway accorded to cable networks that remain, in many ways, less vulnerable to public, political and industry criticism and controversy. As a result, the WB consciously tried to avoid the more serious controversies that would alienate its advertisers or attract governmental and regulatory commentary or intervention. Adopting a more conservative thrust in its programming allowed the network to sidestep a significant degree of social and institutional criticism that would adhere to any "alternative" network.[9]

THE WB AND TEEN-TELEVISION IN THE LATE 1990s

In addition to constructing the WB's teen identity, it is also worth noting that the various WB teen series also consciously adopted a range of characteristics borrowed from mainstream "quality" television, albeit adapting them to the target teen demographic.

One of the notable qualities of the WB's teen-oriented schedule is the overwhelming popularity of the ensemble cast, hour-long, dramatic series format. The WB's teen-oriented, hour-long dramas were the direct descendents of two earlier teen series: the short-lived, critically acclaimed drama *My So-Called Life* (ABC, 1994–95) which treated teen experiences and angst with respect and sensitivity, and the long-running *Beverly Hills, 90210* (FOX, 1990–2000) which dealt with the teenage experiences of close friendships, complicated romantic relationships, and the quest for identity—all presented in a glamorous, attractive, sexy package. Like these antecedents, *Buffy, Dawson's Creek, Roswell, Charmed,* and *Felicity* were all hour-long dramas that effectively blended *Beverly Hills, 90210*'s glossy visual style, and physically attractive ensemble cast with *My So-Called Life*'s honest exploration of the teenage experience. Of course, *Beverly Hills, 90210* and *My So-Called Life* were not themselves the pioneers of the ensemble, hour-long dramatic series. That tradition began with the turn to "quality television" in the 1970s and early 1980s that led to the emergence of hour-long dramatic series such as *Hill Street Blues, Lou Grant,* and *St. Elsewhere* (Williams 1999, 143).

A "quality" television show, as various scholars have noted, was characterized by the use of ensemble casts in an hour-long dramatic format, narratives that replaced the familial milieu with a focus on the familial relationships that existed between friends and colleagues, a tendency towards liberal humanism, a propensity for self-reflexivity, and the adoption of cinematic techniques and aesthetics.[10] Many of these qualities found their way into the WB's teen texts. The WB's teen schedule of *Buffy, Dawson's Creek, Roswell, Charmed, Felicity, Popular,* as well as *Young Americans,* were all hour-long dramas centered around an ensemble cast of teenage friends who provided the familial support and complex interrelationships largely absent from their actual domestic lives.

The shows mentioned above all featured teenagers who were complex, intelligent characters encountering experiences and challenges that characterize the actual teenage years. These WB teen shows actively cultivated the niche teen audience by exploring issues that would resonate with teenagers, such as the complicated, conflicted relationships teenagers have with family and friends. For instance, the teenage Buffy's relationship with her mother is marked by a series of misunderstandings and conflicts, despite the obvious affection they have for each other. In the first two seasons of *Buffy,* Joyce is completely ignorant of Buffy's identity as the Vampire Slayer. Joyce sees her daughter as a typical teenager obsessed with clothes and boys and prone to irresponsible behavior when in fact, Buffy must shoulder the responsibilities of saving the world from myriad monsters and potential apocalypses. On *Roswell,* a group of human and alien teenagers struggle to keep each other safe and protect each other from a threatening adult world determined to uncover their secret and exploit them. In this series, the parents are ignorant of the teenagers' situation and ineffectual in providing any help. On *Dawson's Creek,* three of the teenage characters, Joey, Jen and Pacey, have dysfunctional relationships with their parents; Joey's mother is dead and her father is in prison, Jen's mother has abdicated her maternal responsibilities and sent Jen to live with her grandmother, and Pacey's parents largely ignore and neglect him. The sense of alienation and isolation that these teenage characters experience as they try to negotiate their way in the world, as well as the strong friendship, support, and camaraderie they derive only from each other, may be read as fictional and metaphorical representations of an actual teenager's perception of lived reality.

Like earlier quality television shows, the WB's teen series also adopted an attitude of liberal humanism in its narratives, addressing difficult, often controversial, and significant issues that were particularly relevant to its teen and youth audience. One *Buffy* episode dealt with abusive relationships, highlighting the thin line that exists between love and abusive obsession, and provides an unflinching portrayal of the deadly consequences that can ensue. Another episode in the series addressed suicide and high-school violence and teenage alienation and loneliness. In the episode, Buffy confronts Jonathan, an awkward misfit intent on suicide, and reminds him that all teenagers encounter loneliness, isolation and insecurity and that violence of any form is no solution.[11] *Buffy* and *Dawson's Creek* also explored the issue of sexual identity—in particular, the struggles and prejudices faced by homosexual/lesbian characters. Willow, Buffy's best friend, and Jack, one of the main characters on *Dawson's Creek*, both realize that they are gay. Over the course of several seasons, these series dealt with the confusion that these characters feel about their sexual identity, the implications it has for their friendships, and their fear of their friends' reactions. The series' deliberate decision not to exploit or treat Willow's and Jack's sexuality as "alternative" or aberrant, as well as the attempts to represent their romantic relationships as largely functional, healthy, supportive, and loving, highlights the series' liberal and humanist stance.[12]

The markers of WB's quality teen shows were not restricted to narrative elements or characterization but extended to aesthetic and stylistic elements as well. Stylistically, these shows embraced distinct cinematic qualities by adopting certain "cinematic" (or "film style") visuals. As Gitlin (1985) notes, traditional television visuals emphasize a mechanical, standardized set of techniques based on clarity and efficiency, such as the three-camera method in sitcoms (290). "Quality" television shows in the 1970s and after, such as *M*A*S*H* and *Hill Street Blues*, encouraged the use of more cinematic techniques and styles that rejected the clean and flat television image in preference of "messy" clutter, texture, and momentum (Gitlin, 291). While the WB's teen shows did not share the same cinematic style associated with these earlier quality series, they did embrace the single-camera format and were shot on film, offering the rich, organic visuals lacking in video. The film-trained creative personnel who worked on the WB's shows introduced the cinematic touch. It is noteworthy that the creators of *Buffy* and *Dawson's Creek*, Joss Whedon and Kevin Williamson respectively, had both worked previously on teen-identified feature film projects. Following the WB's success with Whedon and Williamson, the network actively sought out arrangements with filmmakers rather than established television personnel. *Felicity* creators J.J. Abrams and Matt Reeves began in films, the former as a scriptwriter with films such as *Regarding Henry* (1991) and *Armageddon* (1998) to his credit, the latter as the director of *The Pallbearer* (1996). The producers and creative personnel on the WB's *Young Americans* include production designer Vince Peranio, who collaborated with John Waters on all his films, and camera operator Aaron Pazanti (who worked on the Oscar-winning *American Beauty*, 1999). The propensity for cinematic visuals and techniques linked these later shows to the precedent setting strategies associated with quality television shows such as *Hill Street Blues*, *Northern Exposure* and *Twin Peaks*.

While the WB's teen shows obviously owed a significant debt to these predecessors, these shows were not merely copies of quality series reconfigured for a teen audience. In a variety of ways, the WB texts represented the next step in the evolution of quality series' characteristics. For instance, while earlier quality television shows were characterized by self-reflexivity and genre hybridity, the WB shows indulged in a degree of postmodern intertextuality, pastiche, genre hybridity, media mixing, and hyperconscious self-reflexivity, excessive enough to constitute a categorical distinction.[13]

According to Feuer (1984), "self conscious strategies" such as intertextuality and self- reflexivity "operate ... as a way of distinguishing the 'quality' from the everyday product" (44). The unprecedented degree to which the network's shows quote, and frequently spoof, both past and current popular culture made the practice one of the identifying traits of the WB teen television format. The WB's television series were media texts that obsessively discussed other media texts. The WB recognized the 1990s teen audience's heightened media and cultural literacy; theirs was a pop-culture awareness built upon an obsession with popular entertainment in its myriad forms. As a result, many of the WB shows consistently utilized intertextual pop-culture references in an attempt to harness this target audience's interests.

For instance, *Dawson's Creek* habitually paid homage to popular films. In one episode, the *Dawson's Creek* characters referenced the popular teen slasher film *Scream* by engaging in lengthy, often self-conscious, discussions deconstructing the similarities between several incidents that had occurred in the show and the film. In another episode, the four main characters spend the night on a deserted, reportedly haunted island. The episode is rife with stylistic, verbal, and narrative allusions to the phenomenally successful film *The Blair Witch Project* (1999). Each of these episodes portrayed the characters engaged in a significant amount of hyperconscious dialogue revolving around discussions of the films, with numerous self-aware quips regarding the similarities between the films and their experiences. Caldwell notes that the refusal to distinguish between the older and more contemporary films, reducing every citation "to a series of perpetual presents," is central to postmodernism (Caldwell 1995, 206).

In the above cases, the intertextual elements illustrate some noteworthy qualities about late twentieth century teen culture. First and foremost, it highlights the highly intertwined nature of the film and television industries' focus on attracting and harnessing the teen market. The ties that bind the *Scream* film series to the *Dawson's Creek* episode, for instance, allow the film franchise to benefit from the promotional exposure on a hit television show, even as the television show itself actively sets out to attract the very teenagers who were responsible for the success and popularity of the film franchise.

Buffy also consistently cited diverse popular culture texts such as *Jaws* (1975), *The Usual Suspects* (1995), *Dracula* (1931, et al.), and *Star Trek: First Contact* (1996) among others. While *Buffy* tended to restrict these to dialogue references, the series, like *Dawson's Creek*, assumed a high level of media and popular culture awareness in its teen audience. Many of the references tend to be almost glib and sometimes even obscure, with throwaway lines of dialogue comparing the show's characters with characters from other television shows or popular films, or replicating famous movie dialogue.[14] Another teen-oriented WB series, *Popular*, was particularly prone to intertextual citations. In fact, every episode in the series employs film or pop-culture quotations. Entire scenes are lifted from films as diverse as *Psycho* (1960) and *Dangerous Liaisons* (1988). I am not suggesting that shows on other more adult-oriented networks were devoid of any such references; however, they did not approach the intensity and extreme degree that marked the WB shows.

The fact that almost all of the WB's teen-oriented shows engaged in this practice, and did so repeatedly, suggested that the network used the technique to attract the pop-culture-obsessed teenager who visited the movie theaters regularly and who was, therefore, well equipped to recognize and appreciate the references. Interestingly, the intertextual references found in the WB's teen shows were not only restricted to current pop cultural events or primarily teen-oriented trends. *Jaws, Dracula, Psycho,* and *Dangerous Liaisons* all initially belonged to the adult, boomer generation, even though they were also accessible and familiar to teenagers in the 1990s via cable and video. These references, therefore, represented the network's attempt to acknowledge and engage with its media-savvy, target teen audience while simultaneously interpolating them into a more mainstream adult culture. Furthermore, by employing a cultural literacy special (but not isolated) to its key demographic, the network successfully avoided alienating viewers from a broader demographic. Instead, the more mainstream intertextual citations were an attempt to target and "reward" older viewers who could best appreciate these references.

This behavior was distinct from the MTV approach, which actively and overtly alienated and distanced non-teen audiences with its exclusively teen-oriented and teen-targeted content. As a cable network, portions of MTV's revenues were derived from cable subscription fees, making the network less dependent on securing advertising dollars. As such, traditional measures such as high-ratings and a large audience share, which would determine advertising rates, were less important to MTV. In contrast, the WB, as a mainstream, broadcast network, was primarily dependent on advertising for revenue and profits, which meant that ratings and audience share continued to matter.

In addition to these intertextual cinematic references, the WB shows also had a distinctive, hyperconscious, self-reflexive tendency to reference each other, particularly through sly, overtly self-aware, dialogue. For instance, on a *Dawson's Creek* episode, Pacey explicitly referenced key *Buffy* plot-points during a conversation. *Buffy* reciprocated in a scene in which the vampire Spike watches television and addresses the screen with comments and romantic advice for the *Dawson's Creek* characters. On yet another *Dawson's Creek* episode, a character declines a social invitation by pointing out that "*Roswell* is on in five minutes," referring to the impending start of *Roswell*, which followed *Dawson's Creek* on the WB's prime-time schedule.

While it may be tempting to dismiss these occurrences as trivial in-jokes, the cross-series citations bring the WB's varied and various teen-oriented series in contact, uniting them into a distinct corpus of teen texts. Each reference constructs a connection or suggests shared qualities between these texts by building unique links between the network's teenage viewers.[15] The fact that each citation implies that the teenage characters on each show "watched" or were "fans" of the other WB shows worked to encode these shows as teen-oriented products across what teenagers might consider different cliques, thus consolidating the shows' and the WB network's teen brand. These references could also raise different teen audiences' awareness and interests in the other shows and encourage them to tune in by extending their commitment to single shows to become part of a general teen audience with an allegiance to the WB network.

In addition to intertextual, self-reflexive references, WB's teen texts also displayed the postmodern quality of generic blending. In any episode, *Buffy* was at once a high-school drama, a romance, a comedy, a soap opera, and a fantasy-horror-suspense-thriller. This was also true of the "aliens-among-us" series, *Roswell*, which veered from sci-fi/fantasy to high-school romance, from teen alienation to comedy, and from teen drama to soap opera, before circling back again. *Dawson's Creek* was a blend of earnest teen drama, self-aware, postmodern media text, and soap opera. As noted earlier, the generic blending in these shows was not new but a continuation and intensification of the "quality TV" trend that began in the 1980s.

The WB's adoption and adaptation of quality television characteristics across the range of its teen-oriented series helped the network further define and consolidate its teen brand. This strategy subsequently allowed the network to leverage its brand in its publicity campaigns. As Lew Goldstein, a co-executive vice-president of marketing at the WB notes, "The great thing about these shows is that they are a set. You'll notice in our print ads and other areas—tonally—they take on the same impression. Even though they are different shows, they belong together" (quoted in Friedman 1999, S1). The WB network's publicity trailers and advertising campaigns promoting the network were characteristically youthful. The network's promotional spots were built around the most popular and attractive young stars from the network's teen shows. The WB's "Faces I Remember" Image Campaign appeared during the 1998–99 television season. The campaign involved trailers featuring the stars of the hit shows *Buffy, Dawson's Creek, Charmed, Felicity,* and *Roswell* among others. The 2000 Image Campaign that starkly proclaimed "The Night Is Young" subsequently replaced this advertising campaign. Like the previous campaign, it featured the network's stars, showing them partying in a downtown dance club, effectively exalting and reinforcing the WB's teen brand.

The WB's teen-oriented programming was so successful that the network's creative strategies and choices actually transcended the network's boundaries and became markers for teen-oriented television in general. The key qualities that were associated initially with the WB's teen shows began appearing in teen television shows on other networks in later television seasons. Subsequent teen shows, including FOX's *The O.C.* (2003–2007) and UPN's *Veronica Mars* (2004–2007), for instance, display the characteristics of teen quality television (including self-referentiality, intertextuality, and the adoption of a liberal, humanist perspective) that I have examined above.

Kellner's conviction that niche marketing, narrowcasting, programming, and branding would carry the day proved accurate. Indeed, in the 1997–98 television season, the fledgling WB was the only network that saw its audience grow from year to year, increasing their audience share by 25 percent. It also recorded significant gains in advance sales for the 1998–99 season's advertising. That season, *Variety* reported that the WB had successfully attracted more viewers, increasing their viewing households by 24 percent in general. In addition, the network had begun attracting more than just teenagers, seeing its audience share of adults in the key 18–49 demographic rise by 35 percent (Bierbaum 1998, 30). In narrower audience segments, the WB did even better. The WB's programming choices appeared particularly appealing to teenage girls and young women, who quickly became the network's most avid followers. The network was up 43 percent in women 18–34, 48 percent in females 12–34 and 57 percent in female teens. While these numbers may seem negligible by broadcasting standards, it is worth noting that the WB saw increases in each of these categories at a time when every other broadcast network had seen audience numbers decline from the previous year (Bierbaum 1998, 30).

The success of the WB's programming and scheduling decisions enabled the network to double its advertising revenue in a single season. Advance bookings of advertising time on the WB for the 1999 fall season rose to 300 million dollars, up from 150 million dollars in 1998. More than two-thirds of that revenue came from advertisers seeking the 12-to-34-year-old audience (Mifflin 1998, E1). These advertising numbers are particularly significant if we consider the fact that none of the WB's shows ever rose above the 5-to-8 share range in the Nielsen ratings.

Network television is a business, and advertising revenues define the success of a network and its shows. With the WB's teen series successfully attracting the valuable teen audience, advertisers became the biggest fans of the WB. By 1998, the WB was on its way to becoming the number one network among the crucial teen demographic; it was also particularly popular with the teenage girls and young women that advertisers were specifically courting at the time. As Don Aucoin (1998) points out, "[In] TV land ... if you're aged 18–49 and live in or near a city," like many of the WB's key audience, "the networks will cater to you because advertisers will pay premium prices to the networks in order to reach you" (C1). Indeed, by 1998, five of the WB's dramas, *Buffy the Vampire Slayer, Dawson's Creek, 7th Heaven, Charmed,* and *Felicity* all placed in the Top 20 most watched shows among teenagers age 12 to 17 (Lowry 1998, F2).

Conclusion

When it was announced that Warner Bros. was launching a new television network in 1995, the market and industry consensus was less than optimistic. The WB's decision to ignore the established practices of network broadcasting and narrowcast to a niche teen demographic allowed the network to survive and thrive in its first five years on the air. In doing so, the WB showed that, outside of the established networks, "broadcasting" was no longer a viable practice in the late 1990s. The WB's teen focus allowed it to make the most of a key demographic shift taking place in America at the time, when the number of American teenagers began to rise to significant proportions, even as society at large embraced a more teen-oriented lifestyle. Coinciding with a booming American economy, these combined events made the network's target audience particularly vital and valuable. Realizing the opportunities, the WB network consciously began developing programming with a distinct teen-focus. In programming a range of teen-oriented series that consistently borrowed from and adapted a range of quality television characteristics for a teen audience, allowed the network to cultivate a recognizable brand image that gave it a specific identity and helped distinguish WB from other existing and established networks.

Despite the WB's success in targeting a teen audience, the network continued to struggle for profitability. This became even more difficult when UPN, the other newly launched network, also began to target a youth audience.[16] While the teen market was undeniably a significant one, the demographic's numbers were ultimately still insufficient to support two competing television networks targeting the same niche 18–34-year-old demographic, particularly in an environment where teens had access to multiple other forms of entertainment in a variety of (new) media. On January 24, 2006, CBS, UPN's parent company, and Warner Bros. Entertainment, which controlled the WB, announced that the two networks would merge into the CW, a new youth-oriented network that would pool the resources and programming from both the WB and UPN. While this decision confirms the value and viability of the teen market and of the narrowcasting strategy, it also highlights the intensely competitive nature of contemporary television and the limits of targeting any niche market.

Notes

1. See Laurie Thomas and Barry R. Litman (1991) for a concise examination of the Fox network launch, as well as the strategies that Fox used to circumvent FCC regulations.

2. See Jim Bensen (1993); Elizabeth Kolbert (1993); and Bill Carter (1995). The easing of the FCC's "fin-syn" rules began in 1991and underwent gradual deactivation until its suspension in 1995, the year that Warner Bros. and Paramount both launched their television networks.

3. Klady notes that after the early 1980s, studios began ignoring the teen audience, as evidenced by the declining number of teen films produced between the mid–80s and mid–90s (1997). Beck and Smith note that "the teen market has dwindled markedly since the 70s-80s era when films like *Pretty in Pink* and *Ferris Bueller's Day Off* generated big box-office" (Marilyn Beck and Stacy Jenel Smith, "Movies for Teenagers Dwindle with Market," *The Times–Picayune*, July 2, 1995, A30).

4. When FOX was first launched, the network pursued the urban youth audience by programming edgy, racy, and irreverent youth-oriented shows such as *21 Jump Street* (1987–91), *The Simpsons* (1989–), and *Married with Children* (1987–97).

5. *Buffy the Vampire Slayer* debuted on the WB in 1997 and ran for five seasons on the network, until 2001. In its sixth season, the series moved to the UPN network. As the focus of this essay centers on the WB network, comments on the series are restricted to the five seasons it was on the network. Furthermore, it can be argued that by the time the series shifted to UPN, the main protagonists had aged out of their teenage years and the show was, arguably, no longer as teen-oriented since it featured these characters grappling with more adult issues and responsibilities.

6. Representations of the MTV teen can be found in a range of its programs, including *MTV's Spring Break*, a reality show centered around the college-break ritual in which teenagers descend on popular holiday destinations for parties, drinking, and concerts. *MTV Undressed*, a fictional series that centers on a group of teenagers and their various sexual exploits, is another example of the envelope-pushing programming on the cable network that portrays teenagers as anti-authority, amoral individuals who casually pursue sexual and other pleasures with seeming impunity.

7. My thanks to John McMurria for pointing out the distinctive and different constructions of the WB and MTV "teen." It is also worth noting that the WB's white, affluent, "teen" programming ultimately resulted in the marginalization of the WB's commitment to servicing the urban African American audience. With the exception of an occasional African American guest star's appearance on one of the WB's teen shows, those programs tended to be predominantly white. Prior to the WB's decision to target the teen audience in 1997, one show on its schedule, *Sister, Sister* (1995–99), featured teen lead characters and examined teen-oriented issues and concerns. This situation comedy revolved around twin African American teenage sisters. It is worth noting, however, that media discourses about the show consistently and continuously referred to it as an African American family sit-com, with few references to it in any distinctly teen-oriented terms. See Jill Brooke (1998) and T. L. Stanley (1999). The WB seemed to foster this perception. Throughout the show's run, this show was separated from the WB's increasingly popular teen-oriented dramatic hour-long series. Instead, *Sister, Sister* was scheduled with the other African American sitcoms, such as *The Wayans Bros* (1995–99), *The Steve Harvey Show* (1996–2002), *The Jamie Foxx Show* (1996–2001), and *For Your Love* (1998–2002), effectively "ghettoizing," them to a separate single night's programming.

8. By "mainstream network" I mean the broadcast networks such as NBC, ABC, CBS, and FOX, which are distinct from cable networks that function by a different set of rules and are governed by different regulations.

9. Free of the greater constraints placed on broadcast networks to maintain standards of "decency," and less reliant on advertisers' goodwill, The N, a teen-oriented cable network, was launched in 2002. The N re-ran a range of American teen shows such as *Sabrina The Teenage Witch* (1996–2003) and *Dawson's Creek* (1998–2003). However, The N also included in their schedule *Degrassi: The Next Generation,* a Canadian series that actively tackled a range of controversial teenage issues, featuring a pregnant teenager who

considers abortion, and one teenager dealing with a gay father's decision to leave his family for his lover. These issues would not have been seen on a teen series appearing on an American mainstream, broadcast network. In fact, one *Degrassi* episode featuring a teenager having an abortion was banned and never aired on American television.

10. See Jane Feuer, Paul Kerr and Tise Vahimagi (1984) and Thomas Schatz (1999).

11. Ironically, the broadcast of this anti-violence, anti-suicide episode was postponed for several months. A week before the episode's originally scheduled March 1999 broadcast, the Columbine High School massacre occurred, prompting the network to postpone its telecast until September 1999.

12. Interestingly, while the WB network supported the representation of "alternative" sexualities on its shows, it is worth noting that the network's treatment of these issues tended to fall on the conservative side. Willow's romance with her fellow-witch Tara was never explicitly consummated on screen. According to Joss Whedon, the series' creator, the network pressured him to delete a planned kiss between the two women. It was not until the series moved to UPN that the more physical aspects of the relationship were portrayed. In the same way, Jack's character on *Dawson's Creek* was largely relegated to pining for a romantic partner, rather than portrayed as actively pursuing a gay lifestyle. These instances highlight the extent to which the WB network tried to reflect a humanist, liberal perspective while still pursuing a largely conservative tone.

13. Certainly, these qualities of hybridity, postmodern intertextual referencing, and self-reflexivity, are not unique or original to WB shows. FOX's *The Simpsons*, which was also targeted at youth and teens when it was launched, was an early predecessor who actively practiced many of the techniques and aesthetic strategies that came to characterize the WB shows.

14. Acknowledging the obscurity of some of the references, a series of books titled *The Watcher's Guide* have been published. These books conscientiously identify and explain each pop cultural citation for the edification of its (teen)age (or otherwise) audience. See Christopher Golden and Nancy Holder (1998).

15. I would argue that this strategy is different from the traditional practice of having stars or guest stars cross over to appear on different series (for example, as when NBC's *ER* stars, George Clooney and Anthony Edwards, made cameo appearances on NBC's *Friends*, or when *Friends* star Lisa Kudrow made appearances on NBC's *Mad About You*). In these instances, these practices tended to be isolated attempts aimed at increasing the network's ratings. These crossovers did little to enhance the NBC brand identity, nor are they part of a consistent network strategy to attract a specific target audience.

16. Significantly, when the WB cancelled both *Buffy* and *Roswell* in 2001, UPN picked up both series, signaling the latter's growing interest in targeting the same teen audience that had contributed to the WB's success.

References

Aucoin, Don. 1998. "Why the Dr. Is Out: Advertisers, Not Viewers, Dictate Which Shows Live and Which Die." *The Boston Globe*, May 29, C1.

Beck, Marilyn, and Stacy Jenel Smith. 1995. "Movies for Teenagers Dwindle with Market." *The Times-Picayune*, July 2, A30.

Bensen, Jim. 1993. "5th Web Woes: No O & Os." *Daily Variety*, September 6, 15.

Bierbaum, Tom. 1998. "The WB's Getting the Girls." *Variety*, November 2–8, 30.

Brooke, Jill. 1998. "Counterpunch: WB Network's Programming Success." *ADWEEK* (Eastern Edition), March 30, 22–25.

Caldwell, John Thornton. 1995. *Televisuality: Style, Crisis and Authority in American Television*. New Jersey: Rutgers University Press.

Carter, Bill. 1995. "The Media Business: 2 Would-be Networks Get Set for Prime Time." *The New York Times*, January 9, section D.

Farber, S. 1987. "Fox Chases the Ratings Rabbit." *American Film* (March): 33.

Feuer, Jane, Paul Kerr, and Tise Vahimagi, eds. 1984. *MTM: "Quality Television."* London: BFI Publishing.

Foot, David K., with Daniel Stoffman. 1998. *Boom Bust & Echo 2000*, 2nd ed. Toronto: Macfarlane Walter & Ross.

Friedman, Wayne. 1999. "Event-like Promos Build Loyal Young Core for WB." *Advertising Age*, February 1, S1.

Gitlin, Todd. 1985. *Inside Prime-time*. New York: Pantheon.

Golden, Christopher, and Nancy Holder. 1998. *The Watcher's Guide: Buffy the Vampire Slayer*. New York: Pocket Books.

Graham, Jefferson. 1998. "WB & Teenagers Make a Felicitous Combination." *USA Today*, September 29, D3.

Klady, Leonard. 1997. "Taken Unawares, H'w'd Refocuses on Youth." *Daily Variety*, January 15, 10.

Kolbert, Elizabeth. 1993. "Warner Bros. Enters Race for Network." *The New York Times*, November 3, section D.

Lowry, Brian. 1998. "Friday Night Fight Over Young Viewers." *Los Angeles Times*, November 20, F2.

Mifflin, Laurie. 1998. "Where Young Viewers Go (and Ads Follow)." *The New York Times*, September 8, section E1.

Schatz, Thomas. 1987. "*St. Elsewhere* and the Evolution of the Ensemble Series." In *Television: The Critical View*, ed. Horace Newcomb, 4th edition, 85–100. New York: Oxford University Press.

Stanley, T. L. 1999. "Net Gains." *Adweek: Marketers of the Year*, October 11, M86.

Thomas, Laurie, and Barry R. Litman. 1991. "Fox Broadcasting Company, Why Now?: An Economic Study of the Rise of the Fourth Broadcast 'Network.'" *Journal of Broadcasting and Electronic Media* 35, no. 2:139–57.

Williams, Betsy. 1999. "'North to the Future': *Northern Exposure* and Quality Television." In *Television: The Critical View*, ed. Horace Newcomb, 5th edition, 141–54. New York: Oxford University Press.

Zollo, Peter. 1999. *Wise Up to Teens: Insights into Marketing & Advertising to Teenagers*.

3. Defining Teen Culture: The N Network

Sharon Marie Ross

> The N's mission is to be the authentic voice for teens and help them figure out their lives with relevant, topical programming on-air and online at the network's website http://www.the-n.com/.

What is an "authentic" teen voice in the new millennium of the United States, and what role does television play in the creation and maintenance of such a voice? In 2001, The N network emerged on U.S. digital cable television right along with the new millennium to lay claim to this voice, framing themselves publicly (as seen in the mission statement above) in terms of service. This brief but compelling statement reveals an important vision of current understandings from within media industries of not only teens, but also of media industries themselves. In short, teens are a group with a need for media—television and the Internet especially— and the media need teens. Of course, one cannot as a corporate entity offer such a blunt assessment as the driving force behind a network; but The N's mission statement links media and teens inextricably with each other, focusing on teens' need and right to authenticity in their media.

A key component of authenticity for The N can also be seen in the mission statement's inclusion of their website as essential to the television experience of teens. Elsewhere I have discussed the ways in which The N, TheN.com, and the shows of The N effectively immerse themselves, and thus their target viewers, in a digital communication environment that assumes teens and young adults are conversant in Internet and texting protocols (Ross forthcoming). The three terrains of the network—programming, the image of the network, and the website—converge to demonstrate "authenticity" through acknowledging the role of new media in teens' lives—both as a means of interpersonal communication and as an "issue" that teens and their parents face. A significant correlation of this strategy is that it allows the network and its shows to position themselves as "cutting edge" in terms of what teens want. In this essay I will be focusing on how these same three terrains also converge to demonstrate authenticity through acknowledging the role that diversity is playing in millennial teens' lives, and how this, too, assists the network to position itself as cutting edge.

What does this emphasis on being cutting edge provide for a small digital cable network, and what might it provide to viewers? In the following pages, it is argued that The N's authentic teen voice is aggressively multicultural, effectively positioning a real teen as someone aware of and largely respectful of diverse points of view on socially relevant issues. I first examine patterns in the content of The N's main programming, highlighting the show *Degrassi: The Next Generation (DTNG)*, seeking to unravel how this Canadian anchor show of this United States' network set the tone and parameters for "teen" on The N. I then examine how the network, through on-air promos, website content, and subsequent programming choices pursues and negotiates the teen offered up by *DTNG*. Finally, I consider how the authentic teen voice that emerges might be speaking specifically to the millennial demographic in the United States and the value of this for The N and its corporate environment, focusing on the context of the rise and fall of the WB and UPN networks (and the creation of the CW).

The N's Holistic Vision of Teens

In 1999, the roots of The N began with the development of Noggin, a digital cable network for pre-school and elementary school-aged children. Noggin exists under the auspices of MTV Networks, which in turn exists under the corporate umbrella of Viacom. *DTNG* was developed for Canadian television in 2001, and Noggin quickly optioned the show to air in the United States. However, the series was clearly aimed at an older audience than the one Noggin aimed for, leading to the creation of The N, an entity that has the distinction of technically being a *line-up* of programming that nevertheless functions as a network—especially in terms of how The N is presented to viewers. At 5 P.M. EST, Noggin "turns into" The N; at 6 A.M., The N turns into Noggin. (One cannot help but think of Cinderella and her midnight curfew! From 5 P.M. to 6 A.M., the viewer is allowed to be a teenager.)

This marking off of The N from Noggin allows for the purchase and development of programs such as *DTNG*; indeed, given that The N was born to accommodate *DTNG*, it is this show more than any other that sets the tone for the network. For most viewers of *DTNG*, this show was their first exposure to what is actually a franchise of television shows that has existed since 1979, when Canadian public school teacher Linda Schuyler and her partner Kit Hood made a TV movie about kids making their own media (*Ida Makes a Movie*). This movie sparked enough interest in Canada for the development of a series, *The Kids of Degrassi Street*.[1] These programs aired on CBC, the equivalent of PBS in Canada, and as the shows gained popularity among viewers and critics for their frank approaches to teen issues, episodes would appear from time-to-time in other countries (including the United States, on PBS; PBS station WBGH provided some funding as well). In turn, the show came to be seen in Canada as more adult over time, airing first in the afternoon and eventually in prime time.

DTNG was developed for CTV in Canada, a corporate network airing a blend of Canadian and U.S. programming; the show is produced by Epitome Pictures, a small company in Toronto that produces another show on The N, *Instant Star*. *DTNG* returns viewers to the Degrassi Community School, where students attend both junior high and high school. One of the students is the child of characters from *Degrassi High*, and several of that show's cast members have roles on *DTNG* as their former characters grown up. The program follows a large ensemble of teens who can truly be described as multiculturally diverse. Supervising producer Stephanie Williams, who oversees casting, explained in an interview that she attempts to cast "beyond tokenism," seeking to have the cast reflect the diversity of the greater Toronto metropolitan area—a city full of first and second-generation immigrants from a wide array of countries (interview, November 10, 2005).

Because Epitome Pictures receives government funding and tax breaks, their casting must begin with Toronto teens. This restriction, combined with Linda Schuyler's approach to casting for her earlier shows, has contributed to a distinctly different ensemble compared to most U.S. teen shows. (Schuyler had pre-teens and teens become part of a repertory acting troupe, with community kids learning to incorporate their own life experiences into the shows.) Perhaps most noticeable is that the actors are near (often exactly) the age of the characters they play. The actors also look like real teens; Williams stressed that when they cast, they want less of the "beautiful people approach" than one sees in U.S.

television (2005). This is not to say that the characters are unattractive by conventional or even Hollywood standards; but the range of body and facial types is considerably more representative of teens going through puberty—with Williams noting that there has been a concerted effort to maintain body diversity for female characters especially.

This casting environment filters into the content and themes of the show itself, repeating motifs from the earlier series in the franchise. Williams describes Canadian culture—especially in Toronto—as less driven by assimilation than U.S. viewers are accustomed to, offering them characters whose stories are infused organically with their ethnic and national roots, including the tensions that can arise because of this multicultural environment. Thus, when fourteen-year-old Manny Santos has an abortion, her family's Filipino Catholic heritage is underscored as part of her decision-making struggles, and contextualizes later storylines involving her father kicking her out of the family home as she pursues an acting career. Paige Michalchuk's Polish roots emerge in simple conversations about food and dress; Kendra Mason's Asian roots emerge as an issue humorously when a boy pursuing her romantically is confused because her brother is Caucasian. (Kendra is adopted.) Hazel Aden's family story of fleeing Somalia in order to escape religious conflicts there explodes on the school's International Day when an Iraqi Muslim classmate's cultural display is vandalized. (Someone spray-painted the word "Terrorist" on it.)

This approach to multiculturalism is unique for all of U.S. television, let alone teen television. At times characters' racial, national, and ethnic backgrounds are issues—openly discussed and part of the narrative. However, the regular referencing of people's heritages works to offset what many label as the U.S. teen TV cliché of "a very special episode": a special character is brought in (usually never to be seen again) who calls attention to bigotry and ignorance for one day. An offshoot of this is the "within limits" approach to intense teen issues commonly found in U.S. television, particularly those concerning sexuality and/or violence: a main character deals with an intense issue (rape, gay desires, bullying, drugs, pregnancy), the problem is resolved relatively quickly, and once resolved it is never mentioned again—leaving no mark on the characters involved (unless it is that they are punished by being written out of the show). In the United States, this has much to do with the FCC and restrictions that are placed on content aimed at children, which includes teens; it has even more to do with networks' fears of losing advertisers concerned about their product being associated with controversial issues and liberal stands on those issues.

Writers I spoke with from the show (Brendon Yorke and James

Hurst) noted that CTV encouraged the writing staff to push the envelope with content; in Canada, *DTNG* airs in prime-time as part of an adult lineup, less marked as a teen show than in the U.S. (interview, November 10, 2005). Expectations of topicality are in operation, and the writers feel that any tendency towards sensationalism is kept in check by producers' emphasis on exploring reasons and repercussions for the story moments they develop for characters. The show has worked to address almost every issue teens might face regardless of where they live, focusing often on long-term ripple effects. More significantly, the majority of these issues are framed narratively as *social* rather than wholly *individual* concerns, either by emphasizing how one person's problems impact those around them or by emphasizing connections among different people's problems.

A few examples can make this clear. In one story arc, Paige, the most popular girl at Degrassi, flirts with an older soccer player from another school; at a house party he invites her to, the boy rapes Paige, leaving her to unravel the emotional and psychological ramifications across several seasons. The story arc addresses self-blame and the right to anger, as well as the importance of *telling*. It takes Paige some time to reveal what has happened and to seek counseling, and eventually she chooses to press charges against the boy (who has since gone on to college); here the show deals with the legal system and the difficulties young women face in situations of date rape. The boy is acquitted. Throughout Paige's journey, she develops recognition of psychological pain among her classmates as well as signs of abuse; the writers link other storylines to Paige's self-discovery. For example, Ellie Nash is dealing with an alcoholic mother while her father is gone in Iraq, called up for duty in that conflict. Her coping mechanism is cutting, and Paige intervenes when she starts to see Ellie acting in ways similar to Paige's own closed-off behavior after her rape.

In another, more complicated connection, Paige's friend Terri McGreggor develops a relationship with a new student (Rick) who eventually becomes abusive, first psychologically and emotionally and then physically. (Another character, Craig Manning, also recognizes the signs of abuse, having grown up with a physically abusive father.) The show takes pains to link Terri's lack of self-confidence to her abuse, underscoring the ways in which abusers prey upon insecurities; Terri is overweight and very insecure about her attractiveness. Paige becomes infuriated when Terri takes Rick back after he receives counseling, feeling that Terri should be able to stand up to Rick the way Paige has with her attacker; this complicated swirl of emotions and opinions is at work when Rick becomes abusive again and puts Terri in a coma.

This story arc unwinds over two seasons, culminating in another storyline. When Rick returns to Degrassi a year later, Paige and the other students shun him, angry that the school has readmitted him. Bullying of Rick escalates, with otherwise likable characters engaging in hurtful and immature behavior. After a *Carrie*-like bullying prank in which a few students dump paint and feathers on Rick's head while he is on an academic competition TV show, Rick goes on a shooting spree in the school, injuring one student and ending up shot himself. The repercussions of this storyline have continued throughout the run of the show, especially for the injured student. Jimmy Brooks, the school's star basketball player, is paralyzed from the waist down; he was targeted because a friend of his told the shooter that Jimmy was involved in the prank. Another student who came close to being killed (Emma Nelson) develops post-traumatic stress disorder symptoms and begins acting out rashly and without thought for consequences, eventually leading to a story arc about STDs.

There are countless other examples I could provide, but the point is that *DTNG* specializes in weaving together story arcs in ways that emphasize social connections among teens that extend beyond simply socializing—they focus attention on the ways in which personal stories reverberate in a community. The structural and thematic emphasis on how issues and people connect with one another presents authenticity as necessarily holistic. That is, critics and The N position *DTNG* as an authentic show in part because its narratives move beyond simply *presenting* a diverse array of topics and a diverse group of characters. The show presents a central thematic argument that a core component of being a teenager involves coming to terms with the messiness of life in an adult world. In order to survive and then prosper, teens must actively give voice to their thoughts on this messiness (be it messiness concerning race, gender, sexuality, etc.) *and* consider the competing voices of those in their community of teens.

As the writers put it to me, they prefer to present the issues they do in a "totally gray" zone that allows multiple perspectives to be presented (2005). The hope with this approach is that teen viewers will adopt the stance that "if you really understood your neighbors, if you really understood your classmate," one could become a better citizen and contribute more meaningfully to one's community (2005). This mindset is in line with scholar Lorraine Code's discussion of feminist epistemology; Code argues that over generations of patriarchy, women have developed competing ways of coming to understand the world around them that prioritize the group (1991, 1995). The two concepts that Code stresses are second-person knowing and epistemic negotiation. With second-person knowing, individuals attempting to come to grips with some issue or problem turn to those around them, seeking to collect as many perspectives as possible for making any kind of decision. These individuals then come together to examine competing points of view, negotiating with each other while attending especially to the context in which the issue or problem is situated. Such an approach to problem-solving, Code explains, runs counter to patriarchal systems of decision-making rooted in hierarchies, where special individuals can lay claim to the power to hand down decisions; it also runs counter to a philosophy of black-and-white morality, in which clear rights and wrongs exist regardless of context.

It is this emphasis on community and context, combined with the issues addressed and the diversity of the characters, that operates in part to mark *DTNG* as "quality"—particularly among educators, but also among teen viewers (a point I shall return to in the conclusion). In addition, because *DTNG* is the flagship show around which The N built its identity as a network, these elements shaped the design of this "network" as a whole. Building upon a *DTNG* holistic vision of teens, The N has pursued a line-up of programming that collectively reflects this model, positioning the network itself as holistic, and thus authentic.

Programming for Teens: "It (Should) Go There"

With *DTNG* as its centerpiece program, The N quickly worked to market the show in a manner that would also serve to market the network itself. In the early years of the network, when advertising was harder to come by, The N relied on interstitials (network promotional spots between episode segments) to brand the network as holistic and cutting edge, relying on three primary strategies. The first—mentioned in the introduction to this piece—was to emphasize the network's recognition that teens live in an increasingly multi-mediated environment. In between programming segments, viewers could see spots (some animated, some with live actors) featuring texting between "viewers" as they discussed their favorite shows, and even texts about running to the refrigerator for a snack before the show comes back on. One of the more inventive and continuing campaigns involves spots in which teens stuck in annoying circumstances (a boring class, a desired suitor paying no attention, a kid brother barging in his sister's room) receive a text message *from The N*. These messages effectively position the network itself as a person of sorts—an entity that understands the ins-and-outs of teen viewers' lives.

As the network quickly matured, new media interstitials did as well, increasingly directing viewers to visit TheN.com, most often to chat about

DTNG and take quizzes related to the show, and eventually to watch webisodes in which *DTNG* characters were featured in inventive, often comical scenarios. The chat forums and quizzes in particular work with the marketing tagline The N developed for *DTNG*: "*Degrassi* ... It goes there!" On-air promos for the series regularly feature a teen female voice breathlessly describing a character's story arc (often covering more than one season in less than 2 minutes!) as a voice-over for images from the program, ending with the tagline. (Another campaign featured teens sitting in a school hallway discussing characters and events, and ending with the tagline.) By emphasizing conversation and actual viewer investment in story, The N acknowledges to its viewers that they "get them," further branding the network as an understanding entity.

A more serious campaign strategy involving the tagline cleverly uses brief glimpses of scenes from yet-to-air episodes, and overlays these images with non-synchronized soundtrack dialogue that indicates an impending dramatic arc. In other words, because the voices one hears do not correspond directly to the brief images on-screen, viewers cannot tell what is happening to whom. For example, in the months before one character (Liberty Van Zandt) finds out she is pregnant and decides to give her baby up for adoption, and her boyfriend overdoses on drugs, The N used a promo with brief images of *someone* overdosing and *someone* giving birth—but with soundtrack dialogue that indicates almost anyone in the cast could potentially be involved in these events. Likewise, in the weeks before a major character, J.T. Yorke, died on the show, The N ran a promo featuring images of a party out of control, several fights, and a doctor in a hospital saying "he didn't make it"; the soundtrack overlaying this featured a string of characters' voices from potentially any number of scenes.

These more dramatic ads for *DTNG* also emphasize viewer investment in the show, by refusing to spoil what will be happening among the characters. These promos also rest upon the show's established emphasis on community—the events might *happen* to anyone and will inevitably *involve* everyone, thus allowing for the indeterminacy with the images and sound. Research on soap opera fans has shown that the similar emphasis on community found in that genre sustains strong viewer loyalty that often translates to group fandom, with soap viewers regularly talking with each other—increasingly online (see Baym 2000). Thus, it is unsurprising that *DTNG* fans can be found online discussing the diverse community events of the show, mirroring the exchange of perspectives that occurs within the series as they offer their own opinions. As one example, when Emma Nelson, a popular "good girl" character on the show, has oral sex with "bad boy" character Jay Hogart after she was almost shot in the school shooting episode, an intense online debate emerged when one poster labeled Emma a whore before seeing the episode. Viewers began debating whether or not they had the right to label Emma in this way, leading to examinations of context as posters engaged in the process of epistemic negotiation:

> A: I wouldn't say she's a slut. Watch the episode before you go around calling people names.
>
> B: She's not any of that. She was going through a hard time. She watched someone die.
>
> C: Girls face that pressure every day. She just made the big mistake of giving in.
>
> D: It was disgusting what she did but don't go calling her names.... Besides she learned her lesson.
>
> E: What she did in the last episode was really slutty.
>
> F: Even though Manny got pregnant and stole Craig from Ashley, I think Emma is the bigger slut.... She didn't even like Jay, so that is what really makes her the bigger slut.

This debate went back and forth for several pages in the chat room boards for the show, with fans attempting to unravel the circumstances surrounding Emma's actions, pondering the repercussions (Emma develops gonorrhea and an outbreak develops at the school because Jay has multiple partners), and considering the larger community of the show's world (the discussion of Emma's best friend Manny Santos getting pregnant in an earlier season).[2] Another issue emerged from these posts when one person tentatively asked the group to explain what oral sex was, resulting in kind, if awkward, definitions. The web managers of TheN.com anticipate the topics that might emerge as hot points of discussion and information seeking, and accordingly offer quizzes—both educational and more informally social—for site visitors to take. For example, at the same time that the above discussion about Emma was occurring in chat forums, teens could take "The STD? Me? Quiz," which took users through a series of questions aimed at informing young people about how to prevent STDs and what to do if they have symptoms. The quiz (and others like it) is designed so that, as you get a question wrong, you will immediately have your misinformation corrected; and cleverly, if you get an answer right—potentially by random guessing—you are still provided with the same information so that you cannot escape the facts. In addition, at the end of most quizzes, the website provides links to official information sites and forums for more in-depth examination of the subject matter at hand.

Other, less obviously educational topics have created debate in the online forums and emerged within quizzes; at various points in the show's history, quiz and forum topics have included: gay sexuality and gay bashing, religion, drug use and drinking, pregnancy, infidelity, divorced parents.... The list goes on, following the range of topics at work in the show. And like the show, the discussions in the forums and the designs of quizzes promote a diverse range of viewpoints about this diverse array of issues. Other programs that accompanied *DTNG* in its early years on the network likewise had links to forums and quizzes, modeled after the flagship patterns of this original series. While more original dramas have been added to The N's programming slate, early on the network relied primarily on syndicated repeats of teen shows to fill up their schedule. Across the network's short history, a marked emphasis on diversity has emerged in these programming choices also; programs bought have regularly featured African American cast sitcoms from the 1980s and early 1990s (*Fresh Prince of Bel Air, Moesha, One on One*).

The use of syndicated sitcoms from decades past has raised issues among some viewers over the network's identity. Tellingly, those who have complained about these programs being out of date do not focus on issues of diversity—other than in terms of generation. That is to say, complaints do not revolve around the fact that many of these series feature African Americans. Instead, complaints center on the fact that these shows either 1) do not feature teens (specifically, high schoolers) or 2) feature characters who are no longer teens (i.e., these shows are more appropriate for viewing by the older brothers and sisters of those who complain about this lineup). I believe this reveals a significant issue for the network: How do you promote an identity that is cutting edge and millennial friendly while also attempting to retain viewers who may have initially been in high school but are now graduating into college (and potentially beyond)? As several articles in this collection have emphasized, many shows ostensibly labeled "teen" in both industrial and popular parlance are favorites of older viewers (some well beyond college!); it is also not uncommon for shows that begin with teen characters to continue as these characters begin going to college and entering the workforce. *DTNG* in fact graduated its first class of students in 2006; other popular teen series beginning in high school but moving beyond include *Beverly Hills 90210, Party of Five, Buffy the Vampire Slayer, Dawson's Creek* (which also airs in syndication on The N), *Gilmore Girls*, and *Veronica Mars*. Indeed, for U.S. based television, financial success *depends* on characters moving past high school: syndication becomes possible typically after five seasons, traditionally five years of characters' lives.

Nevertheless, some viewers of The N feel that that the network should remain eternally teen, somewhat ironically arguing that they, as a viewer block, should be a temporary audience that will move on to "grown-up" shows and networks. This mindset can be seen in forum discussions concerning the potential regular airing of *A Different World* in 2007, a late 1980s and early 1990s spin-off the 1980s hit family sitcom *The Cosby Show* featuring, originally, Cosby daughter Denise as she begins college at a historically black university. The show appeared to possibly be replacing an hour-long original drama, *Whistler*, that had not succeeded and that had been almost entirely white-cast—and online in TheN.com forums, a contingent of viewers began arguing about this choice:

> A: A Different World belongs on Nick @ Nite not The N ... trust me, not many ppl are going to watch dis show, especially on The N. Now I can understand Fresh Prince cuz that's more vibrant and more teen-ish, but A Different World iz with college studentz, the cast is not all that fine or good looking, and most of The N'z viewers are 13 and older....

> B: I think people are gonna watch this show. I think this is one of the first steps in The N maybe growing up, appealing to an older audience. I've been watching The N since I was like 14 so maybe its target audience is getting older and so they're deciding to grow with them.

> C: I HATE THIS SHOW.... We should petition it and then boycott it. It's the worst show to put on The N right now. I mean if they're losing ratings or something make a new show. Or put on The O.C. or something.

> D: My thoughts, exactly. When I saw this show added to the site, [I thought], "oh no, not ANOTHER outdated comedy that probably isn't funny."

> E: This show is old. And with teens ... they wanna watch more modern shows. Like Degrassi re-runs perhaps?

> F: Yeah. I used to watch A Different World on Nick @ Nite. But I mean it's not much of a teenage show like Degrassi, Moesha and One on One....

> G: My mom said it was on in the 80s, it didn't do well in the ratings at all. It was very stupid. She [Denise Cosby] just goes to her classes and her family comes to visit her and stuff. Just boring stuff....

> H: OMG ... I love this show :) But of course ... no viewers on the-n have ... well ... taste in REAL shows ... and no ... I don't think this show is right for the-n ... it's too mature for y'all :)

> I: Maybe The N is trying to fill-in time slots with certain shows.... You have to remember that A Different World came out in 1987 and its 2007. It still addresses some of the same issues that some of us (in that age group) face today but in an out-dated manner.

> J: ... I don't think it should be on here, but I don't exactly think it shouldn't be on here. I don't really think the viewers are ready for this show, it wasn't really a teen show, but then again that was back then when the themes of the show weren't things that teens were really facing unlike today....

This online argument reveals key dynamics in how teen viewers envision themselves as a market, and what they expect from The N in terms of offering an authentic teen voice. For some, the issue is who exists in the demographic that The N is reaching out to: Is this "network for teens" aimed squarely at 13–18 year olds—or at those who *began* watching while in high school? Do teens only want to watch shows about characters the same age that they are—or are they interested in older characters as well? For others, the issue is one of taste and relevancy: Are younger viewers unable to appreciate more complex, dramatic story arcs and themes? Or is it that the issues present in college-themed series are not relevant to the issues teen viewers face?

Perhaps most telling is the presence in this debate of viewers navigating through two conceptual terrains that have dominated the articles in this anthology. 1) Teen and young adult viewers are increasingly aware of themselves *as* a media demographic; and 2) teen and young adult viewers are increasingly aware of a historical lineage of both "teens" in terms of generation and "teen shows." Thus, some in this discussion wonder about strategies the network might be engaging in, considering ratings, potential shows to buy or produce, growing with the demographic, etc. And others wonder about putting *A Different World* in a historical context, considering whether the issues that college-aged viewers faced in the 1980s are now the issues that *younger* viewers face today.

The last comment in the above forum debate I believe sums up to a degree the issue facing The N today. "J" offers the opinion, "I don't think it should be on here, but I don't exactly think it shouldn't be on here." Much as the experience of adolescence itself is liminal in nature, so, too is the very *concept* of "teen"—and so, too, are understandings of "teen TV." If, as I have argued, a primary motivating force for The N is the positioning of the network as cutting edge via its aggressive multicultural strategies, could it be that this priority is in any way interfering with the ultimate goal of capturing a loyal teen demographic? Sarah Lindman, head of production and programming at The N, emphasized in an interview that diversity of and within content on The N is indeed a priority in program selection (interview, August 14, 2006). "They [viewers] demand it of us," she explained. And additionally, she argued, diversity makes good business sense in a country that will soon see racial minorities collectively becoming the majority. The problem is that, as I have lain out above, U.S. teen-based dramas, both in the past but also currently, are predominantly white-cast. To find programming that allows The N to maintain a commitment to diversity inevitably requires a turn to older sitcoms—or non–U.S. programming.

The N does use interstitials to emphasize issues of diversity, although these have become less common as the network has picked up more advertising; early years featured brief quasi-promotional pieces offering hip-hop poetry, "Viva Latinas!" graphics, and even young African Americans debating the use of the "N-word" (no pun intended) in popular culture. But without programming that reflects a commitment to ethnically and racially diverse viewers, such moves would seem hollow to even the most distracted teen watcher. An alternative, of course, is the development of original programming—a more expensive process than some teen viewers might be aware of. By 2007, The N had developed and aired multiple seasons of three original series beyond *DTNG*, two of which offered diversely cast primary characters (*South of Nowhere*, *Beyond the Break*) and one of which offered diversity among its secondary regular characters (*Instant Star*). Each program can be linked to *DTNG* via narrative strategies that emphasize community and the ripple effects of decision-making; each also addresses issues relevant to teens, presenting multiple perspectives. *Beyond the Break* focuses on the lives of a group of teen-aged female surfers attempting to work together on a sponsored surf team, focusing primarily on romances but also at times on issues of socio-economic status in ways not regularly seen in teen TV. *Instant Star*, a Canadian production from the same studio that produces *DTNG*, focuses on what happens to an independent-minded teen female singer after she wins a *Canadian/American Idol* like contest, examining issues of celebrity, artistic freedom within a corporate framework, friendship, and family—and of course, romance!

The show perhaps closest in spirit to *DTNG* is *South of Nowhere*, a U.S. based series about a family with three teens that moves from Ohio to the Los Angeles area when the mother relocates for her career as a doctor. While the community involved in this show's stories is smaller in scope than *DTNG*'s (following a more traditional teen TV structure), it is a community that relies on epistemic negotiation. The main variation is that *South of Nowhere* regularly shows *failures* in this strategy—episodes can highlight teen characters' lack of power to encourage epistemic negotiation. *South of Nowhere* primarily accomplishes this examination of power through examinations of race and sexual orientation (with sexual orientation receiving more emphasis).

Clay, one of the teens in the Carlin family, is an adopted African American in a Caucasian family—a position that he begins to explore after he and his siblings are thrust into an ethnically and racially diverse high school. The show uses the Carlin family's changed environment to examine definitions of whiteness and blackness as Clay befriends Sean, a fellow African American student who is politically and socially aware regarding issues of race and class in an urban setting. Sean and Clay's friendship rests on epistemic negotiation as they debate the role of racism in their individual lives and how their personal experiences can be extrapolated to the larger communities surrounding them. The show takes pains to demonstrate the role of power in young black men's lives, with Sean and Clay facing situations in which they must confront white society's unwillingness to reconsider what they "know" about young black men. In one episode, the cops harass them; in another, during a school lock-down, they face classmates who assume someone black at the school must have brought in a weapon or drugs. Clay also begins to explore the limits of epistemic negotiation within his own family; his friendship with Sean moves him to ponder his lack of connection to African American history and culture and he eventually seeks out and finds his birth mother, feeling that within his white family there are issues and emotions he cannot fully explore.

The show's primary focus, however, rests with Spencer, the youngest sibling, as she develops a friendship and then a romantic and sexual relationship with classmate Ashley. Mrs. Carlin is appalled by Ashley's "lifestyle," and shockingly appalled when Spencer becomes involved with her over the course of the series' first season. Spencer begins to confront daily her own family's unwillingness to engage in epistemic negotiation, particularly with her religious mother. Mrs. Carlin at one point tries to "cure" Spencer through religious intervention, and variously forbids Spencer from seeing Ashley. Older brother Glenn, the family's popular star athlete, becomes increasingly irate as Spencer comes increasingly out, having to deal with fallout at school over Spencer's actions. Spencer becomes frustrated as she watches Glenn's drug addiction and Clay's getting his girlfriend pregnant garner less anger and outrage than her relationship with Ashley, allowing the show to explore the various weight that teen issues hold in different settings. This central family tension also mirrors issues that Spencer and Ashley confront at school, from straight-out harassment to smaller moments of ignorance. (Spencer especially faces taunts and threats as she becomes more comfortable with revealing her relationship.) The show explores the role of homophobia in stripping teens of power—be that power in the realm of social interactions, familial interactions, educational environment, or physical safety.

Much like *DTNG* then, *South of Nowhere* positions their teen viewers as ready, willing, and able to engage with narratives featuring a diverse array of characters that explore a diverse array of issues that might enter the modern teenager's life. However, as online debates about some of the programming offered on the network reveals, an emphasis on diversity poses problems for a network such as The N that is limited in terms of the program options available for purchase and development. The N's digital cable status—coupled with the fact that it is, in fact, *not* a network—means that it must rely on a heavy slate of syndicated series from previous TV eras in which one would be hard-pressed to find a library of multi-culturally diverse shows featuring teen characters. Ironically, the aggressively multicultural stance of The N that makes it stand out from its competitors is also, at least in its current early years, part of what allows its competition to maintain an edge.

Conclusion

The N, relying on a strategy of program selection that prioritizes multi-culturally oriented series, buttresses the vision of teens that these programs offer—and further supports this vision with a website that promotes discussion of the issues such programs raise. Combined with other strategies—most notably the image of the teen viewer as one immersed and conversant in new media technology—The N has managed to brand itself to viewers and critics as the teen network that "goes there" both in terms of content and in terms of utilizing new media appeals. When this lineup of programming first emerged, The N's direct competition were the networks WB and UPN, the WB primarily in terms of teen and UPN primarily in terms of diversity. As Valerie Wee discusses in this book, the WB's branding of itself rested on the development of a body of teen shows that relied on a cultural and industrial lineage of quality television that defined quality in part as "a propensity for self-reflexivity, and the adoption of cinematic techniques and aesthetics." By focusing heavily instead on a definition of quality that rested predominantly on social relevancy, diversity, and new media literacy, The N was able to selectively appeal to viewers who may have found the WB too narrow in its vision of the teen experience.

As of this writing, The N faces a new competitor—the CW, a corporate blend of WB and UPN. The CW is now aggressively pursuing viewers from one of the same millennial angles that The N has traditionally, emphasizing its website forums and activities heavily in advertising (Ross forthcoming).[3] I believe it is somewhat telling that CW has not (as of this writing) managed to offer their viewers anything substantial in the way of diversity and teens. In its inaugural season, the network placed all its black-cast series on one evening—and only one of those programs featured a teen character (*Everybody Hates Chris*, a family sitcom set in the 1980s—ironically a show that would fit The N's sitcom slate). While network president Dawn Ostroff has publicly emphasized the importance of diversity to the network, noting the same changing demographics of teen viewers that The N has relied on, programming and scheduling decisions have yet to reflect this.

Thus, CW looks much the same as WB—with one night of UPN. In addition, if the network begins to falter in any way due to its "more of the same" approach to defining teen TV, the CW has a budget for original development and purchase that The N does not. While new series are slated for The N in 2007 and 2008, and there is every reason to believe that the network will continue to aim for diversity and multiculturalism in its choices, there are some signs that The N is shifting to a more CW vision of teens. Two recent purchases for the network came from WB, not offering much in the way of diversity (*Dawson's Creek* and *Summerland*). In addition, promos for the network have recently begun speaking to a viewer similar to that described by Valerie Wee: a current campaign uses self-reflexive, comic sketches such as characters from different original series in counseling for problems such as love hexagons and catfight tendencies. Whether The N can successfully incorporate quality elements prevalent historically in less diverse teen programming without sacrificing its quality commitment to diversity and multiculturalism remains to be seen. It also remains to be seen if the network can negotiate the varying demands of what appears to be the ever-broadening teen demographic, which today (2006) can arguably cross from Gen Xers in their thirties to Millennials just beginning high school. Regardless, it will certainly be worth watching to see how the "authentic teen voice" continues to develop—across all these networks.

Notes

1. *The Kids of Degrassi Street* followed elementary-school-aged children, airing from 1980 to 1985; *Degrassi Junior High* (1987–89) and *Degrassi High* (1989–91) followed a new set of characters from junior high to high school (some played by actors from *The Kids of Degrassi Street*). After the initial wrap of *Degrassi High*, the federal government's Health and Welfare Department helped fund a tour of actors from the junior high and high school series traveling across the country and speaking to teens about the issues the series had raised. The result was a talk magazine, *Degrassi Talks*, which aired on the CBC in 1991.

2. Manny's pregnancy also led to an abortion storyline, in which Emma had to grapple with her pro-life stance when Manny goes through with the abortion. The abortion episodes were the only ones The N had not aired at the request of their corporate supervisors at MTV Networks, creating odd moments for viewers as later aired episodes referred back to Manny's "decision," her boyfriend's "actions," and Emma's "support." Eventually The N received permission to air the episodes during a special marathon of the season in which it occurred.

3. See Sharon Ross's *Tele-Participation: Understanding Television in the Age of the Internet.* Malden, MA: Blackwell Press, forthcoming.

References

Baym, Nancy. 2000. *Tune In, Log On: Soaps, Fandom, and Online Community.* Thousand Oaks, CA: Sage Publications.

Code, Lorraine. 1995. *Rhetorical Spaces: Essays on Gendered Locations.* New York: Routledge.

_____. 1991. *What Can She Know? Feminist Theory and the Construction of Knowledge.* New York: Cornell University Press.

Lindman, Sarah. 2006. Interview, August 14.

Ross, Sharon. (forthcoming). *Tele-Participation: Understanding TV in the Age of the Internet.* Malden, MA: Blackwell Press.

Williams, Stephanie. 2005. Interview, November 10.

Yorke, Brendon, and James Hurst. 2005. Interview, November 10.

4. Rocking Prime Time: Gender, the WB, and Teen Culture

Ben Aslinger

Introduction

During a moment of channel surfing on the night of November 2, 2005, I thought I heard Le Tigre coming out of my television speakers, and my remote told me I was watching Warner Brothers' network, the WB. Turns out my ears were right. Le Tigre's "TKO" from their recently released CD *This Island* was featured on the *One Tree Hill* episode titled "A Multitude of Casualties." As a viewer, I did not know how to react. On one level, I was happy that a lesbian punk rock band emerging from the 1990s riot grrrl scene was achieving the level of visibility where a WB teen drama chose to use their song. At the same time, however, I wondered what effect this song had on the narrative. Why had the producers or the music supervisor chosen this song? Were other viewers picking up on the irony created by the disjuncture between riot grrrl–inspired music and obsessively "normal" images of white suburban teenagers exhibiting school spirit at a basketball game?

Le Tigre's song added an additional layer of meaning to the narrative, a layer of meaning encouraged by 1990s trends in both the music and television industries. While the aggressive pursuit of music licenses worked to provide focus to the hazy concept of synergy in the 1990s, Warner Brothers' network the WB (beginning with its early shows, *Buffy the Vampire Slayer* and *Dawson's Creek*) provides an excellent case study of how music licensing works to cement network branding and to open up narrative meanings. This essay examines the ways in which program producers, creators, music supervisors, and the network worked to open doors to new textual possibilities in WB teen dramas. In particular, I argue that industrial pressure to create a compiled popular music sound-track for WB teen dramas allowed music supervisors and producers to include genres and artists previously marginalized in the music industry and to add sonic layers complicating textual readings of gender and sexuality.

While many have lampooned the music on shows such as *Felicity* and *Dawson's Creek*, many of the songs on WB programs function to communicate character interiority, saying what the characters can't say, and often saying what the characters don't know or haven't realized yet. Yet, so many analyses of these teen dramas stop with analyzing visuality via the techniques of mise-en-scène, cinematography, and editing. Will Brooker (2001) goes farthest in his article on cultural convergence and *Dawson's Creek*, arguing for newer understandings of narrative that embrace audience and fan behaviors that move beyond narrow definitions of television textuality. However, while his work opens the door for considering the role of fashion, the soundtrack, and the web in determining the meaning of *Dawson's Creek*, more work on how the soundtrack works within the contemporary media landscape is needed. Given that the music in these shows is so prominently displayed both in terms of the industrial discourses surrounding these programs and the way music functions as sonic wallpaper pervading many episodes, the soundtrack asks for increased interrogation.[1]

"*Can We Sync It Up?*" Getting Music from the CD to the Screen

Contra Simon Frith (2002), I argue that music has palpable effects on television aesthetics. Murray Forman (2002) argues that popular music played a critical role in establishing television conventions during the early days of the medium. Following Forman, my argument is not that music is suddenly important with the rise of the WB in the 1990s, but that the WB's business practices and its programs' textual strategies represent a watershed moment in the history of music licensing for television. However, music in television has been historically under explored, as evidenced by Rick Altman's claim which still rings true today: "Critics have systematically steered clear of TV sound, preferring to dwell on narrative, industrial, or image-oriented concerns" (1986, 39).

In the 1990s, the music industry came to see licensing for film and TV as an integral strategy in keeping labels in the black and in promoting new artists. Licensing is commonly divided into two categories: master use licenses and synchronization licenses. As Jeff Smith explains, "The synchronization license is negotiated with the publishers of a particular song, and this entitles the licensee to use the notes and lyrics to a particular piece of music" (1998, 213). Master use licenses are negotiated with record companies, and the master use license allows licensees to use specific recordings. To use an example from the WB discussed later in this essay, if producers wanted to feature the commercially available recording of Edwin McCain's "I'll Be" on the hit series *Dawson's Creek*, they would pay both master use and synchronization license fees. On the other hand, if Joey (Katie Holmes) were to hum or sing the song, producers would only pay the synchronization license fee, since producers would be using the notes and lyrics but not the recording of the song.

Here, I outline what the WB did to encourage the compiled popular music score in its teen dramas and how production companies and the network took advantage of anxieties rocking the music industry in the 1990s. I also demonstrate how the sometimes friendly, sometimes tense relationship between television and music industries shaped the brand image of the WB as a teen network. Scholars such as Kelly Schrum (2004) have analyzed the ways in which music has played a critical role in rehearsing gender norms and in navigating the transitions between childhood, adolescence, and adulthood. From programs such as *American Bandstand* and *Hullabaloo* in the 1950s and 1960s to contemporary MTV and the use of music in narrative programs, television, popular music, and teen culture have been linked. Below, I outline how the WB re-imagined the economic relationship between television and teen music; in the second half of this essay, I turn to the narrative and representational issues resulting from the WB's strategies.

The WB initiated business practices designed to both expedite music licensing and mitigate costly licensing fees. T.L. Stanley writes:

> The WB plans to pump up the volume for its new TV series *Dawson's Creek* by using cutting-edge music and offering artists a 15-second promo at the end of the show in exchange for a break on licensing fees.... The tags will show the band's album cover and play a five-second music snippet; two or three will air per show. Garth Ancier, the network's entertainment president, said the intent is to infuse the show with hip popular music without breaking the bank. Though a number of TV shows are music-driven, no network has offered to promote artists in such a way [1998, 5].

Such tags at the end of programs, the WB reasoned, were "free" promotions geared to the coveted teen audience, and thus warranted license fee reductions, something newer artists and indie labels were most likely to go along with as radio further consolidated in the wake of the

Telecommunications Act of 1996. By lifting ownership caps on how many stations corporations could own in each market, the Telecommunication Act of 1996 paved the way for a series of mergers and acquisitions within the radio industry. Radio's conglomeration reduced the number of station owners, tightened corporate control over radio play lists, and reinforced format radio's narrow selection of American music for inclusion on the airwaves. At the same time, MTV's turn from video programs such as 120 Minutes, Yo! MTV Raps, and Headbangers Ball to a reliance on lifestyle programs such as Road Rules, Singled Out, and Undressed reduced the number of hours the channel aired music videos and largely pushed music videos out of prime time. Concurrent with radio consolidation's challenges to music promotion, the industry saw the power of music video—which during the 1980s had enabled artists such as Cyndi Lauper, Pat Benatar, Madonna, and the Pet Shop Boys to reach mainstream audiences—decline, forcing it to consider new pathways of distribution and promotion. The WB capitalized on the industry's nervousness, licensing music for broadcast transmission. To note the success of the WB's strategy, Fox's adoption of the same practice for its teen-skewed dramas such as The O.C. demonstrates the business savvy of the WB decision and its broader effect on teen television.[2]

The WB also tried to exploit synergy. Eric Boehlert states that in 1997, "Warner Music Group chairmen Bob Daly and Terry Semel told the heads of all Warner divisions that when searching for music to use in their projects, they should start in-house.... As the only record company with a pipeline to a U.S. TV network, Warner has weekly access to teen viewers" (1998, 31). One example of this use of cross-promotion is Warner recording artist Edwin McCain, an alternative singer-songwriter whose song "I'll Be" catapulted onto radio after its exposure on *Dawson's Creek*. Geoff Mayfield notes that the approximately four minutes of exposure on the "teen-skewed *Dawson's Creek*" netted McCain a "7,000 unit-boost and the Greatest Gainer Award" (1998, 100). Jeremy Helligar of *People* magazine quips, "His CD again seemed headed for the dumpster—until its single 'I'll Be' was featured on the season finale of *Dawson's Creek* last May. Now 'I'll Be' is one of radio's most played singles" (1998, 44). While *Dawson's Creek* was a Sony/Columbia TriStar production and most often featured Sony artists, the WB and Warner Brothers Records aggressively pushed Warner artists such as Edwin McCain and Paula Cole, whose song "I Don't Want to Wait" became the series' theme song. When programs such as *Dawson's Creek* decided to use recordings in the Warner Brothers catalogue, producers saved anywhere from three to ten thousand dollars in licensing fees per song (Ostrow 2000, H1).

During the 1990s, the music industry saw licensing as a revenue stream with the potential to compensate for declining mechanical revenue from CD sales and lost profits caused by downloading and piracy. However, hiccups in the licensing process soon emerged, as DVD distribution caused conflict between television producers and record labels/music publishers/rights owners. Sony/ATV Music Publishing president Richard Rowe comments on the increasing importance of licenses: "As far as we're concerned it's one of the most important growth areas that we have—now and for the foreseeable future—so it's of the highest priority in making up for the decline in mechanical income" (Bessman 2004, 56). In a similar vein, Spirit Music Group President Mark Fried argues: "As record companies, major publishers, and even management companies continue to consolidate and leave writers/artists limited ways and means to break out, we find that smart synch licensing is the best artist-development tool around" (Bessman 56). Rowe and Fried's remarks illustrate the dominant motives behind music industry interest in pursuing television placements, arguments which appear all over the trade press from the mid–90s to the present: 1) that music licensing provides a much-needed inoculation against downloading, piracy, and declining CD sales; and 2) that music licensing has emerged as a major venue for artist promotion and marketing.

Despite the utopian statements regarding licensing, the economic and legal negotiations surrounding licensing hit a major snag over DVD licensing rates. The WB and production companies working with the network angered fans when early seasons of *Felicity* and *Dawson's Creek* were significantly altered in the transition from broadcast to DVD, with original songs replaced with soundalikes.[3] The choice to use soundalikes, tunes that mimic the tone and theme of established artists but are sung and performed by unknown musicians, angered fans who wanted to watch the broadcast versions of shows they had followed over multiple television seasons. The move also angered television viewers who experienced and decoded the narrative based on the specific songs and stars whose music was incorporated into television programs. For instance, teen girl fans of the music of Alanis Morissette or Tori Amos might combine their readings of the music, Morissette's or Amos' stardom, and the visual and dialogic elements of the television narrative. Replacing Morissette or Amos with a musical unknown would significantly alter the sources of viewer pleasure and identification. However, soundalikes became more popular with the rise of DVD distribution.

Hard choices over what to license, what to erase, and what to replace with something cheaper became an economic necessity, especially for risky, edgy, and niche releases. Peter Staddon, senior vice president of marketing for Twentieth Century–Fox Entertainment, argues that when licensing fees for one season may exceed a million dollars, such fees pose a major burden to niche programs that may only sell between 200,000 and 500,000 units (Kipnis 2003, 62). DVD releases of series such as *Freaks and Geeks* were delayed for years, and producers often paid through the nose for the use of classic rock songs, oldies, and established artists. In order to expedite DVD releasing and decrease production and distribution budgets, soundalikes became a popular solution. However, to promote specific artists and albums to a teen audience, the WB moved beyond the soundalike approach by opening doors to younger performers on major labels and independent artists.

The WB network exploited the opportunities of music licensing to introduce teen audiences to new music and to consolidate its image as a network for young, cutting-edge viewers. Using production company and programming strategies to stay "hip" while not "breaking the bank," the WB opened doors to independent and lesser-known artists. Eddie Gomez, Bug Music West Coast creative director, says:

> Being an indie, I'm in charge of a smaller creative department, but a lot of our exploitation efforts go toward film and television and advertising agencies.
> We're the liaison between a lot of the music supervisors in film or TV and our writers, who are looking for that sort of copyright exploitation. The majors are situated more as an A&R force, to acquire new acts.... We turn [supervisors] on to new writers, and I don't think the majors are doing that as much [Henderson 1998, 47–8].

Gomez argues that independent labels and publishers are poised to offer innovative tracks that will appeal to music supervisors desiring a hip sonic charge for their programs. Too, he posits that indie labels and publishers will offer tracks at cheaper licensing rates or will offer blocks of songs at reduced prices.

WB also opened its doors to unsigned artists. Paul Stupin, executive producer of *Dawson's Creek*, states, "Introducing new (musical) artists is what *Dawson's* is about" (Littlefield 1999, 7). John King, the music supervisor for *Buffy* and *Angel*, says, "We established early on, because we were a nobody show and we were usually denied (music) licenses, that we would go to the local music scene and use unsigned artists" (Ostrow 2000, H1).

Because of a confluence of factors including Warner's desire to exploit synergy and attract a teen audience, producers and the network attempted to exploit the affective potential of popular music. While WB executives and producers were primarily concerned with drawing in significant portions of the teen audience and viewed popular music as a promotional hook, the drive toward music licensing—in practice if not in intent—affected how the gender anxieties of adolescence and teen performances of masculinity and femininity were narratively constructed and represented in WB programs. Two such programs, *Buffy the Vampire Slayer* and *Dawson's Creek*, demonstrate how the WB, in its formative stages, showcased music as a crucial part of teen narratives, allowing viewers to rethink the relationship between the visual and the musical.

Music Flowing Through the Buffyverse and Down the Creek

While WB programs such as *Dawson's Creek* and *Felicity* have been associated with music of the angsty teen girl singer-songwriter and the flannel-shirt wearing acoustic troubadour, *Buffy's* musical palette cannot be so easily classified.[4] The credit sequence works to frame Buffy as a strong character with a tough but vulnerable underbelly, and it achieves this effect through its visuals and its post-punk amped guitars.[5] The show's opening, which shows us Buffy kicking the crap out of assorted vampires and demons, also introduces us to the world of psychological torture known as high school that Buffy encounters every day as a teen living in Sunnydale. Accompanying the raucous post-punk music heavily laden with aggressive guitars, Buffy's visual dominance in the sequence works to associate her with the tough sound. Buffy's "punk rock" performance of gender works against the teen girl–angsty music paradigm that many male music critics (and music fans) castigated the WB for endorsing—even feminist rappers Northern State in their song "Dying in Stereo" ask listeners to "save that crap for *Dawson's Creek*." "The post-punk theme also, in line with Sarah Thornton's critiques of Dick Hebdige's notions of subculture, claims a visible presence of female fandom of punk, rock, and masculinized genres of music (Thornton 1994; Hebdige 1979).

As Thornton and other post-subculture studies scholars have argued, female fans (and gay fans) were always there "rockin' at the margins," but the way Hebdige and others drew the boundary lines of the punk subculture worked to obscure the contributions of women and sexual minorities to punk/rock scenes (Coates 2002). This sequence reinforces our image of Buffy as hero, taking the genre of raucous rock music and connecting it to femininity. Not your daddy's "cock" rock, the credit sequence works to counter visual associations that tie femininity to groupie status or victimhood in rock discourses. The audiovisual elements of the opening moments treat the female protagonist as an actor instead of an observer and continue the parallel work of riot grrrl and queercore musical movements in subverting traditional images of gender and sexuality in music.

While rock is used to change the representation of femininity in the credit sequence, it is also used to satirize normative heteromasculinity. "Teachers Pet" demonstrates another way the series connects music, gender, and genre by lampooning the articulation of rock music with aggressive masculinity. In "Teachers Pet," Xander develops a crush on the new substitute teacher. During a rock performance at the Bronze one night, Xander fantasizes about being able to expertly perform on the electrical guitar. In Xander's fantasy, musical virtuosity on the guitar equals a performance of hegemonic masculinity he is unable to perform in his everyday life; in short, rocking the electric guitar enables him to possess phallic power, to become a sexual magnet. Alas, while Xander is hot for teacher, things are not what they appear to be, and Xander finds himself trapped in the teacher's basement waiting to see if the substitute, now known to be a praying mantis, is going to bite his head off.

The episode's use of musical fantasy underscores three themes. First, rock (particularly the guitar) has been articulated with heteromasculinity and sexual power/domination. Second, the inability to perform one's gender correctly leaves one open to violence and danger, although hopefully not decapitation by a giant insect. Third, the idea of the rock musician as sexual symbol is a cultural construct open to contestation. In the series, Xander's inability to perform hegemonic masculinity is what makes his character attractive to viewers and his on-screen compatriots; most of the major male characters who come closest to performing "ideal" masculinity have to leave the diegetic space of the series. While Xander's inability to be a sexual "rock" god places him in danger, it is precisely this quality that allows him to stay in the series as a continuing character in Buffy's circle.

While the guitars thus far rock the cradle of love, the series also uses country music to unsettle gender. At the end of the first season, when Xander finally musters the courage to ask Buffy to be more than friends, Buffy expresses dismay that he would want to transgress the boundaries of their friendship ("Prophecy Girl"). Expressing his pain and frustration to Willow, Xander states he is going to go home and listen to country music, "the music of pain." However, Xander's music is not of the Hank Williams, George Strait, or even George Jones variety—songs of masculine despair resulting from the loss of female affection or the silent suffering from an unrequited love. Instead, Xander's stereo blares Patsy Cline's "I Fall to Pieces." Cline's transgressive performances of femininity in her lyrics, her aggressive sexuality, and her diva status in gay and lesbian subcultures make her inclusion in the narrative an interesting one.

Combining the connotations of Cline's song "I Fall to Pieces" with the televisual narrative, the disjuncture between a woman singing about problems with a male lover and Xander's failed advances towards an older woman opens up room for polysemic and even queer readings of the gender dynamics of this scene. The relationship between sound and image may make it easier for gay audiences to queer the narrative. After all, many gays and lesbians are forced to play the pronoun game some time in their lives, switching gender pronouns to describe personal, social, and sexual lives to hostile audiences so that those more often forced to "code switch" will recognize the signs. At the least, cultural knowledge circulating about Patsy Cline coupled with Xander's wounds in the war of romance encourages viewers to read the scene as another manifestation of how hard it is to perform heteromasculinity correctly. While the dialogue and mise-en-scène elaborate this theme, Patsy Cline's song develops another level of signification regarding how hegemonic masculinity is an ideal that can only ever be approximated.

I now turn to *Dawson's Creek*, another WB flagship program that cemented trends such as the use of promos at the end of episodes and of the compiled popular music score to hook teen viewers. By taking the music of *Dawson's Creek* seriously, I argue that the music has aesthetic, textual, and affective importance, and that those who want to dismiss 1990s female singer-songwriters and their connections to music festival culture want to dismiss fundamental parts of 1990s American media.

Paula Cole's song "I Don't Want to Wait," the theme song from *Dawson's Creek*, is a prime example of how the program's musical selections were lambasted by audiences and critics. Cole's song attracted a great deal of attention, and helped catapult Paula Cole to the national level—Cole even toured with Peter Gabriel's world music tour in the late 1990s. The fact that Cole's song appeared on a program largely marketed to teen girls, and that she achieved exposure at the same time that Sarah MacLachlan's Lilith Fair concerts were beginning to become less fashionable, led to critical dismissal. A critic at the *Toronto Star* dubbed Cole's music as "shrill, life-affirming tripe from a low-level Lilith Fairy" (2004, D3) and another critic described the series as just another low quality show on "The White Babes Network" (*Tampa Tribune* 2003, Baylife 1). While Cole's career may have suffered in the long run from the television connection, her ability to change the visual presentation of her music via the *Dawson's Creek* credit sequence counters trends tying female artists' songs to objectifying images and readings of the artist's body.

Paula Cole could be known for her soundtracking of teen lives, and not just "for her unshaven armpits," or for readings of her concert appearances such as the following:

> Dressed in a sexy tight dress with a slit up the thigh, Cole stayed out front most of the night, rather than hiding at the piano, as she often used to do.... She moved like a cat, sang with striking grace, gestured effectively (throwing her fist in the air to accent "Amen"), [and] stretched vocally on the sultry "Feelin' Love" [Powell 1998, F3].

Cole's move parallels the strategy embraced by some feminist and gay and lesbian artists in refusing to go along with traditional methods of artist representation and visualization. Perhaps television soundtrack inclusion allows artists' work to be visually presented without revealing the artist's body as a text—or at least, in Cole's case, provides a competitive image in determining the visual culture of the music.

At the same time that the program changed the way songs were presented visually, Cole's song introduces a level of psychological interiority cueing viewers into the emotional and mental struggles that are the meat and potatoes of the program. Cole's song about the death of her grandfather expresses emotions of grief, longing, and hope—the kinds of complicated emotions teens are grappling with how to channel and control (Fee and Raposa 2000, 8). Cole's song says much about the attempts to find verbal expressions for the complicated internal struggles for identification and direction that are fundamental to adolescence. If *Buffy*'s ass-kicking post-punk intro argues that women can be just as tough as men, *Dawson's* credit sequence asks viewers to think about how guys might have soft emotional underbellies they are asked to hide in attempts to perform traditional American masculinity. The question in *Dawson's Creek* is not whether Dawson (James Van der Beek) can fight the forces of evil, but what kind of man Dawson will become. Will he be a true friend to Joey (Katie Holmes) and Pacey (Josh Jackson)? What kind of masculinity will he perform? At the end of the series, will we think his psychological journey towards maturity was successful, or does he still have a lot to learn about being a mature adult?

Specific episodes of *Dawson's Creek* in later seasons had diegetic performances of music at concerts and nightclubs. In "Spiderwebs," the eighth episode of the sixth season, Dawson gets No Doubt concert tickets for everyone. Joey's college roommate was in a band, and viewers were exposed to characters on camera talking about musical tastes as well as practicing. In these ways, music became a part of the lives of the characters; shifts in musical tastes, listening, and concert attendance became a way to map characters' emotional growth in addition to the dialogue, mise-en-scene, and cinematography of the program.

These examples from WB programming illustrate larger issues regarding how industrial imperatives pushing popular music into television programs allowed new representations of masculinity and femininity to enter American television targeted to a teen audience in the 1990s. Whether intentional practices by music supervisors and producers or unintended consequences of responses to industrial pressures, the soundtrack's meaning making effects should not be ignored. If teens have had affective relationships with music ranging from the heady days of jazz and swing to the days of Elvis and the Beatles to the present alternative and indie rock boom, music and television industrial attempts to bottle "that teenage feeling" cannot be ignored.[6] Neither can we underestimate the semiotic richness of the music-image combination.

Conclusion

Addressing the role of music in the industrial strategies of the WB, I seek to spark further discussion regarding how concurrent historical shifts in the music and television industries bring increasing amounts of popular music to the small screen. Programs as varied as *Grey's Anatomy*, *The L Word*, *Six Feet Under*, *Queer as Folk*, *Homicide: Life on the Streets*, *Veronica Mars*, *One Tree Hill*, and *Gilmore Girls* all have compiled popular music soundtracks that evidence the shifting role of music in contemporary television narratives. Historically, though, scholars and viewers should remember that this trend was forcefully advanced by the WB network and teen television dramas.

As Anahid Kassabian (2000) argues, the soundtrack has historically been used to track identifications in filmic narratives. Soundtracks tell us how we are supposed to feel about film protagonists and antagonists, what to expect in the coming scenes, and why we should keep our eyes/ears peeled. For Kassabian, popular music soundtracks can create either assimilating or affiliating identifications. Assimilating soundtracks ask us to interpret the narrative in line with preferred narrative and ideological readings, while affiliating soundtracks invite readers to engage in polysemic readings of on-screen action (2–5). The question of how television soundtracks might create affiliating and assimilating identifications in ways unique to the small screen becomes a question of importance to audiences interested both in who owns what and why and audiences interested in seeing and hearing nuanced and novel representations of gender and sexuality. The WB's music licensing push as well as the continuing articulation of popular music, teen series, and teen culture reveal that music plays a critical role in the production and distribution of teen television. While the music of teen television becomes a site for rehearsing cultural norms governing gender and sexuality, it also opens up room for subverting and disrupting these same norms.

Talking about the effect of music on our visual perception remains difficult given our tendency to prioritize some sensory expressions and experiences over others. While music fans trust their ears, for many in media studies, seeing is believing. As film theorist Michel Chion argues, "In continuing to say that we 'see' a film or television program, we persist in ignoring how the soundtrack has modified perception" (1994, xxvi). In the process of writing, what verb does one choose: hear or see? It seems clunky to refer to the "audioviewer" or to use the verb "audioview" (xxvi). Maybe Kassabian's phrase "hearing film" cues us in best to the synaesthesia of engaging with contemporary texts.

Regardless of the verb, scrutinizing the popular music soundtrack in WB teen dramas and contemporary television allows for new avenues of understanding and critically engaging with representations of gender while introducing music to new audiences, even if some people would rather be at CBGB's than Lilith Fair. While studies of teen popular culture have often examined popular music and television as disparate objects of study, the WB's use of music illustrates the importance of considering the use of popular music in teen television and the ways in which popular music in the age of media convergence is apprehended to make particular performances of gender matter.

Notes

1. This is not to say that there are not resources to draw on. Scholars as varied as Kathryn Kalinak (1992), Roy M. Prendergast (1992), Royal Brown (1994), George Burt (1994), Michel Chion (1994), and others have built a body of literature on film music and film scoring that traces many of the historical debates surrounding labor, musical work, payment, and textual practice. Pamela Robertson Wojcik and Arthur Knight's edited collection *Soundtrack Available: Essays on Film and Popular Music* (2001) and Jeff Smith's book *The Sounds of Commerce* (1998) are excellent histories and overviews of popular music in film. However, these models based on film cannot account for the differences between the film and television industries and the ways in which television and film narratives incorporate music differently.

2. The incorporation of music has also become a major part of adult dramas such as ABC's *Grey's Anatomy*, Showtime's *The L Word*, and HBO's *The Sopranos*.

3. While the study of music in television suffers from historical strategies that denigrate the artistic merit of television music (such as the devaluing of music in cartoons with the term "mickeymousing"), the use of "soundalikes" in the commercial distribution of media texts raises an important question of historiographic method. Assessments and analyses of "over–the–air," syndicated, and DVD copies of a series may be analyzing different texts. For media historians for whom primary research materials may be limited to commercially available products, the choice is to analyze the materials that have been successfully licensed and made commercially available to the public or, in attempts to specify original textual materials, to rely on information compiled by fans, which is often incomplete and of questionable veracity. It follows then that shows with a devoted fan base have

traces that are more visible on web and in fanzines. For the purposes of this essay, the following URLs have been especially helpful: the *Dawson's Creek* Music Guide (http:// www.dawsonscreekmusic.com), *Buffy The Vampire Slayer* Music (http://www.buffyworld. com/buffy/music.htm), and *Felicity* Tunes (http://www.felicitytunes.com).

4. For the purposes of this essay, I have chosen not to focus on the Buffy musical episode, "Once More with Feeling." While this episode spawned a successful soundtrack album of its own, this episode's hybridization of the musical and the hour-long television drama proves to be a noteworthy exception to the aesthetic trajectories of music in WB programs.

5. Indeed, many fans of the show appreciated the way that Joss Whedon crafted characters that were simultaneously hard and soft, tweaking dominant constructions of the female heroine.

6. I borrow the phrase "that teenage feeling" from a song title of the same name from Neko Case's 2006 album *Fox Confessor Brings the Flood*.

References

Altman, Rick. 1986. "Television/Sound." In *Studies in Entertainment: Critical Approaches to Mass Culture*, ed. Tania Modleski, 39–54. Bloomington: Indiana University Press.

Bessman, Jim. 2004. "TV, Film Synch Deals Boost Exposure, revenue." *Billboard*, January 10, 56.

Boehlert, Eric. 1998. "The Industry." *Rolling Stone*, August 20, 31.

Brooker, Will. 2001. "Living on *Dawson's Creek*: Teen Viewers, Cultural Convergence, and Television Overflow." *International Journal of Cultural Studies* 4 (December): 456–73.

Brown, Royal S. 1994. *Overtones and Undertones: Reading Film Music*. Berkeley: University of California Press.

Burt, George. 1994. *The Art of Film Music*. Boston: Northeastern University Press.

Chion, Michel. 1994. *Audio-Vision*, trans. Claudia Gorbmann. New York: Columbia University Press.

Coates, Norma. 2002. It's a Man's, Man's World: Television and the Masculinization of Rock Discourse and Culture. Diss. University of Wisconsin–Madison.

"Continental drift." 2002 *Billboard*, September 7, 14.

Fee, Gayle, and Laura Raposa. 2000 "Inside Track; Paula Cole; 'Creek' Buoyed My Song." *Boston Herald*, March 15, News 8.

Forman, Murray. 2002. "One Night on Television Is Worth Weeks at the Paramount." *Popular Music* 21 (October): 249–77.

Frith, Simon. 2002. "Look! Hear! The Uneasy Relationship of Music and Television." *Popular Music* 21 (October): 277–90.

Gorbman, Claudia. 1987. *Unheard Melodies: Narrative Film Music*. Bloomington: Indiana University Press.

Hay, Carla. 2002. "Sound Tracks." *Billboard*, May 11, 17.

Hebdige, Dick. *Subculture: The Meaning of Style*. London: Metheun, 1979.

Helligar, Jeremy. 1998. "Talking with ... Edwin McCain." *People*, September 7, 44.

Henderson, Richard. 1998. "Media Exposure: Indie Pubs Find the Ticket to Getting into the Movies and TV. *Billboard*, December 19, 47–8.

Kalinak, Kathryn. 1992. *Settling the Score: Music and the Classical Hollywood Film*. Madison: University of Wisconsin Press.

Kassabian, Anahid. 2000. *Hearing Film: Tracking Identifications in Contemporary Hollywood Film Music*. New York: Routledge, 2000.

Kipnis, Jill. 2003. "Licensing an Issue for TV DVDs." *Billboard*, November 8, 62–4.

Littlefield, Kinney. 1999. "Teen Tunes Makes the Jump from TV to CD." *Courier Mail*, September 3, 7.

Mayfield, Geoff. 1998. "Between the Bullets." *Billboard*, June 6, 100.

Morse, Steve. 2000. "Paula Cole Turns in Splendid Performance at Avalon." *Boston Globe*, March 17, C20.

Ostrow, Joanne. 2000. "WB Shows and Entrée for Unsung Musicians." *Denver Post*, February 13, H1.

Powell, Betsy. 1998. "Jibes No Big Hairy Deal for Cole, but Singer Is Much Surprised by Angry Letters." *Toronto Star*, April 19, F3.

Prendergast, Roy M. 1992. *Film Music: A Neglected Art, and Critical Study of Music in Films*. 2nd ed. New York: W.W. Norton.

Schrum, Kelly. 2004. *Some Wore Bobby Sox: The Emergence of Teenage Girls' Culture, 1920–1945*. New York: Palgrave Macmillan.

Smith, Jeff. 1998. *The Sounds of Commerce*. New York: Columbia University Press.

Stanley, T.L. 1998. Music Promos Will Flag WB's *Dawson's Creek*. *Brandweek*, January 19, 5.

Tampa Tribune. 2003. "*Dawson's Creek* Fans Don't Have to Wait for Future." May 12, Baylife 1.

Thornton, Sarah. 1994. "Moral Panic, the Media and British Rave Culture." In *Microphone Fiends: Youth Music and Youth Culture*, ed. Andrew Ross and Tricia Rose, 176–92. New York: Routledge.

Toronto Star. 2004. "Tunes to Tune Out." May 9, D3.

Wojcik, Pamela Robertson, and Arthur Knight, eds. 2001. *Soundtrack Available: Essays on Film and Popular Music*. Durham: Duke University Press.

5. "Normal Is the Watchword": Exiling Cultural Anxieties and Redefining Desire from the Margins

Caralyn Bolte

Competing studies of the novel, despite their many theoretical differences, agree that the novel originated as a genre concerned with presenting a culture with a means to interrogate unresolved conflicts that were otherwise impossible to comfortably discuss. The utopian, and seemingly impossible, goal of such an experiment was to purge those unresolved conflicts from the reality of daily living, resolve them easily within the fictional confines of a novel's pages, and transfer those newly resolved cultural answers back into the lives of the novel's readers.[1] The novel, then, has long served as the most honest and unrestrained location for debates about anything that makes us squirm in real life; we marginalize our discussion of the margins of society to fiction in order to keep those fearful issues away from our settled, everyday experience.

Television, especially Teen TV, has emerged as the great-grandchild of this impulse, becoming another genre of increasingly confrontational cultural commentary. In recent years, a few Teen TV shows seem to be creating a niche for such cultural commentary amid programming that elides cultural issues in favor of fantasy, "reality," or forensic science. The top rated shows during the 2005–06 season featured the episodic mystery/fantasy juggernaut *Lost*, the soapy ABC pairing of *Desperate Housewives* and *Grey's Anatomy*, the gritty forensic scientific realism of the *CSI* franchise, and the ever-present reality television ratings winners, *Survivor* and *American Idol*. While certainly addressing cultural issues by incorporating more realistic portrayals of ethnic diversity, a fact especially true in the case of *Lost*, the focus of these mainstream television programs is not on incisive cultural commentary, but rather on reinventing and resuscitating serial and episodic television traditions.[2] Teen TV, often alienated from ratings success both because of its seemingly specific and exclusive audience niche and through its presence on "minor" networks like the WB and UPN, steps into the gap left by these adult-geared programs, and operates in much the same way as the novel did before it as a means to interrogate contemporary cultural ideologies.[3] Emily Nussbaum argues that minor networks offer programmatic freedom, because "[t]he WB and UPN existed to put on shows that were too risky, wonky, or downright weird for the other networks; they *had* to take chances to survive" (2006, par. 3). Programming born of this freedom, specifically shows that focus on alienated teenage protagonists like *Buffy the Vampire Slayer* (*BtVS*) and *Veronica Mars* (*VM*), offer a particularly insightful and powerful narrative perspective, as a view originating from the margins most incisively highlights the fissures in our cultural fabric and, in the process of constructing and presenting such vocal commentary, reevaluates the definition of desire.

She Alone Will Stand: Establishing Exile

Exile, as articulated by Edward Said, is not a state of total abandonment from any personal or social connection. Instead, it is "a median state, neither completely at one with the new setting nor fully disencumbered of the old, beset with half-involvements and half-detachments, nostalgic and sentimental on one level, an adept mimic or a secret outcast on another" (2000, 371). Exile is also not necessarily a separation of one person from a group; as the psychoanalytic theorist Julia Kristeva argues, an individual psychic exile can also cause "the subject [or the person involved] to be reinhabited by a strangeness that is powerfully affective. It exalts and casts down, promotes ungovernable impulses, creates fantasies of horror and delight" (1996, 11). In fact, "[t]he desire for a self at home with itself, even if it must like the prodigal wander still drives our reading of texts," whether those texts be the traditional novel or the new media texts of television, film and video game (17). These desires create a powerful bond between audiences and the fictional figures united with them in a common sense of alienation.

The exiled status of both Buffy Summers and Veronica Mars is established forcefully from the beginning of their respective narratives, the marginalized position of each protagonist becoming an essential part of the mythology of both shows. They both live in sleepy, yet troubled, marginalized communities, Sunnydale and Neptune respectively, safely separate from the nearest California urban center boundaries that both shows seem to orbit around but never transgress. The towns themselves, which seem to resemble but never claim the status of the real-life suburbs that they are patterned after, offer a comfortable sense of distance to the viewer. This is not the Beverly Hills featured so prominently in *Beverly Hills, 90210* that it became like another main character, the Orange County opulence at the center of the soapy goings-on of *The O.C.*, or the hip urban renewal side of the Boston depicted in the college years of *Dawson's Creek*. Buffy and Veronica walk the streets of a purely fictional world, a world that both contributes to the audience's sense of these characters' general alienation and offers the show the freedom to critique a society of which they are, ostensibly, not a part.

As the title character of Joss Whedon's *Buffy the Vampire Slayer*, Buffy Summers arrives in Sunnydale exiled from her previous life and alienated from Sunnydale's established social structure and history. Building on the storyline established by the 1992 film of the same name, the two-part pilot, "Welcome to the Hellmouth," begins with a montage used throughout the first season, a series of scenes highlighting cemeteries and slaying weapons. Over the montage, a voice establishes the mythology of exile that surrounds the main character: she is "the chosen one" who "alone will stand against the vampires, the demons, and the forces of darkness." The montage ends with a close-up on star Sarah Michelle Gellar, alone and centered in the final image, in order to solidify this central plot point—Buffy is, inherently, alone. Buffy has been exiled to Sunnydale, expelled from her previous high school in Los Angeles for criminal behavior necessary to vampire slaying but that establishes for her a somewhat misleading school record described as alternately "dismal" or "colorful." The reputation that follows her to Sunnydale High reinforces her position as an exile, as she becomes the object of gossip and social scrutiny that transcends social status; we see the socially awkward Xander and Jesse lusting after her in the early moments of the school day, and an entire locker room conversation revolves around Buffy's history and inherent difference: "The chatter in the caf is that she got kicked out.... She was starting fights." Her perceived position as a rebellious troublemaker exiles Buffy from other Sunnydale students.

As the new girl in school, Buffy is of course immediately alienated from Sunnydale life; her position as vampire slayer underscores the permanence of this alienation. As the new girl at school, she must negotiate a history and a social structure with which she is unfamiliar. Both Cordelia and Willow must educate her—Cordelia attempts to navigate her away from Xander and Willow and the other "nerds" she deems unacceptable, while Willow educates her about the nature of the relationships that form the nexus of social life in Sunnydale, including her complex relationship with Xander. Giles, as Watcher, must guide her in understanding the history of "odd occurrences" that color Sunnydale's past. Throughout "Welcome to the Hellmouth," Buffy must also confront her inherent difference as the chosen one, as her position as "big news" in "a one-Starbucks town like Sunnydale" encourages questioning about her identity. These moments are compounded as the characteristics accompanying her position as Slayer manifest themselves in her seemingly "morbid" fascination with the "extreme dead guy" found in the girls' locker room and her preference for wooden stakes over pepper spray as a self-defense tool.

While her initial attempts to cover for her "odd" behavior works (her "pepper spray is so passé" line is especially quick-witted and capitalizes on her linguistic difference as well), her inability to integrate into "traditional" high school life, coinciding with her choice to resume her vampire slaying duties, emphasizes and cements her alienation from what is figured throughout the show as "normal" high school life. Buffy herself ruefully recognizes this fact as she fights Darla, destined to become a series-long enemy: "You know, I just wanted to start over. Be like everybody else. Have some friends, you know, maybe a dog. But no, you had to come here. You couldn't go and suck on some other town." Instead of becoming Cordelia's friend and a normal club-goer at the Bronze, her acceptance of her position as Vampire Slayer, and the singular position the mythology ascribes to that role, creates for her a contradictory position: the focus of social alienation, which takes its most obvious form in Cordelia's derision, and a super-heroic figure, manifested in the alternate idol-worship and friendship relationship she maintains with Xander and Willow. Both positions, established clearly in the first episode, solidify Buffy's position as a powerful figure at the margins of society.

Veronica Mars establishes its protagonist's alienation from the established social structure, and her difference from "normal" high school life, clearly and immediately within its pilot as well. Veronica, the daughter of a disgraced former sheriff recalled from office after bungling the investigation into her best friend's murder, lives in Neptune, California, "a town without a middle class" ("Pilot"). The Neptune High social structure that she introduces breaks down into two categories: "your parents are either millionaires or your parents work for millionaires." Because Veronica fits into neither category, she is immediately alienated from both groups. The Mars family, and Veronica in particular, use their private detective work to transcend those rigid social hierarchies, as they work for and with everyone in a seemingly pragmatic but truly economically necessary way. Our introduction to Mars Investigations is highlighted by cases featuring alternately Loretta Cancun, a stripper at the "The Seventh Veil," and Celeste Kane, the wife of the richest businessman in town. Veronica Mars is a character without a place, without a true class position, because she embraces associations with everyone; this attitude becomes her hallmark throughout the series.

Veronica, perhaps as a result of her outsider status, apparently cares little about the opinions of others, whether that be authority figure or peer; the audience is introduced to this detached attitude in the quick succession of scenes that introduce her life at Neptune High. She steps up, in the midst of a mocking high school mob, to rescue Wallace Fennel, a new student being victimized by Neptune's motorcycle gang, a group no one else dares to defy. We learn early in the episode that, although she spends her nights investigating marital infidelity rather than studying for a calculus test, Veronica is a skilled student, able to wake up from sleeping in the middle of AP English to quote Alexander Pope verbatim and immediately return to her nap. She swears comfortably in the midst of her reluctant class participation, banters with the vice-principal, and creates an aura of impenetrability, which culminates in the verbal daggers she exchanges with the motorcycle gang responsible for Wallace's humiliation. These scenes prove her to be a distinctly unusual, and alien, high school student. The audience's sense of her alienation is solidified by the pilot's use of flashbacks, which highlight Veronica's former life as part of the in-crowd. The grayish eight millimeter quality of these flashbacks, and the longing with which Veronica describes them, frames them almost as a dream, a kind of fantasy world that makes the audience wonder if anything remembered so fondly and so vividly could have possibly been real. Reality, in contrast to that inclusive, idyllic world of social harmony, is colored—literally and figuratively within the show—by a distinct sense of alienation from the social and class structure that rules Neptune.

The exiled status of the protagonists within these two teenage television shows is solidified by their choice of friends and their fractured families. Both Buffy and Veronica come from single-parent households, the result of relatively recent parental breakups, and, while both characters demonstrate distinctly different relationships with their remaining parent, they each maintain an independence from the traditional world of domestic teenage duty. Buffy, in the early episodes of the series, struggles to identify and bond with her mother, a result of the secrecy with which Buffy leads her life. In "Prophecy Girl," the first season finale, the gap between Buffy and her mother becomes evident. In a scene contrasting one in which Buffy discusses her prophesied death honestly with Giles and Angel, Joyce tries to analyze her daughter's silent pensiveness, eventually attributing her lack of appetite and reticence to talk to Buffy's failure to get the right date to Spring Fling. Satisfied with her own perceptiveness, Joyce tells Buffy "See, sometimes I actually do know what you're thinking." Buffy's facial expression as she looks up at her mom in a cross between surprise and dejection, combined with the audience's knowledge of what Buffy is facing, emphasizes the great gulf between the reality of Buffy's everyday experience and the fiction that her mother constructs about her normal teenage life. Veronica Mars, fiercely loyal and quite close to her beleaguered father, also demonstrates a similar silent distance from him as she keeps the most fundamentally difficult experience of her young life, her drugging and rape at a high school party, a secret.[4] The deliberate distance that Buffy and Veronica maintain from their parental authority figures contributes to their exiled narrative perspective, keeping them alien and unembraced by any accepted hierarchical social structure.

Friendships, within both *BtVS* and *VM*, solidify this sense of exile. While both Veronica and Buffy establish close friendships within the course of their first seasons, these friendships work to solidify their exile rather than to subvert it. Xander and Willow establish themselves early as embodying the fringes of the social world, and Cordelia calls Buffy's association with them "downward mobility." While Buffy doesn't seem to care about this fact—a testament, perhaps, to her own realization of her exiled status and her desire to choose what she wants rather than what is socially acceptable—the reality of her association with Xander, Willow, and, to a certain extent, Giles assures her position on the margins of Sunnydale society. Wallace, at least initially, does the same for Veronica; his position as the new kid in school offers no real social caché to Veronica. In fact, her quick befriending and defense of Wallace seems to reify her as the defender of the downtrodden, friend of the friendless. While Wallace goes on to become a successful Neptune High basketball star in the later episodes of the first season, Veronica remains his exiled, outsider friend, always keeping his popularity separate from their friendship.[5]

Despite developing deep friendships, both protagonists remain distinctly isolated. Buffy is quick to point out that her responsibility is one her friends cannot share; in one particularly comical scene, as Buffy is about to fight, Willow recognizes Buffy's predominance by saying, "You're the Slayer—we're like the Slayerettes" ("The Harvest," Season

One). While Xander, Willow, Buffy, and Giles certainly become one in purpose in saving the world from an apocalypse every season, the categorization of Xander and Willow as Buffy's backup band of demon hunters emphasizes the primacy of Buffy and, by extension, her singular responsibility as the Slayer. Veronica ascribes much the same position to herself as detective, endowing her investigation into her best friend Lilly's murder a kind of mythic importance, and on herself, by extension, the responsibility for completing it successfully. While she does, halfway through the season, begin to share her information with her father, she keeps both her father and Wallace out of the loop during much of her investigation, asking them to supply her with pieces of information or play roles without ever privileging them with the whole story. Only at the end of the season does Veronica confide in Wallace about her drugging and rape, at the same time as Keith and Veronica join in solving Lilly's murder. Throughout the episodes, however, in her daily life, Veronica operates as much the lone wolf as Buffy does, solidifying for the audience and for the mythology of both series that these women are alone in their responsibilities.

The Power of the Exiled Perspective

> "Mark me down as skeptical."—Veronica Mars,
> "Meet John Smith," Season One

The enormous power of the exiled narrative perspective comes from its ability to see, and critique, the world differently and more cogently than a perspective originating within the established social structure. Both *Buffy the Vampire Slayer* and *Veronica Mars* embrace this power, consciously and conspicuously critiquing the seedy underbelly of "what's cool" and exposing the underpinnings of social, gender, and class dynamics. The ability of each protagonist to stand outside of, but not be completely alien to, those social structures offers credibility to their critique that normally wouldn't exist. These former insiders can see, now that they are outside the world that they once occupied, what doesn't work; their unique perspective encourages their audiences, through the audience's association with these exiled protagonists, to similarly interrogate the worlds in which they live.

One especially powerful weapon of the exiled protagonist is the witty verbal assault. Much has been written about the hyperverbalism of *Buffy the Vampire Slayer*. Critics have argued that Buffy's ability to "play with language in this way" is "tied to Slayage" and "it is not a role that just anyone can fill" (Overbey and Preston-Matto 2002, 75). Veronica is no slouch, either, when it comes to witty banter and amazing one-liners. *BtVS* creator Whedon himself lauds the series for its "deft, glorious wit," an essential ingredient that "give[s] *VM* more laughs than many sitcoms, and ... never grate[s] against the emotional brutality" that becomes one of the many thematic characteristics of the show (2006, par. 4). Not only do these exiled protagonists view the world differently, with more truth (or, as Whedon terms it in the case of *VM*, with "a knack for seeing through people and their inevitable fictions"), but also both Buffy and Veronica have the ability to articulate that truth when others cannot (2006, par.3). Both of these women demonstrate the power that comes from the margins in their language, and Veronica Mars, as "a complex, savvy outcast" demonstrates that "[t]he two Americas can only become one when those who are marginalized outthink and outlast those at the center"; part of their ability to do this comes from their humor, wit, charm, and brassy sense of verbal confidence (Abernathy 2004, pars. 1 and 8). These qualities offer them the powerful opportunity to comment, literally, on the world around them. No one can match them, and no one really tries.

Both shows, focused as they are on teenage life, take aim most obviously and clearly on the violent and dangerous world of the "in-crowd," demonstrating the ways in which each show's distinct mythology shapes its cultural commentary. Buffy's approach to the world, colored by occult lore, permeates her vision of the in-crowd and establishes the series-long metaphorical approach to social issues. In a first season episode appropriately named "The Pack," *BtVS* characterizes the behavior of the in-crowd, both before and after their accidental possession by the scavenging spirit of African hyenas, as inhuman. The high school students in question are the victims of an ancient Masai ritual gone wrong, which transfers the traits of the hyenas into the bodies of the students. Interestingly, however, we are introduced to the main members of this "pack" before their possession; their later "possessed" behavior is not much different than their self-satisfied cruelty as members of the in-crowd, an essential component of the episode's critique. The writers' choice to include Xander, a perpetual outsider, as the newest member of this new in-crowd, viscerally engages both audience and characters. Xander is unwittingly included when he enters the hyena exhibit to defend another student from the cruelty of the group. This inclusion of Xander, and the vast disparity between his actions before the possession and after, calls specific attention to the violence of such unkind behavior. Xander, Willow, and Buffy are on the margins of Sunnydale High society, and Xander's new position—and alarmingly different behavior—emphasizes the violent and personally devastating effects of the "in-crowd" of which everyone seemingly aspires to be a member.

The obvious animal characteristics aside, including an increasingly hyena-like laugh and a peculiar penchant for raw meat of any kind, the interpersonal violence exhibited by the pack is a clear critique on the common social impulse to "prey on the weak." As Buffy expresses concern to Giles about Xander's behavior, sure that some supernatural force must be responsible for the dramatic change in her friend, Giles downplays the behavior as a result of natural adolescent development. After chronicling his newly wretched behavior, Buffy waits for Giles's assessment, which he offers in one of the episode's funnier moments; "Ahh, it's devastating. He's turned into a 16-year old boy." Giles's argument that to "prey on the weak" is natural turns the supernatural into a more immediately accessible social phenomenon. This interpretation of the group's behavior makes their activities that much more resonant, and Buffy's desire to eliminate it rises to the level of explicit social critique.

The pack moves as one, and the episode demonstrates both their single-minded lack of individuality and the negative effect of that lack. In one slow-motion scene, the pack, now all wearing the same dark, earth-tones amid the bright patterns and unique colors worn by the other students on the quad, walk through the crowd with critical, smirking looks on their faces. The episode is full of these kinds of group staredowns of other students; each member of the pack seems to feed off of the negative actions of the other. Most poignantly, we see this when Xander viciously insults Willow in a scene that foregrounds the two longtime friends against a backdrop of the pack. They all look on, almost hypnotized by his actions, and seem to gain power and pleasure from the act. No one member seems to be able to act individually; when they are separated, the group is intent on seeking the missing member out.

In a scene set in gym class, the episode focuses attention on the real potential for emotional violence that such behavior creates. The members of this popular group systematically pick off the slow and the weak during a game of dodge ball, eventually leaving just Buffy and the male student they had been harassing early in the episode. Dodgeball is an interesting choice for this particular episode, as it elevates to sports metaphor the systematic alienation and Darwinian social selection inherent in high school life. Leaving Buffy alone, implicitly recognizing her power, the group bands together, literally, into a circle to "eliminate" the less popular student in a stunning and viscerally disturbing scene of group victimization. Buffy's ability to stare them down, her status as one strong enough to *not* be preyed upon by the in-crowd despite her alienated status from their social structure, offers her the ability to narrate this version of the violence of the social world without being caught up in it either as victim or perpetrator. The obvious message of this episode is that the in-crowd can be cruel, and the common experience of teenage alienation creates a resonant shared experience of exile within the audience that encourages disdain for such behavior. More interestingly, the episode's unique metaphorical approach to this issue subtly calls attention to the simultaneously shared desire for inclusion within this crowd while critiquing it as the mentality that results in such negative behavior.

Veronica Mars picks up where *BtVS* leaves off, elevating the incisiveness of the cultural commentary by stripping the metaphor and integrating the same issues within a realistic context of ethnic and socioeconomic separation. The class-based social hierarchy, transparent in its construction, indicates the unique *VM* approach toward these issues of inclusion—they're real, they're messy and complex, and they're at the heart of all of the show's storylines. Veronica becomes the interpreter of this class and social status language for Wallace, explaining the coined term "09er" to him and literally "reading" the party flyer that he finds undecipherable, explaining in the process that "it's in code so that undesireables—which, by the way, is you and me—don't show up" ("Credit Where Credit is Due," Season One). Veronica's ability to take on this task of cultural interpretation, to see and read the way Neptune's hierarchies are established and reinforced through the lens of her past experience, gives her a uniquely critical perspective.

As with the critique of the "desireable" and socially powerful in-crowd in *BtVS*, *Veronica Mars* highlights how a rigidly established and enforced social structure elides individual agency and how the lockstep behavior resulting from such groupthink becomes dangerous and emotionally devastating. Veronica, the only person equipped to transcend rigid class boundaries to see truth, reveals the issue at the heart of the episode's mystery, the clandestine relationship between Chardo, a PCH biker from the other side of the tracks, and Caitlin, Logan Echolls's rich girlfriend.[6] This exposure elicits a violent reaction from both groups as they attempt to contain the transgression. The initial confrontation finds Caitlin allowing the 09ers, a pack of white, overprivileged teenagers, to beat up Chardo for his transgression of their sexual territory; the confrontation is interrupted by the PCHers seemingly riding to Chardo's rescue as, after a brief conversation between the group leaders, the 09ers leave Chardo alone. Rather than resolving the situation peacefully, the leaders of the two very distinct social groups choose to keep their worlds completely separate, confronting the issue within their social groups. Chardo is exiled from the PCH Bike Club, abandoned by his cousin

Weevil, and beaten by his former friends as punishment for his betrayal of their social order.

The 09ers, while less overtly violent in their reaction, punish Caitlin nonetheless, exiling her in a typically high school manner. Logan refuses to look at her, and the entire group, without speaking, refuses to allow her entrance to their lunch table. Her exile, it seems, is as complete and as clearly communicated as Chardo's was through body blows. While Caitlin's catty behavior and Chardo's criminal acts seem to make their eventual punishment somewhat appropriate, the level to which their respective social cliques react to their transgressive affair borders on the ridiculous. The social critique implicit here is not focused on the rigid social hierarchy of high school or the cruelty of teenagers. Veronica's gaze, which originates from the outside of both of these groups, surveys a structure established by social stereotyping and maintained by mutual fears of miscegenation, issues critiqued again and again throughout the show's first season.

Confronting Gender and Identity in Buffy the Vampire Slayer

> "I'm an old-fashioned gal. I was raised to believe that men dig up the corpses and women have the babies."—Buffy Summers, "Some Assembly Required," Season Two

Buffy's role as a young woman negotiating two identities allows her particular insight into the issues of identity that permeate any depiction of adolescent life. Interestingly, *BtVS* concerns itself most with exposing common myths about socially proscribed identities, especially those related to gender and youth, and demonstrating the power of each individual. While we often see Buffy rebelling against the constrictions of being a Slayer, sometimes with quite negative consequences, the second season brings for both the audience and Buffy a recognition that her choice to abandon expectations associated with either of her identities (the high school Buffy and the Slayer Buffy) results in a further marginalized but much more powerful composite identity. Kendra, the second Slayer that we meet halfway through the second season, provides an interesting foil to Buffy in this regard. Kendra's limited approach to her role as Slayer, characterized by unquestioning obedience to the same rules and regulations that Buffy eschews, creates in her a technical mastery but a passionless approach to her calling.

As a result, Kendra is unable to see the world in the perceptive way that Buffy does, to negotiate the gray areas of the underworld effectively within her role as the Slayer. She lumps Angel, for example, in with every other vampire who deserves to be slayed, an assessment so glaringly off the mark at this point in the series that the audience is shocked by a lack of the perception they have come to expect. We share Buffy's view of the world, which asserts both the viability of maintaining a balanced life and the appropriateness of abandoning rigid, mindless, uninterrogated obedience to restrictions. We see normality in Buffy's ability to multitask, to choose to be normal amid the insanity of her world; her plan for a "pineapple pizza and teen video movie fest ... [p]ossibly something from the Ringwald oeuvre" after her showdown with Spike and Drusilla serves to alienate her further from both traditional teenage and the very untraditional Slayer worlds ("What's My Line? Part 2," Season Two). While Buffy's choices alienate her further from social norms, they also demonstrate how an individual, regardless of age or gender, has the power to choose one's destiny and, as a result, subverts myths of identity formation and of gender restriction.

BtVS consistently critiques traditionally held notions of gender as another facet of its examination of identity. The most obvious incarnation of this is Buffy's role as Slayer. Joss Whedon envisioned a character that would reverse traditional expectations. He wanted to recreate the "blond girl in the alley in the horror movie who keeps getting killed.... Literally, I just had that image, that scene, in my mind, like the trailer for a movie—what if the girl goes into the dark alley. And the monster follows her. And she destroys him" (Udovitch 2000, 60). We see the inversion of these gender expectations, obviously, through Buffy's strength and power as the Slayer, but this is especially true because she appears to be just a normal girl. Surprise at Buffy's role as Slayer for characters in the show is connected not to Buffy's inherent lack of intellect or ability, but strictly to her size. Stereotypes dictate that small equals weak, that women can be seen as objects, and that men are in control. In *BtVS*, those expectations are consistently reversed in an attempt to interrogate the validity of such unexamined stereotypes. Despite the strength that Whedon offers his Slayer, the strength is the strength of a metaphorical superhero; while engaging and resonant to viewers, that inversion of gender expectations remains somewhat distant from real-life experience.

While *BtVS* projects a remarkably homogenized society with regards to class and ethnic diversity, the series does take care to address how the marginalized groups depicted have limited access to social power. Being young, in Buffy's world, automatically means alienation from social power. Despite her ability to consistently save the world, Buffy still falls under the purview of the gatekeepers of cultural power. Buffy's narrow-minded nemesis, Principal Snyder, is constantly at odds with her, unable to see her as anything other than a rebellious troublemaker. When Giles, a relatively fair, impartial, and flexible adult role model, suggests that Principal Snyder give her the benefit of the doubt, the principal scoffs and calls Giles's faith in the students "weird." Christine Jarvis, in her analysis of teenage horror, argues that teachers, the figureheads of social power, "may be well-meaning but out of touch, or grotesque buffoons.... They are often revealed to be dangerous" (2001, 257). Such is certainly the case with Snyder. He interferes constantly with Buffy and her slaying duties, seemingly oblivious to the strange activities centered in his school, with an eye only towards her expulsion and metaphorical destruction.

Snyder is also exposed as a person unable to use power wisely or fairly. In "Band Candy," the teenaged Snyder misuses his power freely, threatening to reprimand a fellow teacher whom he sees intoxicated, gleefully announcing that he will use this information in her next performance evaluation—just because he can. His power, whenever it is wielded, is exercised unfairly. The choice of the Sunnydale Mayor as the major villain of Season Three furthers this critique of social power, seemingly coloring all figureheads of social structures as inherently evil. Buffy's interactions with these figures of power illuminate the true nature of corruption, making her role as exiled protagonist essential to the cultural commentary of the series.

While the show on the whole seems to carefully avoid issues of race and class, stereotyping is a topic interrogated as an extension of this abuse of social power. Being young, in Buffy's world, is the source of prejudice, as is being female and being associated with the occult. In one of the series' few direct attacks on stereotyping, prejudice, and the perils of mob rule, "Gingerbread" focuses its critique on prejudice born of fear. Buffy's mother, reacting to some tragic violence in the neighborhood that she believes results from occult activities, forms a community advocacy committee which begins, quite literally, a witch hunt. Joyce Summers degenerates from a relatively understanding, compassionate woman who wants to be supportive of her daughter's vampire slaying into a single-minded, unyielding woman who sees visions of dead children, orders school raids, and nearly executes the innocent in her mission to rid the world of the evils of witchcraft. Lockers are searched, books and personal belongings confiscated, and all civil liberties seemingly abandoned in favor of increased safety.

The fact that this strand of cultural commentary resonates, even nearly ten years later, in our current political climate testifies to the universality of its approach and delivery. Only Buffy and her friends, who recognize the irrationality of the mob's decisions, keep trying to find the truth, efforts that lead to the discovery of an alternate explanation for both the tragedies and Joyce's behavior. The literal witch-hunt in "Gingerbread" comments on all the similar metaphorical witch hunts present in society, campaigns of mob fervor that unfairly stereotype and castigate large groups of people because of fear. In a community charmed by the seeming justice and virtue of a mobocracy, only Buffy and her similarly alienated figures can see through the fog of assumption and panic to find the truth.

Class, Ethnicity, and Identity in Veronica Mars

> "I am projecting a ghetto aesthetic. Word."—Veronica Mars, "An Echolls Family Christmas," Season One

While *BtVS* contains its social commentary within a fantasy-framed mythology, *Veronica Mars* amplifies the resonance and accessibility of its social critique by removing the metaphorical distance and dealing directly with issues of ethnicity and class prejudice, along with the typical adolescent issue of identity formation. Veronica, like Buffy, is charged with balancing two different identities—high school student and detective. While both protagonists seek to integrate their identities, Veronica does a much better job of achieving this successfully, possibly because neither of her identities is dependent upon secrecy for its success. Her successful integration of these two identities into her everyday life is also a result of Veronica's belief in fluidity of identity, her unwillingness to be shackled by categories established by the social structures from which she is alienated.

Veronica occupies many different identities, many aliases, in her work as a detective. She seamlessly moves, in "The Wrath of Con," for example, from Veronica as detective into as many identities as it takes to solve her case without losing any sense of who she is. She becomes the dippy blonde Amber who "falls" for the con under investigation, the knee-sock wearing, black-wigged Gamegirl, and the sweater-wearing "nerd hag" to Wallace's math nerd persona among others. Wallace attempts to adopt this attitude of identity fluidity in the same episode but comically recognizes that, despite his disguise, he is still essentially himself: "pocket protector and I'm still full of pimp juice!"[7]

Identity is, in Veronica's eyes, complex, unique, and ever changing. That Wallace, her best friend, can say that he still doesn't understand her and that he has stopped trying is a testament to this philosophy. *VM*'s articulation of "identity" as a series of subject positions to be occupied temporarily rather than rigidly pre-constructed roles to adopt permanently argues a belief both in social mobility and individual change. In fact, Veronica's ability to transcend borders of identity while solving cases reflects her attitudes, and by extension the show's attitudes, towards the more complex issues of class and ethnic identity.

The cultural commentary of *VM* depends on the interconnectedness of class and ethnicity and the transparency of that connection within Neptune society. The establishment of Neptune as a fictional space depends upon the audience's understanding of the class divisions and the population of those within each class strata, and our recognition of Veronica's transgression of those structural borders is dependent on the same. *VM*'s elevation of the discourse on race and socioeconomic status by making such divisions so obvious—eliminating the middle class—is a distinctly unique position in teen TV. While some other shows have addressed the gulf between the classes (the glaringly upper-class-centric *Beverly Hills, 90210* and its descendent, *The O.C,* come to mind, as does *One Tree Hill,* all of which feature a token working class character to demonstrate the disparity between the two worlds), few come close to addressing the real issues underpinning such divisions. If Sunnydale is a remarkably white, upper middle-class, political issue-free zone, Neptune is its polar opposite. The 90909 zip code, white, rich, and spoiled, is juxtaposed against the multiethnic, distinctly working class neighborhoods on the outskirts of town.

The divisions are clear in the interactions between the residents, which in many episodes take on a distinctly "West Side Story" vibe.[8] While violence does occasionally play a part in maintaining the social distance between the two disparate groups, the gulf is widened by the stereotypes that each group embraces about the other. Despite their mutual penchant for biting one-liners and a shared lack of respect for authority, Logan Echolls and Weevil Navarro, the leaders of their respective groups, refuse to see their commonalities even when their actions demonstrate how well they work together. Even after bonding by punishing the teacher who gave them detention, they maintain comical, but distinctly stereotypical, attitudes. When discussing the potential of adding Weevil to his high-stakes poker game, which Weevil sees as an easy opportunity to scalp the rich boys, Logan says, "My only concern is property values going down if anyone sees you in my house without a leaf blower or a skimmer," of course capitalizing on the stereotypical attitude of Latinos as good for nothing but as outdoor service workers. Weevil plays off that stereotype, inverting it to reflect his own attitudes towards the rich 09ers: "You're concerned? I'm the one that's got to go up into the hills, all by myself. What if I run into a pack of you white boys, huh? On some clean, well-lit street? I could be bored to death" ("An Echolls Family Christmas," 2004). Veronica's ability to cultivate friendships with each, relying on both of them equally to help her in times of trouble, demonstrates her ability to bridge the gulf between class positions. She, because of her exiled status and belief in the fluidity of identity, does not adopt class as her defining identity marker and, as a result, demonstrates a great deal of freedom.

VM is concerned, throughout its first season, with accurately and realistically confronting issues that are confined to "very special episode" status on other shows. One of the most viscerally difficult issues that *VM* portrays is the violence that seems to permeate real life. Logan Echolls, despite being the big man on campus, is frequently beaten by his father; this truth is not discovered until the end of Season One and is never resolved. In its failure to resolve the issue, *VM* demonstrates that complex problems, even when confronted and eliminated, have long-lasting effects. Logan, while occasionally the villain and often the comic relief, is also broken. Violence extends to the world of romance as well: Veronica is date-raped; Lilly is murdered by her much-older lover; Carmen is videotaped during an indiscreet display and blackmailed; the details, fictional or true, of the sexual life of every student at Neptune High is up for sale to anyone willing to expose a fellow student for $10; and, at the end of the second season, a series of rapes at Hearst College seems to offer up a preview of the third season's complex mystery.[9]

Nothing is safe, nothing is sacred in Neptune, and Veronica's involvement with Mars Investigations makes that fact abundantly clear. Her desire to achieve truth at all costs—even when it involves being personally hurt in the process—comments carefully on the fact that such an impulse, however painful, is essential to recognizing the real ills of society. No true good can come from a cursory portrayal of deep and difficult issues. Like *Buffy*, *VM* will never have a "very special episode," because its entire philosophy of storytelling focuses on interrogating, carefully and skillfully, the violence, stereotypes, and divisions that infect Neptune society and, by extension, ours as well (Wilcox 1999).

The Price of Being Included

> "Don't forget. You're a high school girl. Do some high school girl things every once in a while."—
> Keith Mars, "Ruskie Business," Season One

> "Relax, Dad. I'm cutting pictures of Ashton out of *Teen People* as we speak."—Veronica Mars

Despite their embrace of the power and perception that comes from narrating from the margins, and their seeming successful mediation between two worlds, both Veronica and Buffy continue to seek inclusion within the traditional social worlds of high school life. Buffy, for example, when she realizes that she has been excluded from participating in that social world in any meaningful way, takes conscious steps to reintegrate herself. After approaching her favorite teacher for a recommendation and learning that the teacher didn't know her name, Buffy begins to desire her life before her days as the Slayer: "At Henry, I was prom princess, I was fiesta queen, I was on the cheerleading squad. The yearbook was, like, the story of me. Now it's senior year and I'm going to be one crappy picture one and one-eighth of one crappy page" ("Homecoming," Season Three). Buffy funnels this distress into a vicious campaign with Cordelia for homecoming queen. Cordelia scoffs at her decision, attributing Buffy's alienation from traditional high school rites of passage, in typical Cordelia-speak, to Buffy's involvement with "monsters, blood, and innards." Clearly, Buffy's motivations are to become a part of the established structure of high school society; for all intents and purposes, she wants to be a "normal" high school girl. Despite all of her efforts, however, as Cordelia skillfully points out, her Slayer status thwarts her quest. The homecoming race is no exception, as it degenerates into what the villains of the episodes termed "Slayerfest '98," a hunting game featuring Buffy and Cordelia (mistaken as Faith, another slayer) as the prey. Nothing in Buffy's world will ever truly be normal, despite her best efforts. Her Slayer status will always create an impenetrable gulf between her and the social world to which she seeks entry.

Veronica, by the beginning of the second season, craves the reinstatement of the normal teenage life she had before her best friend's murder, only to find that quest impossible. The second season premiere, aptly named "Normal Is the Watchword," chronicles Veronica's attempts to abandon the exile of her junior year and begin with a clean slate of social inclusion. Her best friend's murder now solved, Veronica believes that, perhaps she, too, can return to life before her marginalized existence. As if chronicling the ingredients of a "normal" life, Veronica tells the audience in voiceover: "Normal—that's the watchword. Sounds good, doesn't it? Senior year begins tomorrow and all appears hunky-dory. Best friend—check. Boyfriend—check." The ingredients are all there, but Veronica's life will never be normal. The girl that even the less-than-genius Sheriff Lamb recognizes as "pretty hard-boiled" can never be truly content to sit back and let the mysteries of Neptune be solved (or, more than likely, remain unsolved) by someone else with less capacity for wit, intelligence, and special insight. She can't possibly, just as Buffy can't, allow the people she cares about to be hurt when she has the capacity to do something about it.

Veronica recognizes this in that same episode, saying, "Just when I

think I'm out they pull me back in." The truth of Veronica's life can actually be articulated more powerfully by reversing that sentiment—just
when Veronica, Buffy, or any other powerfully marginalized figure
attempts to reintegrate within a social structure that will strip her of her
ability to see and act outside of those boundaries, her desire to be more
than a rigid stereotype and to be endowed with agency pulls her back
out to the margins where she can retain the most power. In demonstrating this desire for inclusion, an almost universal desire that resonates with
Teen TV audiences of any age, and its ultimate failure to truly motivate
Veronica or Buffy to abandon their powerful positions at the margins,
these series successfully redefine this desire to be included. Veronica and
Buffy may not be a part of the normal social structures that they comment on, but they certainly are a part of something larger, more important, and ultimately much more mature. These teenage impulses, then,
are abandoned in favor of a more mature approach to individual choice,
encouraging all who are pressured to be a part of something larger at
any cost to really consider the weighty consequences of that self-sacrifice.

Ultimately, for Buffy and Veronica as protagonists, the contradictory pairing of accepted alienation with a deep desire for inclusion mirrors the status of the series themselves. *BtVS*, while popular with its base
of dedicated fans, was never successfully integrated within the mainstream television community. The recipient of two Emmy awards, in
makeup and music, the series was nevertheless consistently passed over
for recognition for its writing and acting amidst massive fan lamenta-
tion (Laureman 2004). Anthony Stewart Head, who portrayed Giles during the entire seven year run of the series, commented on the series'
alienation from such recognition: "We're never going to get a bloody
award, because they don't know whether we're a comedy or a drama,
and you have to be one or the other" (Udovitch 2000, 60). *Buffy*'s desire
to transcend generic conventions, as well as its ability to combine fantasy with cultural commentary, is precisely what the creators and producers had in mind despite the fact that it resulted in alienation. Marti
Noxon, supervising producer, said, "You can get to the emotional truth
of things almost by sleight of hand, while people aren't really looking.
It's sort of like 'Here, look at the shiny vampire,' and behind that, there's
something really raw going on" (Udovitch 2000, 60).

Veronica Mars, often acknowledged by critics and viewers alike as
a "worthy *Buffy* heir," faced much the same reception from TV audiences (Nussbaum 2006, par. 4). While critically lauded and praised by
cult figures like Stephen King, Joss Whedon, and director Kevin Smith,
the show simply didn't find a large following, often only coming in sixth
place out of seven broadcast shows being rated on Wednesday nights

(NeptuneSite.com, April 6, 2007). Despite hoping that the timeslot after UPN's top-rated show, *America's Next Top Model*, would help pull in viewers for the 2005–06 season, show creator Rob Thomas recognized that the Wednesday night timeslot would be difficult, saying, "I just pray that the people with the TiVOs watch us and tape the other show, because we need it" (quoted in O'Hare 2005). Recognizing that competing against the ratings and fan-following juggernaut *Lost* was not a good idea, UPN decided midway through the second season to move the show, once again, to Tuesday nights at 9 P.M., demonstrating both a desire for the show to find a following and a recognition of its failure to do so. Despite their inability to achieve traditional methods of recognition, both of these series have cultivated a passionate fan base, solid DVD sales, and active academic interest.[10]

Just like the exiled perspectives of the protagonists, which offer so much fodder for cultural commentary for their respective series, *Buffy the Vampire Slayer* and *Veronica Mars*, like Teen TV in general, originate from the margins of established broadcast television. The unique, perceptive view of life, because of its marginalized status, offers Teen TV the opportunity to creatively and, often surreptitiously, communicate with an audience often underserved or pandered to by traditional attempts at such social critique. Rather than proverbially wagging their fingers at the audiences they appeal to, these shows slyly present the contradictions, hypocrisy, and tragedy of everyday life with a wink or a look of concern. Recognizing the intelligence of its audience, shows like *Buffy the Vampire Slayer* and *Veronica Mars* negotiate an outsider status with an ability to appeal universally to their audiences. While targeting teenagers by portraying them on the screen, these series often resonate with larger, broader, and older audiences than the demographic of the on-screen characters might suggest. One online fan, devoted to *BtVS* and a fan of *VM*, put it best:

> [*BtVS*] deals with milestone life experiences: first loves, family deaths, forbidden relationships, absentee parents, transitioning into adulthood, etc., in a context that is completely unlike our own lives. It is a way to examine, explore, and relive the moments that make us who we are in a way that is just removed enough to not be overwhelming.... But really, I just like it [misti, E!online.com, April 6, 2006) (http://www.eonline.com, accessed April 8, 2006].

The ability of these series to present a worldview that seems so parallel to our own, to let us experience, or re-experience, all of those firsts from a safe distance, makes these Teen TV shows far more powerful as cultural texts than audiences or critics have perhaps recognized before. They have become, in our increasingly high-tech and multimedia world, our newest serialized novels, with complex characters and culturally relevant plot points that engage viewers the way that great literature always does. We, like this fan, "like one liners ... [and] ... sassy broads" but we also like feeling that, for an hour or two every week, we can see the world in a much more perceptive way. For us, as audiences and for the protagonists we connect with, alienation means power.

Notes

1. I refer primarily here to the critical dialogue between Ian Watt (1957) and Michael McKeon (1987). Nancy Armstrong (1987) takes an interestingly similar position in her *Desire and Domestic Fiction*, arguing in part that the fictional construction of the domestic space in novels led to the changing of those same worlds in British society.

2. One could certainly argue for this revisionary impulse for *Lost*, with its embrace of the (sometimes literal) cliffhanger, but shows like *Desperate Housewives* are also revising the nighttime soap opera model by incorporating Gothic elements.

3. I don't include FOX in my consideration of "minor" networks since many of the top-rated shows on television are shown on FOX, even in the Teen TV market. According to ratings reported by TV Week, for the week of March 6, 2006, the highest rated Teen TV program was FOX's *The O.C.* with a 5.5 share (2nd place in its timeslot); that show is by far the highest rated of the programs commonly thought of as marketed toward teens. *Seventh Heaven* (2.5 share), *Smallville* (1.8 share), and *Gilmore Girls* (2.0 share) were the only other Teen TV programs that approached *The O.C.*'s dominant market share. While the highest rated show that week was FOX's *American Idol* (with a remarkable 17.9 share), the highest rated minor network show was the UPN's *America's Next Top Model* Cycle 6 premiere (with a 3.6 share) and the highest rated WB show was *Beauty and the Geek* (1.5 share). The numbers clearly indicate a wide gulf between the performance of highly rated mainstream programming on major networks and the ratings performance of the minor networks and Teen TV (http://www.tvweek.com/page.cms?pageId=10 [accessed April 23, 2007]).

4. While we learn in the penultimate episode of the first season that Veronica's "rape" was actually "consensual" sex while under the influence of drugs, Veronica believes it to be a rape until the moment of that discovery. I will, then, refer to it as such, since the psychological trauma of such a belief emphasizes the uniqueness of Veronica's choice to remain silent. The writers' decision to, at the end of the second season, revisit the "rape" and establish that, in addition to having consensual sex with Duncan under the influence of GHB, Veronica was also raped by Cassidy Casablancas, highlights the importance of this event to Veronica's identity at the margins.

5. Subsequent episodes of the first season of *Veronica Mars* chronicle Wallace's increasing popularity. When offered the opportunity to join Wallace's new version of the in-crowd, the athletes, Veronica refuses, keeping her relationship with Wallace separate and further demonstrating her position as an outsider.

6. Remarkably, the real-life, tabloid posterchild of the rich elite, Paris Hilton, plays the role of Caitlin; this casting choice emphasizes the characterization of the 09er group and engages with the audience's understandings of real-life American class distinctions.

7. This fluidity of identity, the ability to transition from alias to alias while remaining in control, is a fairly interesting gendered portrayal in current television programs. Veronica's performance of identity in this episode parallels that of Sydney Bristow on the *Alias*, who also routinely and successfully integrated disparate identities into one cohesive whole. No male character is so obviously charged with this primary task in current television programming, leading one to wonder why women are recognized with the ability to negotiate disparate identities seamlessly.

8. This underlying connection, along with a connection to the S.E. Hinton novel *The Outsiders* (1967), is slyly mentioned within the show itself through witty one-liners spoken by Logan and Veronica, respectively.

9. See Season One episodes, in order: "A Trip to the Dentist," "Leave It to Beaver,"

"M.A.D.," and "Like a Virgin." The final reference comes from the end of Season Two, "The Rapes of Graff."

10. Online campaigns for a second season encouraged fans to send dollar bills with "Veronica Mars is smarter than me" written on them to UPN executives, a reference to "The Clash of the Tritons," an episode in the first season.

References

Abernethy, Michael. 2004. "Control." *PopMatters*, 4 (October), available at http://www.popmatters.com (accessed January 21, 2006).

Armstrong, Nancy. 1987. *Desire and Domestic Fiction: A Political History of the Novel.* New York: Oxford University Press.

Hinton, S.E. 1967. *The Outsiders.* New York: Puffin (1997).

Jarvis, Christine. 2001. "School Is hell: Gendered Fears in Teenage Horror." *Educational Studies* 27, no. 3: 257–67.

Kristeva, Julia. 1996. "Stranger to Ourselves." In *Julia Kristeva: Readings in Exile and Estrangement,* ed. Anna Smith, 11–50. New York: St. Martin's.

Laureman, Kerry. 2006. "Introducing ... the Buffy!" *Salon.com,* September 17, available at http://www.salon.com (accessed April 8, 2006).

McKeon, Michael. 1987. *The Origins of the Novel: 1600–1740.* Baltimore: Johns Hopkins University Press.

Nussbaum, Emily. 2006. "Revenge of the Niche." *New York,* February 13, available at http://www.nymag.com (accessed April 8, 2006).

O'Hare, Kate. 2005. "The Cool Kids Hang with 'Veronica Mars.'" *The Buffalo News,* October 2.

Overbey, Karen Eileen, and Lahney Preston-Matto. 2002. Staking in Tongues: Speech Act as Weapon in *Buffy.* In *Fighting the Forces: What's at stake in Buffy the Vampire Slayer,* eds. Rhonda V. Wilcox and David Lavery, 73–84. Lanham, MD: Rowman and Littlefield.

Said, Edward. 2000. "Intellectual Exile: Expatriates and marginals." In *The Edward Said Reader,* eds. Moustafa Bayoumi and Andrew Rubin, 369–81. New York: Vintage.

TV Week. 2006. Weekly television ratings chart, March 6-March 12, available at http://www.tvweek.com/page.cms?pageId=10 (accessed April 23, 2007).

Udovich, Mim. 2000. "What Makes Buffy Slay?" *Rolling Stone,* May 11, 60.

Watt, Ian. 2001. *The Rise of the Novel.* Berkeley: University of California Press.

Whedon, Joss. 2005. Ace of Case. *Entertainment Weekly,* October 14, 131.

Wilcox, Rhonda V. 1999. "There Will Never Be a 'Very Special' *Buffy: Buffy* and the Monsters of Teen Life." *Journal of Popular Film and Television* 27, no. 2: 16–23.

6. Riding the Third Wave: The Multiple Feminisms of *Gilmore Girls*

Francesca Gamber

"She named me after herself ... she says her feminism just kind of took over." These words help introduce viewers to teenaged protagonist Lorelai "Rory" Gilmore during the pilot episode of the CW series *Gilmore Girls*. She said it: the F word. Almost as soon as the second wave of feminist activism arose in the mid–1960s, commentators began pronouncing its death; *Time* magazine alone has done so more than one hundred times since 1969 (Pozner 2003; Baumgardner and Richards 2000). At the dawn of the twenty-first century, feminism seems to be faring badly. Long gone is the clear-headed leadership of women like Gloria Steinem, and the sense of purpose and identifiable policy goals that galvanized women around the passage of the Equal Rights Amendment for a decade. Most women born after 1970, charged Ginia Bellafante in a widely-cited 1998 obituary for feminism, define women's empowerment in such vacuous terms as "fashion spectacle, paparazzi-jammed galas, mindless sex talk ... a whole lot of stylish fluff" (54). Perhaps even more damage has been done to the survival of feminism as a political movement not by the public discourses created by women who would gladly call themselves feminists but by the tendency of other women to refuse that label all together. These women often begin statements with, "I'm not a feminist, but ..." because to be a "feminist" means never shaving your legs, never wearing makeup or a bra, and to the extent possible, being a lesbian.

In the midst of this debate, Rory Gilmore's statement indicates that there is at least one place where feminism unquestionably lives: Stars Hollow, Connecticut, the fictional town in which *Gilmore Girls* is set. While many observers bemoan the tendency of young women to find their feminism in the "stylish fluff" of popular culture, recourse to *Gilmore Girls* at a historical moment in which few can agree whether or not feminism is alive, let alone how it should be defined, is understandable. For its part, *Gilmore Girls* doesn't disappoint. The series, which premiered in 2000, centers on the relationship between single mom Lorelai Gilmore and her daughter Rory, whom Lorelai had at age sixteen. The dual focus on both adult and adolescent characters has enabled the series to appeal to an audience not solely composed of teenagers. This essay, however, will concentrate on the ways in which the series represents feminism to its teen viewers as it follows Rory through high school and college.

Gilmore Girls is indebted to the success of second-wave feminism in bringing issues like teen pregnancy and single motherhood to mainstream television. From that foundation, it goes on to depict the most recent iteration of feminism, a so-called third wave that arose in the early 1990s, not as a uniform program but as a matter of choice from among several different models of womanhood. Throughout the series, Rory confronts the feminisms inhabited by her mother, grandmother, and her peers, trying them on for size through two key televisual means: dress and language. Yet Rory never exactly mimics any one of these models, instead crafting her own feminism from her experiences. This self-fashioning is especially prominent after Season Four, in which the series takes Rory's first year of college as the start of her transition from acting out different feminist models to creating her own. By depicting third wave feminism to young viewers as the process of encountering multiple feminisms and choosing one's own, *Gilmore Girls* provides a valuable window onto the current state of feminism, both for cultural analysts and its impressionable teen audience.

Defining the Third Wave

Before engaging with *Gilmore Girls*, a brief foray into the history of feminism in the United States will contextualize the sort of representation the series offers. In the 1950s and 1960s, women fueled the burgeoning movement for racial equality and civil rights as well as the parallel student movement emerging on college campuses. By the mid–1960s, however, civil rights organizations like the Student Nonviolent Coordinating Committee had embraced a Black Power philosophy that required the ejection of its white members and elevated African American men over women as movement leaders. Within the student movement, women tended to be relegated to such traditionally gendered chores as getting coffee and making copies and were largely shut out of higher levels of leadership and decision-making (Evans 1980).

Around the same time, women who were not involved in these movements were galvanized by Betty Friedan's *The Feminine Mystique* (1963), which voiced the dissatisfaction felt by thousands of Cold War suburban housewives confined to domesticity. These disaffected women forged their own organizations, magazines, films, and other cultural means of expressing their demand for equal treatment in the workplace as well as in the home. By the mid–1970s, however, the movement's popularity ironically brought about its decline. Members of varied racial, ethnic, and class backgrounds criticized the middle-class white women who led the movement for reproducing racism within feminist organizations and defining movement priorities only on their terms. Many of these women founded their own groups, and by the late 1970s, there seemed to be as many feminisms as there were feminists. There were groups for African Americans, Latinas, Asian Americans, lesbians, and sex workers, and they could seldom agree with each other on goals and priorities. In the meantime, what Susan Faludi has famously described as a conservative "backlash" followed in the 1980s that veritably made feminism a dirty word. The Equal Rights Amendment failed to secure ratification in 1982, and films like *Fatal Attraction* (1987) vilified feminists as unnatural women whose preference for career over family could have homicidal consequences (Evans 1980; Rosen 2000; Springer 2005; Faludi 1991; Felsenthal 1981; Critchlow 2005).

Historians usually identify fragmentation over racial differences as the primary cause of the disagreements that sapped feminist momentum by the 1980s. The daughters (and sons) of second-wave feminists who grew up during the 1980s have cited reasons of their own for their sense of alienation from their mothers' movement. "For many of us it seems that to be a feminist in the way that we have seen or understood feminism is to conform to an identity and way of living that doesn't allow for individuality, complexity, or less than perfect personal histories," wrote Rebecca Walker, the woman credited with coining the term "the third wave," in 1995 (xxxiii).[1] Rather than mimicking the second wave, young feminists of the 1990s created a third wave that continued second-wave critiques of gender inequality but made room for women's varied racial, ethnic, class, and sexual identities and allowed women to enjoy all of the elements of what Jennifer Baumgardner and Amy Richards term "pink-packaged femininity." Many second-wave feminists would argue that this implied characterization of them as joyless, bra-burning man-haters is an unfair one. But so the perception goes, and so has third-wave feminism defined itself against it.[2]

Despite the underlying imperative in third wave feminism to right the wrongs of the second wave, most of its practitioners acknowledge not only their inheritance of a political agenda from the second wave but also their upbringing in a culture transformed by second wave agitation. For third wave feminists, a woman's right to reproductive freedom or the ability to combine both work and domesticity is a matter of course, and this ubiquity represents a hard-won struggle pursued by the second wave. "For our generation, feminism is like fluoride," write Baumgardner and Richards. "We scarcely notice that we have it—it's simply in the water" (2000, 17). In this way, *Gilmore Girls* itself is descended from feminist battles in the realm of culture and their demands for more realistic depictions of women in film, television, the press, and other media. In the 1970s, *The Mary Tyler Moore Show* acquainted mainstream audiences with the character of the single professional woman that was a sitcom staple by the 1990s; *Julia* familiarized viewers with the single working mother. For all the criticism the medium receives, television continued to achieve notable successes in the depiction of women in the 1990s, and *Gilmore Girls* reflects many of these advances: the wisecracking working mom of *Roseanne*, the frank depiction of teen sexuality that characterized *Beverly Hills, 90210* and *My So-Called Life*, the intelligent and fast-paced dialogue of *Dawson's Creek*, the strong teen girl heroine of *Buffy the Vampire Slayer*.

Gilmore Girls makes its own contribution to positive depictions of women in television through its feminist consciousness (even if its main characters are, as in so many programs, conventionally beautiful middle-class white women). Many reviews of the program refer to the show's creator, Amy Sherman-Palladino, as a feminist. One critic described the series as a "smart, vibrant woman's world" (Tucker 2003, 87). Within Stars Hollow, men continue to occupy the elected office of town selectman, but many town businesses are owned by women, married women or women with children work, and even the town mechanic is a woman. When Rory goes to college, her dorm room is adorned with pro-choice posters and another featuring Gloria Steinem dressed as a Playboy bunny, referencing Steinem's 1963 investigation into working at the Playboy clubs that became a well-known news article (Steinem 1995b). Other commentators cite *Gilmore Girls* when ticking off series that feature women in prominent roles or non-traditional positions, and in 2001, the National Organization for Women placed the series at the top of its list of recommended programs.[3]

Yet *Gilmore Girls* may be described as a "feminist" series not simply because its central characters are women. It also operates within a third wave landscape that acknowledges the multiplicity of feminisms among women and presents them all rather than attempting to reduce them to a single program. According to the chronology that the show establishes, Lorelai was born in the late 1960s, positioning her within the age group responsible for crafting third wave feminism. Indeed, women born around this time have written many of the foundational works of third wave feminism. Yet, the series also makes feminism an issue for Rory, who would have been born in the mid–1980s, thus pushing third wave feminism into what remains a largely uncharted age group. The show uses distinctively third-wave tools to represent Rory's engagement with multiple feminist models—dress and language. The series pilot establishes the primacy of these two elements when it refers to Lorelai's skills in making and altering clothing and Rory's love of books.

Many third wave feminists have identified popular culture as a crucial ground for the articulation of feminist messages. Some feminists—both younger and older—have criticized this aspect of third wave feminism as frivolous and apolitical; what does it matter that a CW series focuses on a single mom when there is still no Equal Rights Amendment? Yet third wave feminists see their emphasis on culture as political in and of itself through what Baumgardner and Richards define as "Girlie" feminism (2000, 135–38). Girlie feminism revels in the bric-a-brac of traditional femininity that second-wave feminists rejected, including clothes shopping, nail polish, makeup, and gendered toys. "For Girlie girls," writes Rebecca Munford, "'femininity' is not opposed to feminism, but is positioned as central to a politics of agency, confidence and resistance" (2004, 148). Rather than acknowledging that, for example, dress is one of many ways in which society assigns and perpetuates arbitrary gender designations, Girlie feminists reclaim it as a means of exercising ownership and choice over their bodies. Indeed, as the epitomal second wave feminist Gloria Steinem puts it, "Feminism has always stood for the right to bare, decorate, cover, enjoy, or do whatever we damn well please with our bodies" (1995, xvii).[4]

Dress becomes a less problematic means at the disposal of a television series for exploring different models of womanhood and feminism precisely because feminist theorists have argued its artificiality so persuasively. As Judith Butler asserts in *Gender Trouble*, "Gender is an identity tenuously constituted in time ... a performative accomplishment which the mundane social audience, including the actors themselves, come to believe" (1990, 140–41).[5] Historians of children's dress in the United States have buttressed this assertion of performativity by demonstrating that clothing for boys and girls underwent periods of sharp differentiation at times of heightened anxiety over the disruption of accepted gender roles, particularly in the 1890s and 1950s (Paoletti 1997; Rubinstein 2000; Bederman 1995). *Gilmore Girls* makes use of the performativity of gender through dress as well as language as Rory crafts her own feminism from the models she encounters. This sense of flexibility and play are, indeed, characteristic of third wave feminism, too.

"You're me"/"I'm not you"

The immediate task facing Rory in the navigation of multiple feminist models is that of distinguishing herself from her mother. The premise of *Gilmore Girls* is that Rory and Lorelai are extremely close; the age difference is not great, they share the same name, and they often share the same wardrobe, leading one reviewer to beg, "Someone please remind them they're not a peer group" (Bellafante 2004; Ostrow 2004). Lorelai is certainly Rory's initial and probably most influential feminist model. Lorelai's feminism manifests itself in her dogged insistence on her independence from her parents, Emily and Richard. When she became pregnant as a teenager, she refused her wealthy parents' urging to marry Rory's father. She later left her parents' home with an infant Rory and moved into the aptly-named Independence Inn, rejecting her family's money and privilege to work as a maid. Lorelai eventually became the manager of the inn and, in Season Five, opens her own inn with her best friend. Lorelai is also in no hurry to get married, calling off one engagement in Season Two; when she does get engaged at the end of Season Five, it is she who pops the question to boyfriend Luke Danes.

For her part, however, Lorelai is conscious of the mistakes she has made and takes pains to keep Rory from repeating them. In the pilot, Rory objects to leaving Stars Hollow High School to attend the exclusive prep school Chilton, and Lorelai discovers this is because she has a crush on a boy. "You're me," she tells Rory sarcastically. When Rory protests, Lorelai reports, "Really? Someone willing to throw important life experiences out the window to be with a guy? It sounds like me to me" ("Pilot"). When Rory stays out all night with her boyfriend Dean after attending a school dance, Lorelai's mother Emily salves what must be years of hurt feelings by taunting Lorelai with the idea that Rory will repeat Lorelai's reckless past. Despite the doubts she expressed in the pilot, Lorelai tells Emily, "Rory is a good kid, mom. She's not me" ("Rory's Dance").

Rory attempts to mimic Lorelai's behavior several times, and the result usually is not a good one. In the first season, Rory and Dean's breakup is precipitated by Rory's inability to say, "I love you," a stumbling block Lorelai blames herself for passing on to Rory. "When it comes to love and relationships, I don't necessarily want you to be like me," Lorelai tells her ("P.S., I Lo..."). When Rory loses her virginity to Dean, who is married to someone else at this point, at the end of Season Four, she fires back at a disappointed Lorelai that Lorelai had her own tryst with Rory's father Christopher while he was engaged to another woman. "So this is all my fault?" Lorelai asks. "I set one crappy example for you and you have no choice but to follow in my footsteps?" ("Raincoats and Recipes"). In the fifth season, Rory again mimics her mother's forwardness in the realm of sexual behavior after Christopher glowingly describes his and Lorelai's first kiss as teenagers at the reception following Emily and Richard's renewal of vows. "Said she just wanted to know what it would be like," he says. Equipped with this example, Rory corners her latest crush, Logan Huntzberger, in an empty room and kisses him. "I just wanna know what it would be like," she says, repeating Lorelai's phrase. It would be tempting to read this encounter as Rory practicing an inversion of gender roles; when it occurs, she is serving as her grandfather's best man for the renewal ceremony and wearing a pantsuit and tie. But the exchange with Christopher and her use of the same words Lorelai used indicate that Rory is trying on her mother's model for size, not trying to be a man. Things end badly: Lorelai, Christopher, and Luke interrupt Rory and Logan with much shouting ("Wedding Bell Blues").

Gilmore Girls thus makes the point that simply assuming her mother's model of feminism will not suffice for Rory. This point mirrors one that is made by third wave theorists as well. Many of them challenge the wave model itself for positing the second and third waves as separate and oppositional generations, a construct that leaves young feminists with only the choice of rejecting or accepting their mothers' feminism and shuts older women out of third wave feminism all together. These critics argue that this framework invites conflict rather than cooperation, and reassert common interests across feminist generations. "As Third Wave women," write Baumgardner and Richards, "we no longer have to measure our success by how far away we got from our mothers' lives. A feminist daughter who lives her life differently from her mom has really learned feminism, not just passively inherited it" (2000, 214–15). Lorelai's insistence on ensuring that Rory's life will be different from her own, then, is also problematic, for Rory's feminism cannot be defined solely in accordance with or in opposition to that of her mother's.

Seasons One–Three: "I don't wish to be her, exactly"

The first three seasons of *Gilmore Girls* find Rory actively engaging different feminist models and demonstrate this process of trial and error through means of dress and language. Yet just as she does when confronted with her mother's example, Rory tries on these other models of feminism but ultimately modifies them in her own way, and the instances in which she simply mimics them usually produce conflict. From the start, the series presents Rory as smart, thoughtful, and certain about her ambitions. Both Lorelai and Rory identify her transfer to Chilton as a necessary step toward eventually attending an Ivy League school and becoming a journalist. When Rory begins attending Chilton in the first season, her transition from one school to another and what that transition signifies to Rory are communicated through her new requirement of wearing a school uniform. She understands that in attending Chilton, she will be surrounded by students who are as dedicated to their studies as she is: "And we get to wear uniforms," she tells her best friend, Lane Kim. "No more having people check you out to see what jeans you're wearing 'cause everyone's dressed alike in boring clothes and just there to learn" ("Pilot"). Clad in her new uniform, she meets the headmaster on her first day at Chilton and describes her career goal as "being" journalist Christiane Amanpour. When the Headmaster questions why Rory doesn't want to "be" Cokie Roberts, Oprah, or Rosie O'Donnell, he is quick to point out the implication that Rory simply wishes to imitate someone else. Rory is equally quick to point out that while Christiane Amanpour is a feminist model for her, she does not intend to replicate it "exactly," only "to do what she does." Rory begins Chilton with concrete goals and a role model she has deemed more appropriately feminist than others ("The Lorelais' First Day at Chilton").

Rory's subjection of feminist models in popular culture to her own feminist standards is also apparent in her appreciation for *The Donna Reed Show* in a memorable episode in the first season. At the outset, Lorelai and Rory ridicule the show's ideal of the "perfect 50s family" as the fabrication of "a script/Written by a man." Later in the episode, Rory and Dean get into an argument over what the show represents, which to Rory is "the whole concept that [a woman's] one point in life is to serve somebody else." But when Rory surprises Dean by dressing up in an old-fashioned shirtdress, heels, and pearl necklace and cooking him dinner, she reveals that the model of womanhood Donna Reed represented was more forward-thinking than it appeared on television. Rory informs Dean that Reed "was an uncredited producer and director on her television show, which made her one of the first woman television executives"

("That Damn Donna Reed"). Before literally trying on the model of womanhood represented by Donna Reed, Rory first uncovers Reed's hidden defiance of the very subordination in whose service her television character was employed. It turns out that Donna Reed is not the same person as "Donna Reed," and just as she does with Christiane Amanpour, Rory decides that the real-life Donna Reed is acceptably feminist.

Her encounter with feminist models outside of popular culture is more complicated. While Lorelai pointedly rejected her parents, their social world, and their expectations for her, Rory is more willing to experiment with the model of womanhood represented by her grandmother. At first glance, Emily seems an unlikely feminist model for a young woman: she does not work outside of the home and is very much a society matron, planning parties and participating in a social circle populated by other members of the Daughters of the American Revolution (DAR) and the wives of Richard's business colleagues. After Emily and Richard agree to pay for Rory's tuition at Chilton, Lorelai and Rory renew their relationship with the elder Gilmores in the form of a weekly dinner and thereby re-enter their social world. For both mother and daughter, presence in this world has a dress code; they always wear nice, often frilly, dresses when attending dinner. Rory goes even deeper into the Gilmores' elite social setting to please her grandmother, and this is again symbolized by conforming to a dress code. In the second season, Rory dons a white dress and long white gloves to participate in a DAR debutante ball. Clearly, however, Rory does not approach the coming-out as the other girls do, making her involvement in it less imitative and more tongue-in-cheek, as seen in Rory's astonishment when one girl tells her gravely that "the two minutes you are standing on those stairs tonight will determine the social status for the rest of your life" ("Presenting Lorelai Gilmore"). Unlike the other debutantes, Rory is not concerned with cementing her own social status and participates in the event only because, as she puts it to a critical Lorelai, "it's just really, really important" to Emily. Rory's willingness to try on Emily's model of womanhood (figured literally in her debutante ball get-up) nonetheless exemplifies a third-wave perspective that understands there are lessons to be learned from your mother's—or your grandmother's—feminism.

Even more influential than her forays into the Gilmores' elite social world, however, is Rory's observation of her grandparents' relationship. Although Emily is in many ways a traditional wife, her interaction with Richard in fact does not resemble the "feminine mystique" model of the 1950s in which the man is king of the proverbial castle. Their marriage seems to belong to a much older tradition, one that the historian Laurel Thatcher Ulrich has identified as existing in colonial America before the rise of stringent separate spheres for men and women. These marital relationships recognized distinct areas in which husbands or wives exercised authority, but they were also predicated on mutuality, respect, and obligation, not domination and subordination (Ulrich 1982). At various points in the series, Emily prevails upon Richard to make peace with Lorelai and Rory in order to preserve their relationships with them, like insisting that he take Rory golfing even when he protests. Conversely, when Lorelai turns down a second date with the son of one of Emily's society friends, Richard instructs her to change her mind because the aftermath of the refusal could mean that Emily loses her prominence in the DAR. Indeed, when Richard ignores one of these entreaties in the fourth season, Emily separates from him briefly.

Rory comes to expect the same mutual obligation in her relationships with her boyfriends. Although he visibly does not want to, Dean dutifully attends dinner at Emily and Richard's home, enduring a tongue-lashing from Richard, and escorts Rory to her debutante ball in a tuxedo. The absence of mutuality is what ultimately dooms Rory's relationship with Jess, the brooding ne'er-do-well nephew of Luke Danes, in Season Three. Jess reluctantly goes to dinner at the grandparents' home but leaves in the middle of it after an argument with Rory. He also never makes concrete plans to see her. By the end of the season, Jess fails out of high school and leaves town without escorting Rory to her prom.

Another feminist model comes into Rory's life in the form of her father's girlfriend, Sherry, a successful cosmetics sales executive. When Sherry becomes pregnant unexpectedly, her baby shower is a prime opportunity for elaborating on the feminism she represents. Lorelai is the only shower attendee who has had children; all of Sherry's friends are busy career women who say they have neither "the time" nor "the guy" to have children. They also recall how surprised they were to hear that Sherry, who is as career-driven as they are, was pregnant, compliment her on staying so slender during her pregnancy, and throw around phrases like "green's the new pink" when discussing baby trends. Sherry's ill preparedness for pregnancy and motherhood becomes apparent as she describes scheduling her C-section around a presentation for work. "A half hour before I had Rory, I was eating a pepper sandwich and watching TV," Lorelai marvels in response ("Take the Deviled Eggs").

Sherry, who also prints up invitations to her Cesarean, goes into labor prematurely, and none of her friends can join her at the hospital because they are all working. When Rory arrives, Sherry moans, "This wasn't supposed to happen until next week. I wrote it down." She enlists Rory to help her rearrange her work responsibilities to accommodate the early labor, and Rory symbolically tries on this career-centered feminism by putting on an cell-phone headset, making phone calls, and tracking down a fax machine. Yet, when Sherry asks Rory to don a hospital gown and gloves and join her in the delivery room when Christopher is late, Rory's playacting comes to an end. She desperately calls Lorelai, exclaiming, "I don't want gloves. I don't want a gown. I don't want to be in there" ("Dear Emily and Richard"). Rory's process of trying on different models of womanhood stops when she is asked to assume the costume reserved for the baby's father. The ways in which the career-driven woman embodied by Sherry and her friends is caricatured in these two episodes provide a negative example for Rory, one that reaches its fruition in the fifth season when Lorelai and Rory discover that Sherry has left Christopher and their infant daughter to take a job in Paris.

A final feminist model in the first three seasons does not come from someone older than Rory. A strong counterpoint to the problematic generational model of feminism comes from acknowledging the influence that one's peers can wield. For Rory, this influential peer is Chilton classmate Paris Geller, whose feminism comes in the form of a superhuman work ethic and commitment to gaining admission to an Ivy League college. In the second season, Paris sets Rory straight about what it takes to get into Harvard. "You need more than good grades and test scores to get you in.... It's the extras that put you over the top," Paris explains ("Hammers and Veils"). On the same afternoon that Rory receives this revelation, she breaks plans with Dean to work on her resume in language given to her by Paris: "Good grades aren't enough." Another fight ensues between Rory and Dean, and gradually Rory comes to see the flaws in Paris's thinking. By the time they graduate from high school, it is Rory who exercises influence over Paris, encouraging her to relax and reminding her that there is more to life than school.

The technique of trying on different feminist models through dress and language, as part of a young woman's development of her own feminism, is not confined to Rory in *Gilmore Girls*. Rory's best friend Lane also tries out different models of womanhood, although her process is largely defined in opposition to the strict rules imposed by her devout Korean Christian mother. When viewers first see Lane in the pilot, she is walking to school with Rory and, now safe from her mother's surveillance, pulling a rock music t-shirt over the shirt she is already wearing. Lane deceives her mother by hiding clothes and makeup her mother would find objectionable beneath the floorboards in her bedroom. She even makes a brief attempt at asserting herself by dying her hair purple but loses her nerve and dyes it back to its natural color. Only when Lane's mother discovers her stockpile of contraband clothes, makeup, and CDs and forces her to move out can Lane fully inhabit the feminist model she has crafted for herself.

Season Four and Beyond: "It's what I saw. So I wrote it."

Third wave feminism, its founding writers have claimed, refuses to prescribe a single means of being a feminist but rather recognizes "paradox, conflict, multiplicity, and messiness" (Dicker and Piepmeier 2003, 16). As a result, there seem no longer to be hard-and-fast rites of passage that deliver all girls from childhood to feminist womanhood. Third wave feminists have rejected the idea that feminism is only for adults, broadening their appeal through teen magazines like *New Moon* and events like Take Our Daughters to Work Day to foster empowerment in girls and young women. Not even the loss of virginity stands as a certain departure from adolescence to adulthood, with today's young women deciding for themselves when and whether to have sexual activity. They foster a respect for "sexual individualism" that refuses to invest virginity, and the loss of it, with the heavy significance with which it is usually associated (Baumgardner and Richards 2000; Kamen 2000). For Rory, *Gilmore Girls* selects her transition from high school to college in Season Four to initiate a shift in her engagement with multiple feminist models. In Season Four and beyond, Rory becomes much less invested in the use of dress and language as means of inhabiting other women's feminist models and much more active in using them to forge her own model. Her college years are marked by an emphasis on linguistic integrity and originality. Dress, while less prominent in these seasons, comes to signify Rory's deeper involvement in the aristocratic social world occupied by her grandparents.

Dress is central to presenting the start of Rory's college career as a portentous rite of passage. Shortly after arriving for her first year at Yale, Rory no longer has to wear her Chilton uniform. She also cuts her long hair, a change that was so controversial when it was done by the title character on the WB series *Felicity* that Amy Sherman-Palladino had declared to a newspaper in 2001, "No one on 'Gilmore Girls' will cut their hair, ever" (quoted in Fazzone 2001, 16). At the start of Season Four, Rory signals the declining importance that dress, as a form of play-acting, will assume. In the first episode, Rory turns down an opportunity to dress up as the Ice Cream Queen for the grand opening of Taylor Doose's ice cream shop. After rattling off a list of the costumes Rory has put on for other town events, a chagrined Taylor says, "You belong to the Ivy Leagues right now. It's time to cut those small-town ties and ... have one of those high-class naked parties with that Bush girl" ("Ballrooms & Biscotti"). Tellingly, when Rory is no longer available to put on a costume and participate in town events like always, Taylor's response is to imagine her attending a "naked" party. It seems that in the first three seasons, as Rory was engaging other feminist models in search of her own, she was already inhabiting a Rory model that involved, in part, wearing her Chilton uniform and wearing costumes for town events. Now in college, she gives less thought to dress, even seeing it as an inconvenience.

Rory reiterates her departure from this earlier model of herself in Season Five when Anna, a Chilton student interested in applying to Yale, comes for a visit and expresses excitement at the prospect of no longer having to wear a uniform. "Wait 'til you're late for class and it takes you twenty minutes to put together an outfit," Rory replies ("But Not as Cute as Pushkin"). This exchange occurs as Rory is showing an overstimulated Anna her favorite campus library, indicating the increased significance that language has assumed for Rory in crafting an authentic feminism. Rory begins writing for the *Yale Daily News*, and one of her first pieces is a critical review of a student dance performance. Lorelai, Emily, and Richard all agree that the piece was quite harsh. "It's what I saw. So I wrote it. That's what the editor told me to do," Rory insists ("Die, Jerk"). In Season Five, Rory hopes to impress her editor with a story on illegal downloading, but Paris casts doubt on the originality of such an article. In response, Rory proposes an exposé on the Life and Death Brigade, a secret student society that no previous reporter has been able to penetrate. "I want to do this story," she says. "I want to find this club, track them down, get on the inside" ("Norman Mailer, I'm Pregnant!"). Rory's investment of language with her sense of self is so strong that when Mitchum Huntzberger, a newspaper executive, tells her that she doesn't have what it takes to be a journalist, she briefly decides to drop out of college. Later, she overcomes this self-doubt, returns to Yale, and becomes editor of the *Yale Daily News*.

As Rory formulates an individual feminist model no longer based on trial-and-error of other models, dress functions as an index to her growing comfort in Emily and Richard's elite world, a world that also dovetails with the social setting she encounters at Yale. In the fourth season, Emily and Richard throw an aforementioned party to introduce Rory to the sons of their Yale-alumni friends. Emily and Richard similarly threw a birthday party for Rory in Season One, even giving her a dress to wear (which, true to form, Lorelai then alters). In the first season, Rory is uncomfortable at this party because Emily and Richard have invited Chilton classmates whom Rory still doesn't know well; when Emily instructs her to give a speech to thank her guests for attending as the "responsibility" of the "hostess," Rory refuses and storms off. By Season Four, that discomfort is gone. Rory allows Emily's makeup artist and hairdresser to ready her for the party and accepts Emily's offer to wear her diamond necklace, earrings, and tiara. She is dismayed to learn the true nature of the party, which she had thought was only for Emily and Richard's alumni friends, but she stays and even enjoys herself.

Rory's participation in the aristocratic environment Lorelai rejected is furthered by her relationship with Logan Huntzberger, the son of the aforementioned newspaper publisher. Initially, Rory interacts with Logan and this social world as a spectator in pursuit of her story on the Life and Death Brigade, of which Logan is a member. Logan allows Rory to accompany him to a Life and Death Brigade event, even providing her with a fancy evening dress to wear. But when Logan reminds her that legendary journalists such as George Plimpton, Ernie Pyle, and Hunter S. Thompson were great because they were willing to participate, Rory is convinced to take part in a stunt. This event marks the start of Rory and Logan's courtship, thus combining her pursuit of linguistic originality with the role of dress as a signifier of her new comfort in elite social settings.

By the second half of the fifth season, discussions of Rory's maturation occur in ways that are more abstract. Instead of watching Rory literally try on different models of womanhood, various characters refer to what "kind" of "girl" Rory is. Though both Logan and Lorelai have their doubts, Rory willingly begins casually dating Logan, assuring him that she's uninterested in having a steady boyfriend. She ultimately admits that the casual scenario ultimately isn't for her. "I'm a girlfriend girl, Logan," she tells him. "I have boyfriends, not escorts" ("But I'm a Gilmore"). When Logan takes his now-girlfriend Rory to his parents' home for dinner, the kind of girl Rory is becomes an issue again. Logan's grandfather chastises him for selecting an unsuitable future wife, and his mother agrees: "She wants to work.... A girl like Rory has no idea what it takes to be in this family, Logan." While this discourse suggests that Rory, and others around her, have come to see her occupying a certain essentialized womanhood, the process of engagement, practice, trial-and-error, and adaptation that has preceded it argues otherwise. Before arriving at this moment, in which Rory has established herself as a "girlfriend girl" and career woman, she has experienced a number of alternatives. When she describes herself in these terms, she can do so because she has crafted a sense of self, an individual feminist model, from out of her previous experiences. The appearance of a feminine and feminist essence is, ironically, derived from a long and ongoing experience of performance.

"Look what Jane Fonda hath wrought"

There is much at stake in the representation of contemporary feminism offered by a teen TV series like *Gilmore Girls*, and not simply for adults searching for signs of feminist life in the twenty-first century. Media scholars link the ever-present concerns of parents, politicians, and policymakers regarding depictions of violence and sexuality on television to the crucial role that television plays in acculturating teens to their peers, their families, their society, and themselves. Yet they add that viewers in general and young people in particular use what they see on television to "make meaning." Television, argues David Buckingham, figures "not as a powerful source of dominant ideologies, but on the contrary as a 'symbolic resource' which young people use in making sense of their experiences, in relating to others and in organizing their daily lives" (1993, 13). Indeed, as Sue Murray argues, the teen TV series *My So-Called Life* fostered intense identification among teen girls with its depiction of alienation, insecurity, and a desire for love as elements of what it's like to be an adolescent girl (1999). What meaning might teen viewers, male and female, make of the representation of feminism that *Gilmore Girls* offers?

"Look what Jane Fonda hath wrought!" exclaims Taylor Doose when Lorelai ignores his warnings to move her car from a no-parking zone at the end of Season Five ("A House Is Not a Home"). Lorelai and Rory clearly owe much to second wave feminists like Jane Fonda; they are smart, independent, career-minded, and not afraid to show it. Yet, *Gilmore Girls* does not simply engage in a facile celebration of the strong woman. Much of the tension in the series comes from Lorelai's and Rory's efforts to balance their work with their romantic and familial relationships. Critics of second-wave feminism chide it for its focus on politics, the workplace, and other public-sphere issues, ostensibly positing them as antithetical to wifehood and motherhood and suggesting that a woman cannot be a feminist and be devoted to her family at the same time (Fox-Genovese 1996). Yet, Lorelai challenges this interpretation, confiding to Luke:

> I just—I feel like I'm never gonna have it, the whole package, you know? That person, that couple life. And I swear, I hate admitting it because I fancy myself Wonder Woman, but I really want it. The whole package ["Lazy-Hazy-Crazy Days"].

Gilmore Girls as of this writing has yet to show its viewers whether either Lorelai or Rory obtains this "whole package." But in third wave fashion, it has already demonstrated that a young woman like Rory can combine both femininity and feminism. She can be a girlfriend and a student/journalist-in-the-making. She can wear frilly dresses, participate in a debutante ball, and still be true to her ambitions. She can pursue a writing career and not be depicted as masculine. She also lives in a world where other women recognize this, too. Part of growing up is confronting the models of feminist womanhood presented by other women, determining which elements work for you, and devising your own model accordingly. This emphasis on choice, multiplicity, practice, and revision also characterizes third wave feminism. *Gilmore Girls* challenges all those pronouncements of the death of feminism, all those critiques of the second wave, by presenting a vital feminism whose only requirement of young women in order to remain vital is not that they parrot a single feminist model but rather that they make a feminism of their own. This was the most important lesson that the third wave learned from the second. The plurality that once spelled the end of second wave feminism is, ironically, its most important legacy.

Notes

1. For what is understood as the first articulation of the "third wave" designation, see Rebecca Walker (1992).

2. There has been a flurry of recent writing on third wave feminism. It is beyond the scope of this essay to parse all of the varied definitions of it that exist; the one I have distilled here derives from the following authors' work: Findlen (1995); Heywood and Drake (1997); Baumgardner and Richards (2000); Dicker and Piepmeier (2003); Munford (2004); and Zack (2005).

3. For example, see: De Vries (2001); Fazzone (2001); Bryson (2002); Press (2004); Ross (2004); *USA Today* (2004); Owen (2005); and Press (2005).

4. Dress has certainly been employed against feminist goals; when members of Phyllis Schlafly's Stop ERA groups marched in the late 1970s, they made sure to dress in ways that signified traditional womanhood and femininity; see Felsenthal (1981) and Critchlow (2005).

5. Also see Thorne (1993) and Morris (1995). Dress is so central to the performance of gender identity that refusing to wear gender-typed clothing is included among the symptoms of Gender Identity Disorder in children; see Minter (1999).

References

Baumgardner, Jennifer, and Amy Richards. 2000. *Manifesta: Young Women, Feminism, and the Future.* New York: Farrar, Straus and Giroux.

Bederman, Gail. 1995. *Manliness & Civilization: A Cultural History of Gender and Race in the United States, 1880–1917.* Chicago: University of Chicago Press.

Bellafante, Ginia. 1998. "Feminism: It's All About Me!" *Time*, June 29, 54–61.

_____. 2004. "The Power of Adult Clothes in a Youth-obsessed Culture." *New York Times*, March 28, sec. 4, 14.

Bryson, Jodi Lynn. 2002. "Gilmore Girl's Life." *Girls' Life*, 9, issue 1 (August/September): 42.

Buckingham, David. 1993. Introduction. In *Reading Audiences: Young People and the Media*, ed. David Buckingham, 1–23. New York: Manchester University Press.

Butler, Judith. 1990. *Gender Trouble: Feminism and the Subversion of Identity.* New York: Routledge.

Byers, Michele. 2003. *"Buffy the Vampire Slayer:* The next generation of television." In *Catching a Wave: Reclaiming Feminism for the 21st Century*, eds. Rory Dicker and Alison Piepmeier, 171–87. Boston: Northeastern University Press.

Critchlow, Donald T. 2005. *Phyllis Schlafly and Grassroots Conservatism: A Woman's Crusade.* Princeton, NJ: Princeton University Press.

De Vries, Hilary. 2001. "In Comedies, Signs of New Women's Movement." *New York Times,* February 25, sec. 2, 19.

Dicker, Rory, and Alison Piepmeier. 2003. Introduction. In *Catching a wave: Reclaiming feminism for the 21st century*, eds. Dicker and Piepmeier, 3–28. Boston: Northeastern Univ. Press.

Evans, Sara. 1980. *Personal Politics: The Roots of Women's Liberation in the Civil Rights movement and the New Left.* New York: Vintage.

Faludi, Susan. 1991. *Backlash: The Undeclared War Against American Women.* New York: Crown.

Fazzone, Amanda. 2001. "Boob Tube: NOW's Strange Taste in TV." *The New Republic,* 225, issue 5 (July 30): 16–17.

Felsenthal, Carol. 1981. *The Sweetheart of the Silent Majority: The Biography of Phyllis Schlafly.* Garden City, NY: Doubleday.

Findlen, Barbara, ed. *Listen Up: Voices from the Next Feminist Generation.* Seattle: Seal Press, 1995.

Fox-Genovese, Elizabeth. 1996. *"Feminism Is Not the Story of My Life": How Today's Feminist Elite Has Lost Touch with the Real Concerns of Women.* New York: Nan A. Talese.

Gillis, Stacy, and Rebecca Munford. 2004. "Genealogies and Generations: The Politics and Praxis of Third Wave Feminism. *Women's History Review* 13, no. 2:165–82

Henry, Astrid. 2004. *Not My Mother's Sister: Generational Conflict and Third-wave Feminism.* Bloomington: Indiana University Press.

Heywood, Leslie, and Jennifer Drake. 1997. Introduction. In *Third Wave Agenda: Being Feminist, Doing Feminism*, eds. Leslie Heywood and Jennifer Drake, 1–20. Minneapolis: University of Minnesota Press.

Kamen, Paula. 2000. *Her Way: Young Women Remake the Sexual Revolution.* New York: New York University Press.

Kinder, Marsha. 1999. "Kids' Media Culture: An Introduction." In *Kids' Media Culture*, ed. Marsha Kinder, 1–28. Durham: Duke University Press.

May, Elaine Tyler. 1988. *Homeward Bound: American Families in the Cold War Era.* New York: Basic Books.

Minter, Shannon. 1999. "Diagnosis and Treatment of Gender Identity Disorder in Children." In *Sissies and Tomboys: Gender Nonconformity and Homosexual Childhood*, ed. Matthew Rottnek, 9–33. New York: New York University Press.

Morris, Rosalind C. 1995. "All Made Up: Performance Theory and the New Anthropology of Sex and Gender." *Annual Review of Anthropology* 24:567–92

Munford, Rebecca. 2004. "'Wake Up and Smell the lipgloss': Gender, Generation, and the (a)Politics of Girl Power." In *Third Wave Feminism: A Critical Exploration*, eds. Stacy Gillis, Gillian Howie, and Rebecca Munford, 142–53. New York: Palgrave Macmillan.

Murray, Susan. 1999. "Saving Our So-called Lives: Girl Fandom, Adolescent Subjectivity, and *My So-Called Life.* In *Kids' Media Culture*, ed. Marsha Kinder, 221–35. Durham: Duke Univ. Press.

Ostrow, Joanne. 2004. "TV's Female Stars Just Can't Fill Void Left by Carrie & Crew." *Denver Post,* March 14, F-16.

Owen, Rob. 2005. "Women on TV: More Than Equals." *Pittsburgh Post-Gazette*, October 25, C1.

Paoletti, Jo B. 1997. "The Gendering of Infants' and Toddlers' Clothing in America." In

The Material Culture of Gender, the Gender of Material Culture, eds. Katharine Martinez and Kenneth L. Ames, 27–35. Winterthur, DE: Henry Francis Du Pont Winterthur Museum.

Pozner, Jennifer L. 2003. "The 'Big Lie': False Feminist Death Syndrome, Profit, and the Media." In *Catching a Wave: Reclaiming Feminism for the 21st Century*, eds. Rory Dicker and Alison Piepmeier, 31–56. Boston: Northeastern University Press.

Press, Joy. 2004. "The Sunshine Girls." *Village Voice*, November 2, 113.

_____. 2005. "This Is Your Mom on Drugs." *Village Voice*, August 9, 52.

Rosen, Ruth. 2000. *The World Split Open: How the Modern Women's Movement Changed America*. New York: Viking.

Ross, Sharon. 2004. "Dormant Dormitory Friendships: Race and Gender in *Felicity*." In *Teen TV: Genre, Consumption, Identity*, eds. Glyn Davis and Kay Dickinson, 141–50. London: British Film Institute.

Rubinstein, Ruth P. 2000. *Society's Child: Identity, Clothing, and Style*. Boulder: Westview Press.

Springer, Kimberly. 2005. *Living for the Revolution: Black Feminist Organizations, 1968–1980*. Durham: Duke University Press.

Steinem, Gloria. 1995a. Foreword. In *To Be Real: Telling the Truth and Changing the Face of Feminism*, ed. Rebecca Walker, xiii–xxviii. New York: Anchor Books.

_____. 1995b. "I Was a Playboy Bunny." In *Outrageous Acts and Everyday Rebellions*, 2d ed., 32–75. New York: Henry Holt.

Thorne, Barrie. 1993. *Gender Play: Girls and Boys in School*. New Brunswick, NJ: Rutgers University Press.

Tucker, Ken. 2003. "The Good 'girls.'" *Entertainment Weekly*, April 4, 87.

Ulrich, Laurel Thatcher. 1982. *Good Wives: Image and Reality in the Lives of Women in Northern New England, 1650–1750*. New York: Knopf.

USA Today. 2004. "The Winding Path of TV's Woman of the House." October 1, 2E.

Walker, Rebecca. 1992. "Becoming the Third Wave." *Ms.*, January/February, 39–41.

_____. 1995. "Being Real: An Introduction." In *To Be Real: Telling the Truth and Changing the Face of Feminism*, ed. Rebecca Walker, xxix–xx. New York: Anchor Books.

Zack, Naomi. 2005. *Inclusive Feminism: A Third Wave Theory of Women's Commonality*. Lanham, MD: Rowman and Littlefield.

7. "That girl of yours— she's pretty hardboiled, huh?": Detecting Feminism in *Veronica Mars*

Andrea Braithwaite

The "Chick Dick"

A neon vacancy sign flickers starkly against the black night sky. A silhouetted couple writhes ecstatically behind thin curtains. A man in a partially closed bathrobe walks barefoot to the ice machine. Over such iconographic imagery of illicit liaisons and fleeting lust, the detective's voice muses sardonically about trust and betrayal, motels and money shots. Watching impatiently, the detective twists the telephoto lens, glances at the dashboard clock, and counts down the hours until her calculus exam the next day. Slouched behind the steering wheel sipping from a thermos is the petite, blonde Veronica Mars—part high school student, part private eye.

The female detective has become an increasingly visible and profitable popular culture phenomenon. Playing a central role in the resurgence of crime and mystery fiction in the 1980s, characters like Sara Paretsky's V.I. Warshawski and Sue Grafton's Kinsey Millhone helped establish the female investigator as a formidable—and feminist—cultural figure (Walton and Jones 1999). As Linda Mizejewski notes, women detectives are now highly valuable commodities across fiction, film and television, yet these characters are often bound by postfeminist ideologies of feminism and femininity (2004). The woman detective both reproduces and comments on the double bind characteristic of postfeminist popular cultural representations: female characters are defined by their freedom to choose, yet these popular narratives continually individualize and depoliticize the very notion of "choice" to a narrow range of socially acceptable identities and options. *Veronica Mars* negotiates this position by providing a deliberately different iteration of the "female dick." Veronica is a "chick dick."

Using the term "dick" in relation to a woman detective seems to be almost as provocative as the figure herself; Linda Mizejewski, for example, tells of her failed attempt to use the phrase "female dick" in the title of her 2004 book *Hardboiled and High Heeled: The Woman Detective in Popular Culture* (2005, 121). Some authors refer to their narratives as "tart noir," and define their protagonists as "neofeminist women, half Philip Marlowe, half femme-fatale, who make their own rules, who think it's entirely possible to save the world while wearing a drop-dead dress and four-inch heels" (Henderson and Duffy, http://tartcity.com, 2004). This chick dick is an emergent pop cultural trope that highlights the performative nature of gendered identities through the intersection of differently gendered genres—most often romance and crime narratives.[1]

Veronica Mars' opening scene described above emphasizes to the chick dick's dual articulation: Veronica is immediately constructed as both a stereotypical private eye and as an ordinary teenage girl through her concurrent cynicism about romantic love and her concern for her grades. By identifying how *Veronica Mars* engages with postfeminism and postfeminist representational strategies, I hope to draw attention to the chick dick's commercial and political leverage—how this character highlights some of the contradictions inherent in televisual articulations and commodifications of feminism and feminist issues. Not entirely congruent with the female investigator, the chick dick's distinctively postfeminist baggage influences her interrogation of generic and cultural expectations.

More than a repopularization of the woman detective, the chick dick reworks and reframes feminist issues for a target audience that is coming of age when popular postfeminism has declared feminism "dead." Popular culture's "post-ing" of feminism relies on a limited interpretation and incorporation of feminism's central goals—female freedom and equality—and a depiction of independent and successful female professionals to imply that these goals have been achieved, thus making feminism redundant. Angela McRobbie argues that postfeminist portrayals of women's social status and achievements present a social sphere

> in which female freedom and ambition appear to be taken for granted, unreliant on any past struggle (an antiquated word) and certainly not requiring any new, fresh political understanding, but instead merely a state into which young women appear to have been thrown, or in which they find themselves, giving rise to ambivalence and misgiving [2004, 6].

Little consensus exists regarding the definition and shape of postfeminism. Popular postfeminism is significantly different from academic postfeminism, for, as Ann Brooks makes clear, academic postfeminism "is fundamentally about, not a depoliticization of feminism, but a political shift in feminism's conceptual and theoretical agenda" (1997, 4). For the purposes of this argument, I am focusing on media representations of postfeminism as the discursive framework in which *Veronica Mars* operates and is understood. This is not to dismiss the insights and critiques that academic postfeminism offers, but to distinguish how *Veronica Mars* is situated within a particular set of popular meaning-making strategies and what they offer young women in terms of their relationships to feminism and what feminism entails. As Sarah Projanksy points out, "The way postfeminist discourse defines feminism is now part of what feminism *is*" (2001, 14).

Dual generic resources inform Veronica Mars' depictions and explanations of young women's roles in the public and private sphere: detection and teen TV. The chick dick's political preoccupations are articulated both through and against these discursive and representational frames, which the series' first season uses to foreground anxieties around gendered experiences of school, employment, and sexual violence. While her appearance is certainly enabled by postfeminism, the chick dick's work is often critical of its constraints on young women's freedom and equality.

The Double Architecture of Veronica Mars

As Tzvetan Todorov has influentially argued, mystery narratives have a double or "dual architecture" in which "the story of the crime and the story of the investigation" eventually converge (1977, 44). Todorov's formulation also describes the confluence of hardboiled and teen drama in *Veronica Mars*. In this instance, the series' double architecture is particularly gendered, and its structure is central to understanding the chick dick's cultural work. *Veronica Mars* draws upon the hardboiled tradition's representations of power, knowledge, and authority, a masculine form epitomized and popularized by characters like Dashiell Hammett's Sam Spade and Raymond Chandler's Philip Marlowe, and iconographically embodied by Humphrey Bogart in film adaptations. At the same time the program invokes the feminine melodrama and popular culture's typical "representations of girls as figures of social redemption and salvation," a pattern Jenny Bavige traces back to nineteenth century novels for girls that championed traditional feminine virtues like altruism and compassion (2004, 42). Both heroic and vulnerable, the girls who possess such traits enrich not just themselves but their community as well.[2] Veronica's dual life as both a high school girl and a private investigator problematizes this familiar performance; the imbrications of a hardboiled narrative within teen drama politicizes the criteria for social redemption by resolutely insisting that violence is constituted by its cultural context. Postfeminism's rhetoric of personal agency falters in the face of such conditions, for Veronica's season-long investigations suggest that salvation requires more than a blonde teenaged girl is able to achieve on her own.

The investigations that structure *Veronica Mars'* first season—finding out who raped her at a party and who killed her best friend Lilly—confront and contradict postfeminism's proclamations of gender equality. As the "genre most likely to expose both the limitations of the postfeminist heroine and the nasty sex and gender issues that her presence supposedly precludes," the crime narrative's political potential is accented by serial television's industrial and narrative logic (Mizejewski 2005, 125). *Veronica Mars* raises and resolves small narrative incidents on a weekly basis while generating a sustained audience by unraveling major storylines over the course of the season. Television's economic imperative—to create the compulsive viewing audience so attractive to advertisers—enhances the familiar hardboiled conclusion that crime is endemic to and embedded in contemporary social conditions. The chick dick narrative recasts this hardboiled crime trope into an indictment of violence against women. An often violent sexual exploitation and domination of women thus pervades *Veronica Mars'* first season on several levels.

One of television's numerous and varied inflections of the soap opera, the teen series is culturally figured as feminine. Rooted in the family melodrama (Banks 2004, 18), teen television addresses stereotypically "feminine" concerns about family, interpersonal relationships, and identity from an ostensibly teenaged perspective. The genre's emphasis on dialogue, emotion, and dialogue about emotion further genders teen television as feminine. With its themed dances, championship basketball games, and catty lunchtime gossip *Veronica Mars* clearly identifies itself as teen television and Veronica as a teenaged heroine. Veronica exists on the fringes of her wealthy high school's social order; after her father, the town's former sheriff, accused computer software magnate Jake Kane of murdering his daughter Lilly, Veronica finds herself cast from the elite clique and must navigate high school, a microcosm of the larger Neptune community, on her own.

Teenagers' liminal social position provides a powerful allegory when considering the series' focus on female agency and vulnerability. As the program's narrative center, the audience is asked to align themselves with Veronica, who is marginalized at multiple levels. Not only is Veronica an outsider in her high school's hierarchy, but also, as Glyn Davis and Kay Dickinson point out, the teenage experience itself is one of otherness and disenfranchisement (2004, 11). Like the postfeminist female, teenagers' social position carries the appearance of increased rights, yet they are still bound by legal and social restrictions on their mobility, agency, and expression. These "contradictory forces are negotiated through the school and its televisual representations," an environment in which the private and public spheres relentlessly collide (Davis and Dickinson 2004, 11). As episodes such as "Like a Virgin" demonstrate, however, the genre's emphasis on interpersonal and romantic entanglements can easily override the teen drama's potential to address the gendered power dynamics of these relationships.

In "Like a Virgin," each Neptune High student receives a "purity test" via email, a quiz that assesses sexual promiscuity. With questions like "Have you ever done it in a car? Have you ever had a fling while on vacation? Do you lie to protect your reputation?" the quiz assigns a purity rating that labels sexual activity beyond an invisible threshold as "slutty"—unless, of course, the student is male (as Wallace's consternation at his score of seventy attests). Any student's test results can be purchased online, and the school halls quickly become the site of angry confrontations and devastating breakups. Despite not having taken the test, Meg, one of Veronica's casual acquaintances, has a score of forty-eight. Meg's boyfriend, with whom she has been sexually chaste, indignantly deserts her after her score is spray-painted across her locker, and Meg's public life—her involvement in a variety of academic and extracurricular activities—is plagued by her peers' viciously personal harassment. This persecution illustrates what Bonnie Dow describes as the "doubleness" of postfeminist television representations: "an affirmation of women's progress and ... a reminder of the problems such progress has created," as the visibility of Meg's success makes her the target of such abuse (1996, 139).

This episode focuses on the complicated network of high school friendships and the sexual politics at play in the purity test and its aftermath. "Like a Virgin" thus draws attention to the ways in which, for women, the distinction between the public and private spheres does not parallel their lived experience, for their presence in one is always determined and judged by their behavior in the other. Veronica's own experiences make this explicit; her personal and school life are inextricably linked to her investigative work—at school she is regularly asked to solve other students' problems, while at work she is constantly treated like nothing more than a teenaged girl. The first season's underlying preoccupations underscore the negligible demarcation between private and public spheres. In uncovering the circumstances of both Veronica's rape and Lilly's death, the trope of "investigation" reveals the continued relevance of one of feminism's central arguments: the private is *never* private, and personal experiences are conditioned by women's subordinate political position in male-dominated social structures (see Dow 1996, 209). By repeatedly dragging private transgressions into public view, *Veronica Mars'* "narrative reinterprets the initial crime as evidence of something else": for women the distinction between public and private life is spurious at best (Walton and Jones 1999, 209).

As numerous feminist critics have noted, the hardboiled detective is a particularly appealing figure for feminist appropriation.[3] Symbolizing agency, authority, and subversion of the dominant social order, the hardboiled detective is traditionally a masculine position, facilitated by a male prerogative. Tough and aggressive as a literary form as well, the hardboiled novel swaggered onto the American crime writing scene in the 1920s and 1930s as deliberate reaction against the "soft" or "feminine" British "cozy" mysteries popular at the time. Through its gritty and dark realist aesthetics, archetypal hardboiled fiction consciously and explicitly critiques its cultural context; instead of considering crime an aberrant act by a solitary damaged individual, the hardboiled novel presents it in causal relation to wider patterns of social and political corruption, as a response to complex and changing social conditions.[4]

Already imbued with an aura of oppositional politics and centering on the prowess of a powerful protagonist, hardboiled conventions offer a rich resource for feminist rewritings. As a form which "actually prescribes that a marginal figure lay claim to the narrative's central perspective," the presence of hardboiled elements in texts like *Veronica Mars* offers a way to work through the genre's gendered ascriptions of authority in order to foreground an empowered *female* perspective (Walton and Jones 1999, 40). *Veronica Mars'* incursions into the hardboiled pattern serve as instances of what Linda Mizejewski refers to as "the wrong body in the expected place" (2004, 12). Veronica's wrong body is not only female but teenaged as well. This use of the hardboiled masculinist discourse in the chick dick narrative confronts popular understandings of the links between genre and gender, assumptions that circulate alongside postfeminist constructions of femininity and feminine behavior.

The hardboiled detective is easily identified and made masculine by his toughness, reacting to dangerous situations with a quick wit and even quicker reflexes. Veronica's diminutive stature prevents her from physically confronting others; she instead uses her intellect to assert her authority. Her sardonic and aggressive attitude has earned her a reputation, in the words of one teacher, of being "unique, gifted, unsettling" ("Mars vs. Mars"). Veronica actively negates the image of a bubbly and inevitably compliant "girl" through her shrewd, often harsh comebacks, what Priscilla Walton and Manina Jones term "tough talk as resistance" (1999, 131). As she tells a male student who has been gleefully harassing an awkward, unpopular girl, "Shut up. If I want you to speak, I'll wave a snausage over your nose" ("Hot Dogs"). She chases two students out of a classroom by saying, "It's all fun and games until one of you gets my foot up your ass" ("M.A.D."). And when the school's guidance counselor admonishes Veronica, saying, "You know, you're never going to come to terms with Lilly's death if you keep all that pain bottled up inside you," Veronica retorts: "Wow. I have that exact same platitude-a-day calendar at home. It's how I know beauty comes from within" ("Clash of the Tritons").

The private investigator is often a loner, unencumbered by familial or romantic ties and fiercely proud and protective of his autonomy. Such a characteristic is at odds with the teen series, which continually mines interpersonal relationships for dramatic conflict. Through its double architecture, *Veronica Mars* explores both individualism and community as gendered ideals, as Veronica attempts to achieve a balance between her burgeoning sense of independence and her commitments as a friend and daughter. Veronica deliberately creates distance between herself and others, initially resisting new kid Wallace's overtures of friendship and keeping him emotionally at an arm's length throughout most of the first season.

This strategy is often validated—just when Veronica and fellow outcast Wanda Varner begin to enjoy their shared interests in "Return of the Kane," Veronica discovers that Wanda is working as a snitch and has told the local law enforcement that Veronica is holding illegal drugs. In "Ruskie Business," when Veronica and popular cheerleader Meg have managed to form a friendship in the face of their high school's strict social hierarchy, Veronica is devastated to learn that her ex-boyfriend Duncan is interested in dating Meg. Veronica's self-sufficient veneer briefly cracks in "A Trip to the Dentist"; she finally lets Wallace in, filling him in on her investigations into her own rape and Lilly's death. She tells him, "This is so not an 'I told you so,' but do you see why I kinda keep things to myself?" Her autonomy is not merely a reenactment but instead a recasting of a typical hardboiled trait, now a buttress against the kinds of betrayal and loss she experiences as her public and private lives entwine.

Like many female detectives, Veronica's most meaningful relationships do not mimic traditional ones (Reddy 1988, 118). Her friendship with Wallace is surprisingly platonic for teen television, and as a daughter, she evades the redemptive function of popular culture's familiar "heroic girl" figure (Banks 2004). Veronica can never fully realize the heroic girls' function as her family's salvation. Veronica's mother left Neptune, along with her husband and daughter, after Veronica's father Keith Mars was rousted from his post as town sheriff. When Veronica eventually tracks her mother down, she discovers she has become an alcoholic. Selflessly sacrificing her entire college tuition savings to pay for her mother's treatment, Veronica at first seems to have accomplished her goal of reuniting her family. The idyllic scenes of mother and daughter singing and preparing dinner together as an indulgent father watches are only temporary, for Veronica's mother never completes her treatment and is clandestinely drinking. Realizing that her mother's presence is jeopardizing a secure and supportive home environment rather than creating it, Veronica tells her to leave ("Leave It to Beaver").

While constantly concerned about his daughter's welfare, safety, and academic success (generally running background checks on the boys she dates), Keith Mars recognizes and supports Veronica's independence. As he tells Wallace's mother, Veronica is "not your average seventeen year old" ("A Trip to the Dentist"). Often interacting as equals, Veronica and her father share business and domestic duties, and his respect is made clear in "Mars vs. Mars" when the two find themselves on opposite sides of a case. Even though Veronica is eventually proved wrong her father encourages her tenacious moral convictions, telling her, "If I were in trouble I'd want you on my side." Veronica's moral code significantly revises the hardboiled detective's unerring belief in freedom and justice.

Interested in more than just solving the crime as a means of upholding legal definitions of right and wrong, Veronica frames her function as helping those she sees caught by circumstance. For instance, when a routine background check on a woman's lost love turns up empty in "Ruskie Business," Veronica perseveres, telling her father, "I just thought it would be nice if, instead of breaking people up, we brought them together for once." Her sympathy for rich kid Logan Echolls when he refuses to believe that his mother has committed suicide overrides her resentment of his cruelty toward her after Lilly's death, and she doggedly follows any clues to provide him with a sense of closure. In "Mars vs. Mars," Veronica defends a teacher she believes to be falsely accused of impregnating one of his students. When she learns that the accusations are accurate, she not only drops the case but also ensures that he is removed from the high school. Veronica's investigations are "rooted in a concern for relationships and for life," an emphasis on situational victimization that often identifies spaces in which young women are most susceptible to sexualized power differences (Reddy 1988, 118).

This concern is also articulated through the series' insistent and compelling use of the voiceover. A staple in fiction, film, and television crime stories, first-person narration and voice-overs draw the audience into the detective's experiences, a "focus on the world as perceived by the private eye" (Horsley 2005, 274). By appropriating this representational strategy, the series positions the audience to see the world through Veronica's teenage female eyes, creating a space for the "recovery of female subjectivity" that is otherwise absent from the hardboiled form (Horsley 2005, 224).[5] The female voice at the program's narrative center reworks generic convention to reveal the gendered dynamics of home, school, and employment. Intimate in tone, these confessional moments frame the audience's entry into the conditions young women face as they navigate and interrogate their personal and professional relationships.

Veronica's subjective narration highlights the program's double architecture, for her perceptions of both past and present experience demonstrate how, as a chick dick, she is caught between and determined by the competing demands of girlhood and detecting. For instance, in "Ruskie Business" Veronica's voice-over intones, "When I've had my fill of soul mates, glitter, and puppy love, I always find a private detective's office a refreshing change of pace." Her sleuthing culminates in an emotionally charged revelation at the high school dance later in the episode. She reflects that "Between getting fooled by the Russian bride and finding out Duncan has the hots for Meg, I've had my fill of surprises for tonight. J. Geils was right. Love stinks. You can dress it up with sequins and shoulder pads but one way or another you're just gonna end up alone at the spring dance strapped into uncomfortable underwear." Such interior dialogues are telling illustrations of Veronica's own perspective on both the perils of and parallels between her public and private lives.

Confounding the roles of the male hardboiled detective and the girlish teen heroine by simultaneously playing both, Veronica's voice-overs also articulate her sense of agency, reclaiming and rewriting the detective's authoritative voice from a "position of subjectivity embodied in the feminine autobiographical voice" (Walton and Jones 1999, 152). For

Veronica, detecting is more than just a job; it is a means to assert control over the forces that determine her social position. As she tells us: "Tragedy blows through your life like a tornado, uprooting everything, creating chaos. You wait for the dust to settle and then you choose. You can live in the wreckage and pretend it's still the mansion you remember. Or you can crawl from the rubble and slowly rebuild. Because after disaster strikes, the important thing is that you move on. But if you're like me, you just keep chasing the storm" ("Meet John Smith"). By speaking of her social environment as a site of struggle, Veronica establishes from the start her refusal to simply accept her circumstances as capricious twists of fate—one of the many ways in which resistance pervades the chick dick's character.

Veronica's voice-overs frequently draw attention to political and social corruption and their impact on individuals' lives. Neptune's rigid hierarchy is echoed in its high school, and by existing on its fringes, Veronica can interrogate its significance. In Neptune, there is no such thing as a personal life, for everyone knows everything about everybody else. Veronica frequently makes use of this network of knowledge to follow clues, rarely needing to speak to more than a few people to find the information she seeks. The trope of investigation reveals the deep connections that structure Neptune, incriminating the entire town in the systemic exploitation of women represented by Veronica's rape and Lilly's death.

The most hyperbolic expression of Neptune's incestuous social order is the lurking suspicion that Veronica is Duncan's sister, the illegitimate offspring of Jake Kane and Liane Mars, who were once king and queen of the Neptune High prom. Duncan's belief in this possibility creates the conditions for Veronica's rape: when she is slipped a date-rape drug at a party months after Duncan's desertion and Lilly's death, she has consensual—albeit unremembered—sex with Duncan who had also been drugged. Although a paternity test confirms that Veronica is Keith Mars' biological daughter, the incest narrative's implication remains: that Neptune's social networks negate the distinction between public and private life, leaving Veronica continually exposed.[6] Her vulnerability comes not from choice but from circumstance, for Veronica's attempts at autonomy and agency are limited by being a teenaged girl in a society that, despite postfeminist proclamations of women's equality, still targets and humiliates them for their sex and sexuality.[7] Detecting is one means of exerting power over these circumstances, an appropriation of agency "not just within the confines of or despite the conventions of the genre, but *through* those very conventions," that rewrites the genre's gendered discourse in the process (Walton and Jones 1999, 86–87).

Interrogating Postfeminism

Veronica Mars' double architecture—its combination and contestation of the gendered discourses of teen drama and hardboiled detection—foregrounds the show's engagement with postfeminism. Postfeminism's articulation in North American popular culture "assumes that feminist goals have been achieved, for the most part, by women's access to the public sphere" (Dow 1996, 99). Women are thus "liberated" from feminism's strident ideology; their equality now a cultural given, they can work, go shopping, attend school, raise a family, and assert their sexuality free from the oppressive confines of patriarchy. Or, as Veronica quips in "Betty and Veronica," "Whoever said it's a man's world had no idea how easy it is sometimes to be a girl." Still, *Veronica Mars* cannot simply be claimed as either a feminist or postfeminist text. As Jenny Bavige comments, "The debate around the feminist credentials of ... any TV show which depicts girls made strong ... is understandably caught up in unraveling the problematic politics of a show which demonstrates many of the contradictions and complexities" of postfeminism (2004, 43).

In *Veronica Mars*, these complexities are most apparent in the fusion of Veronica's professional and private concerns. As many commentators on the female detective note, by occupying a male position the female detective is a woman in drag.[8] *Veronica Mars* compounds this typical formula, for Veronica's most effective sleuthing is accomplished not by assuming the private eye's air of authority, but by adopting an overtly feminine demeanor—a "high drag" in which this chick dick acts as a detective by playing a "girl." When Neptune High's mascot is stolen right before the championship basketball game, she goes undercover as Betty the perky cheerleader at the school across town ("Betty and Veronica"). To ingratiate herself with Lilly's confessed killer, Abel Koontz, she pretends to be a college journalism student from his hometown—complete with a convincing southern accent, spiral-bound notebook and sensible heels ("Like a Virgin"). In "The Wrath of Con," Veronica quickly switches her feminine comportment as the situation warrants. She poses as an inexperienced gamer in knee-high socks, a short kilt and black bob wig to infiltrate the local video-game bar; dons reading glasses, a high-collared shirt and three-quarter length skirt to appear as an eager academic just checking out the local college; and giggles as a ditzy blonde in a sultry red dress and curled tresses to lure a trust-fund scam artist.

This high drag highlights the performative nature of both the detective and the "girl" as gendered roles. An extension of postfeminist "girling" in which the independent and successful woman is "made safe by being represented as fundamentally still a girl," *Veronica Mars* insists that girlhood itself is a performative position (Tasker and Negra 2005, 109). These multiple layers of performance mark the limits of the acceptable identities women must embody in order to pass in different social contexts. Veronica constantly mimics social ideals of femininity and feminine behavior by routinely engaging in such charades; they are her means for taking over the typically male position of detective, for the threat of her "wrong body in the expected place" is mitigated by her parodic performance of girlishness.

The array of appropriate femininities from which Veronica can select her most effective teen girl identity also alludes to what Elspeth Probyn refers to as postfeminism's "choiceoisie": "choice freed of the necessity of thinking about the political and social ramifications of the act of choosing" (1990, 156). One of television's prominent rhetorical strategies for depicting feminist issues, "choiceoisie" draws on and dilutes feminism's call for collective freedom and equality. Rather than culturally influenced and potentially political choices, prime-time obstacles like relationships, families or careers become individual and personal dilemmas. This individuation is powerfully articulated and repudiated in *Veronica Mars'* treatment of teenage romantic relationships and the failure of heterosexual romance. Intimate and sexual relationships are repeatedly portrayed not just as teenage tribulations but also as emotionally and physically dangerous interactions in which women are not equal despite struggling to be recognized as such. With its culturally resonant imagery of agency and authority, the series' use of the hardboiled narrative re-politicizes issues that teen TV raises and postfeminism sanitizes, particularly "the most radical aspects of feminism, those centered in sexual politics and a profound awareness of power differences between the sexes at all levels and in all arenas" (Dow 1996, 88).

Veronica's attempts at a relationship with her best friend Lilly's former boyfriend Logan Echolls illustrate not only the typical teenage tropes of infatuation and lust but also Veronica's awareness of and reactions to the dangers young women face when dating. When Veronica learns Logan procured the GHB that incapacitated her on the night of her rape, she immediately tries to distance herself from him in social and educational environments that make such security profoundly difficult—she stands him up on their first real date and deliberately avoids him at school ("M.A.D."). Logan presses Veronica for an explanation. He unexpectedly shows up at her house just as she has stepped out of the shower, and her white terry-cloth bathrobe suggests a vulnerability that her words sharply contradict. She tells him: "I'm gonna find out who did this to me and I'm gonna make them pay. Even if it was you" ("A Trip to the Dentist").

Yet, what was portrayed and experienced by Veronica as rape throughout the first season, was actually mis-remembered consensual intercourse. Veronica even assuages Logan's guilt when he confesses to his part in providing the drugs. Her sexuality is the real perpetrator, and the fraternal house party at which teenage boys drugged their dates in order to have sex is forgotten. This turn away from date rape to consensual sex illustrates the confusion around rape that postfeminism implies feminism itself has produced (see Projansky 2001, 92–94). By emphasizing the expression of female desire, feminism—specifically the more commercially viable elements of feminism adopted by popular culture—has confounded what constitutes consent. As Ariel Levy comments, commodified images of active female sexuality create a climate in which women feel obligated to acquiesce to sexual overtures, "a repercussion of the very forces [second-wave feminists] put in motion—they are the ones who started this" (2005, 45).

This indeterminacy around feminism's impact on young women's lives illustrates the contradictory and "problematic politics" Bavige sees as characteristic of postfeminist television (2004, 43). *Veronica Mars'* relation to these politics remains complex, reiterating female vulnerability while continually searching for culprits and explanations.[9] For instance, once she is told that her rape was apparently consensual sex with Duncan, Veronica apologizes to Logan and tries to trust him again. However, sprawled on the bed in the Echollses' pool house waiting for Logan to return with refreshments, she notices electrical cables running from the overhead fan to disappear behind what seems to be a bookcase. The cables lead to a hidden video camera, and rather than risk any further sexual exploitation Veronica escapes out the Echolls estate's back entrance ("A Trip to the Dentist").

When Veronica figures out that Logan's father Aaron killed Lilly, sexual intimidation becomes more than just a threat. Veronica finds a cache of videocassettes in Lilly's secret hiding space that detail Lilly and Aaron's sexual encounters, and she surmises that Aaron murdered Lilly when she refused to return the tapes. Lilly's death at the hands of her powerful older lover directly resulted from resisting her own sexual exploitation, and when Veronica tries to bring this truth to light Aaron almost kills her as well, screaming "I'm not going to let a seventeen-year-old piece of ass *ruin my life*!" ("Leave It to Beaver"). Both girls refuse to let themselves be made victims of sexual abuse and are punished—Veronica is ridiculed and further ostracized for what her peers see as promiscuity while Lilly is brutally beaten to death—and the first season's preoccupation with unraveling rather than quickly resolving these two cases reiterates the violent and long-lasting impact of such crimes.

Veronica and Lilly are not the only girls in Neptune that struggle with the gendered power dynamics of intimate sexual relationships. By contrasting Veronica's relentless pursuit of her rapist and of Lilly's killer with the choices other girls feel they must make, the program highlights "the profoundly disturbing silences of mass-mediated postfeminist discourse on issues such as male responsibility, female solidarity, [and] sexual politics" (Dow 1996, 160). In "M.A.D.," fellow student Carmen tries to break up with her boyfriend Tad. He refuses and threatens to put on the internet a sexually suggestive video he made of her at a party. Feeling trapped, Carmen begs Veronica for help. Veronica decides to play off Tad's homophobia by creating a website detailing Tad's fictional love affair with another male student. Tad sends the video out to the entire school anyway, yet Carmen decides not to retaliate, figuring "I'd rather have the entire world think I'm trashy than let a guy like Tad push me around." Such is the problem of postfeminist "choiceoisie": Carmen can only choose between a forced sexual relationship with Tad or sexual harassment from other students as a slut. Whether she remains silent or speaks out, she is demeaned because of her gender and sexuality.

In "Mars vs. Mars" Veronica's favorite teacher, Mr. Rooks, is accused of impregnating Carrie Bishop, one of his students. Despite the compelling evidence against him, Veronica is convinced he is innocent and succeeds in discrediting Carrie. Later, stopping by Mr. Rooks' house on an errand, she notices striking similarities to the circumstances of Carrie's seduction, such as his black silk sheets and The Rolling Stone's *Tattoo You* playing softly in the background. She learns that Carrie was acting on her best friend's behalf, attempting to speak out against Rooks because her friend was too afraid. Like Veronica and Carmen, Carrie is mercilessly belittled by her peers, a vivid depiction of the problems with a postfeminist media environment in which "the new female subject is, despite her freedom, called upon to be silent, to withhold critique in order to count as a modern, sophisticated girl" (McRobbie 2004, 9).

These storylines clearly contend that power differences still structure sexual relationships, that males can lay claim to an authority based on their gender, and can have that authority culturally validated by wider social attitudes toward young women's sexuality. As Maureen Reddy argues, "All legal improvements in women's status mean very little without a fundamental reimagining and reordering of women's position within the family and within other 'personal' relationships" (1988, 106). While Veronica can make a difference on a small or episodic level, the recurrence of such situations throughout the first season suggests that the individualization of women's issues into one particular woman's issue does nothing to resolve the social conditions that enable ongoing sexual oppression and abuse. By structuring its myriad stories around how these issues intersect with high school girls' lives, *Veronica Mars* critically underscores their systemic nature and the need for their continued interrogation.

Conclusion

Veronica Mars' combination of the gendered discourses of teen melodrama and hardboiled detection highlights one of feminism's central tenets: that women's choices are regulated by cultural norms around sex and gender (see Dow 1996, 95–96). As a chick dick, Veronica actively addresses these limits; her performances of both the masculinist imperatives of crime narratives and the teen drama's construction of an ideal femininity confront the gender expectations that circulate within and around these popular formulas. Such negotiations extend beyond the boundaries of generic change in television programming, however, for Veronica does not just find lost dogs or school mascots but also investigates the circumstances and culprits that belittle, demean, and abuse young women. By adapting the private investigator's characteristic authority and agency, and by transforming teen female life into a serial crime story, *Veronica Mars* challenges popular postfeminism's easy dismissal of feminism's relevance. The program's trope of investigation scrutinizes claims of individual freedom and choice by making public the multiple ways in which young women are constructed, conditioned, and exploited on the basis of their gender and sexuality.

Veronica Mars' first season foregrounds the sexual politics of adolescence in a way that suggests that for young women there is no clear distinction between public and private struggles for equality. The series thus resonates with other teen texts, for while the chick dick is often explicitly coded as a detective, her central concerns are also compellingly dramatized in programs like *Buffy the Vampire Slayer* and *Roswell*.[10] Although Buffy, Liz, and Maria are not aligned with hardboiled traditions, like Veronica they continually interrogate agency and norms of femininity in sexual relationships, work, and school. The presence and popularity of these investigative girls across teen TV suggest that their representations of young women's experiences are tapping into wider discourses about and contestations of ideal girlhood, and that these representations may have a particularly revealing relationship with real life. *Veronica Mars* offers its audience a heroine that refuses to stay silent about popular postfeminism's political ambivalence and that tries to rework generic and cultural expectations about what it means "to be a girl." As Veronica herself notes, "The real tragedy happened long before I came along. I just brought it to the surface" ("The Girl Next Door").

Notes

1. Through novelistic series such as Janet Evanovich's bestselling Stephanie Plum series and Sparkle Hayter's Robin Hudson series, and through movies such as *Head Over Heels* (Mark Waters 2001) and *Perfect Stranger* (James Foley 2007), the chick dick is quickly becoming a commercially successful articulation of the female detective.

2. Bavige points to novels like Louisa May Alcott's *Little Women* (1868), Frances Hodgson Burnett's *A Little Princess* (1905), and Lucy Maud Montgomery's *Anne of Green Gables* (1908) as paradigmatic narratives that promote an ideal of girlhood through sweetly cheeky young female role models.

3. See: Munt (1994), Cranny-Francis (1988), Clark (1990), Emck (1994), and Mizejewski (2004).

4. See: Chandler (1944), Porter (1981), and Horsley (2005).

5. This is not to imply that *Veronica Mars'* use of the voice-over is uncommon; series like *Ally McBeal* (FOX 1997–2002) and *Sex and the City* (HBO 1998–2004) also rely on this technique to highlight their heroines' perceptions and experiences. As Amanda Lotz (2006) argues, this device is often used in female-dominated dramatic programs to emphasize postfeminist ambivalence and misgivings over conflicting desires that arise from trying to "have it all." The voice-over's role in series popularly acknowledged as postfeminist thus make the reflexive impulses of *Veronica Mars'* hybrid narrative structure more apparent (*Redesigning Women: Television After the Network Era* [Urbana: University of Illinois Press]).

6. While such storylines are a familiar gambit of "feminine" forms like the soap opera and romance novel, they recur in hardboiled narratives as well. In *Chinatown* (Roman Polanski 1974), for instance, incest functions as a metaphor for the city's pervasive political and social corruption. See Gans [1974] and Shetley [1999].

7. This emphasis recurs throughout *Veronica Mars'* subsequent seasons. Episodes like Season Two's "One Angry Veronica" and "The Rapes of Graff," and Season Three's "Spit and Eggs" and "Poughkeepsie, Tramps and Thieves" clearly depict young women's physical vulnerability and their struggle to be treated as autonomous individuals.

8. See: Littler (1991), Munt (1994), Wilson (1995), and Walton and Jones (1999).

9. Seasons Two and Three of *Veronica Mars* demonstrate a continued preoccupation not only with establishing the parameters of what constitutes rape, but also determining who can set these criteria. Both seasons feature narrative arcs in which it is not entirely clear what were actual incidents of sexual assault and what were misunderstandings or even acts staged by vengeful feminists ("Lord of the PIs"). Veronica's determined investigations in these storylines place her in the role of "avenger," a figure Jacinda Read sees as a "key site through which the current feminist moment can be understood" (2000, 182) (*The New Avengers* [Manchester: Manchester University Press]).

10. See: Helford (2002), Byers (2003), and S. Levy (2003).

References

Alcott, Louisa May. 1868. *Little Women*. London: Puffin Classics (1994).

Banks, Miranda J. 2004. "A Boy for All Planets: *Roswell, Smallville* and the Teen Male Melodrama." In *Teen TV: Genre, Consumption, and Identity*, eds. G. Davis and K. Dickinson, 17–28. London: BFI.

Bavige, Jenny. 2004. "Chosen Ones: Reading the Contemporary Teen Heroine." In *Teen TV: Genre, Consumption, and Identity*, eds. G. Davis and K. Dickinson, 41–53. London: BFI.

Brooks, Ann. 1997. *Postfeminisms: Feminism, Cultural Theory and Cultural Forms*. New York: Routledge.
Burnett, Frances Hodgson. 1905. *A Little Princess*. New York: Ace Books (1975).
Byers, Michele. 2003. "*Buffy the Vampire Slayer*: The Next Generation of Television." In *Catching a Wave: Reclaiming Feminism for the 21st Century*, eds. R. Dicker and A. Pipemeier, 171–87. Boston: Northeastern University Press.
Chandler, Raymond. 1944. "The Simple Art of Murder." *The Atlantic Monthly* (December): 53–59.
Clark, Danae. 1990. "*Cagney and Lacey*: Feminist Strategies of Detection." In *Television and Women's Culture: The Politics of the Popular*, ed. M.E. Brown, 117–33. London: Sage Publications.
Cranny-Francis, Anne. 1988. "Gender and Genre: Feminist Rewritings of Detective Fiction." *Women's Studies International Forum* 11:69–84.
Davis, Glyn, and Kay Dickinson. 2004. Introduction. In *Teen TV: Genre, Consumption, and Identity*, eds. G. Davis and K. Dickinson, 1–16. London: BFI.
Dow, Bonnie. 1996. *Prime-time Feminism: Television, Media Culture, and the Women's Movement Since 1970*. Philadelphia: University of Pennsylvania Press.
Emck, Katy. 1994. "Feminist Detectives and the Challenges of Hardboiledness." *Canadian Review of Comparative Literature* 21:383–98.
Gans, H.J. 1974. "*Chinatown*: An Anticapitalist Murder Mystery." *Social Policy* 5: 48–49.
Helford, Elyce Rae. 2002. "'My Emotions Give me Power': The Containment of Girls' Anger in *Buffy*." In *Fighting the Forces: What's at Stake in Buffy the Vampire Slayer*, eds. R. Wilcox and D. Lavery, 18–34. Lanham: Rowman and Littlefield.
Henderson, Lauren, and Stella Duffy. 2004. Tart City, available at http://tartcity.com (accessed April 15, 2007).
Horsley, Lee. 2005. *Twentieth-century Crime Fiction*. Oxford: Oxford University Press.
Levy, Ariel. 2005. *Female Chauvinist Pigs: Women and the Rise of Raunch Culture*. New York: Free Press.
Levy, Sophie. 2003. "'You Still My Girl?' Adolescent Femininity as Resistance in *Buffy the Vampire Slayer*." *Reconstruction* 3, available at http://reconstruction.eserver.org/pastissues.html.
Littler, Alison. 1991. "Marele Day's 'Cold Hard Bitch': The Masculinist Imperatives of the Private-eye Genre. *Journal of Narrative Technique* 21:121–25.
Lotz, Amanda. 2006. *Redesigning Women: Television after the Network Era*. Urbana: University of Illinois Press.
McRobbie, Angela. 2004. "Notes on Postfeminism and Popular Culture: Bridget Jones and the New Gender Regime." In *All About the Girl: Culture, Power and Identity*, ed. A. Harris, 3–14. New York: Routledge.
Mizejewski, Linda. 2004. *Hardboiled and High Heeled: The Woman Detective in Popular Culture*. New York: Routledge.
_____. 2005. "Dressed to Kill: Postfeminist Noir." *Cinema Journal* 44:121–27.
Montgomery, Lucy Maud. 1908. *Anne of Green Gables*. Toronto: Seal Books (1983).
Munt, Sally. 1994. *Murder by the Book? Feminism and the Crime Novel*. New York: Routledge.
Porter, Dennis. 1981. *The Pursuit of Crime: Art and Ideology in Detective Fiction*. New Haven: Yale University Press.
Probyn, Elspeth. 1990. "New Traditionalism and Post-feminism: TV Does the Home." *Screen* 31:147–59.
Projansky, Sarah. 2001. *Watching Rape: Film and Television in Postfeminist Culture*. New York: New York University Press.
Read, Jacinda. 2000. *The New Avengers: Feminism, Femininity and the Rape-revenge Cycle*. Manchester: Manchester University Press.
Reddy, Maureen. 1988. *Sisters in Crime: Feminism and the Crime Novel*. New York: Continuum.
Shetley, Vernon. 1999. "Incest and Capital in *Chinatown*." *MLN* 1, no. 14:1092–1109.
Tasker, Yvonne, and Diane Negra. 2005. "In Focus: Postfeminism and Contemporary Media Studies. *Cinema Journal* 44:107–10.

Todorov, Tzvetan. 1977. *The Poetics of Prose*, trans. Richard Howard. New York: Cornell University Press.

Walton, Priscilla, and Manina Jones. 1999. *Detective Agency: Women Rewriting the Hardboiled Tradition*. Berkeley: University of California Press.

Wilson, Ann. 1995. "The Female Dick and the Crisis of Heterosexuality." In *Feminism in Women's Detective Fiction*, ed. G. Irons, 148–56. Toronto: University of Toronto Press.

8. The Portrait of an Artist as a Young Fan: Consumption and Queer Inspiration in *Six Feet Under*

Barbara Brickman

Nearly from its first episode, the HBO original series *Six Feet Under* has earned the devotion of a cult fan following. This dedication has often been remarked upon in reviews of the series and is at least partly fueled by an official HBO website, which includes bulletin boards, obituaries for each funeral at Fisher and Sons, and a complete episode guide with soundtrack listings attributed to specific scenes. With bulletin boards available "all day, every day" on topics such as "Episodes," "Characters and Relationships," "Predictions," and "About the Music," HBO has given these fans an outlet and a sanctioned community (www.hbo.com/sixfeetunder). In turn, the fans of this "full-blown cultural phenomenon" have shown extreme dedication, going so far as to write to actual funeral directors who share the (unfortunate) name of "Fisher" for stationery, pens, etc (Peyser 2002, 60). Reviewers have even admitted being fans, although not all have been so approving.[1] The show, now having concluded after five seasons, offers these viewers and fans a complex character study in which questions of identification, desire, and fluid subjectivities haunt every character in the program, including the teen member of the Fisher clan, Claire. More significantly, Claire alone provides another vital element for these fans—a surrogate within the program itself.

From the pilot episode, written and directed by Alan Ball, Claire Fisher is distinguished by the program's creators as a privileged spectator, as well as a frequent television viewer. While several critics (and even Claire herself) have commented on her relative invisibility before her father's death, for the viewer of the first episode, she becomes quite visible as a subject empowered to see. [2] Having returned from the morgue after her older brother Nate has had to identify their father's body, Claire retreats to her room, where her mother finds her absorbed in a Christmas special on television. Without turning around and barely taking her eyes off the screen, she does not engage with her mother, who awkwardly blurts out, "We have to eat, Claire. We didn't die!" Instead, Claire glares past her crystal meth haze at "Mister Magoo's Christmas Carol," and this popular show is revealed to the viewer in a reverse shot from Claire's point of view. (Interestingly, the 1962 Christmas special was the last hurrah for the famous cartoon character only to appear ever after in reruns, perhaps like Nathaniel Fisher, Sr., for whom this episode dramatizes an exit from the world of the "living.") Moreover, this scene will not be the last time the series self-reflexively offers Claire Fisher as a model and mirror for the television viewer, as I will discuss further below.

Yet, perhaps more importantly, the pilot episode also presents Claire as a privileged spectator who gains the power to know. Although David has introduced his partner Keith to his unwitting mother as a friend with whom he plays "racquetball," Claire scoffs at this explanation and then recognizes their intimacy from across the crowded room at her father's viewing, smiling at a view of their physical contact. Shortly thereafter, when Ruth is confessing her adultery to her son Nate, she agonizes about the ability of her deceased husband (and God) to "see" her and know everything that she has done, which wracks her with guilt. Moreover, I would suggest, Ruth's discussion of privileged sight might extend to Claire, who is the only person to see her ghost-father at his own funeral the next day, although he will "visit" other family members in later episodes. In accordance with this privilege, one might note that in the very next episode, Gabe, Claire's friend and suitor, insists that what makes Claire different is that she can "see through walls" ("The Will," 1:2). In a program bursting with ghostly visitations, intertextual allusions, and moments of postmodern self-reflexivity, Claire stands out as one apart, as the one who sees.

In this essay, I argue that Claire, the central adolescent subject in the series, is distinctly marked by the program as a fan and spectator, and, in her fandom, she reflects the fluid subjectivities and continuum of sexualities championed by the series as a whole. Moreover, the inspiration drawn from this fandom (of female objects, generally) encourages

Claire to become more than a consumer, instead, translating her fandom into artistic expression. Throughout the first season of the series, the fan/viewer-surrogate role suggested for Claire in the pilot continues, as she is shown watching *The Partridge Family* (1970–74), playing video games on-line, or sharing a video of *The Nutty Professor* (US, 1996) with her mother. Of course, by foregrounding her viewing practices and avid consumption of popular culture, visual media, and music, the program alludes to her place within the most coveted and anxiously courted demographic in the second half of the twentieth century: teenagers. Since the 1950s, the corporate sector in the United States, including the film industry, according to Thomas Doherty (2002), has seized upon the teen market as seemingly boundless and insatiable, yet powerfully unpredictable (see also Hine, 2000). The rise of this market force perhaps has reached its zenith in the generation (of which Claire is a member) sometimes called the "boom echo," dwarfing the buying power and influence of their parents' generation, the "baby boomers." However, Claire also represents a troubling figure for these models of consumption, as she exhibits an ability to read against the grain, to reject some forms of mass-produced popular culture (through "alternative" music, for example), and to manipulate these products for her own ends and, ultimately, toward her own art. In other words, she represents both teenaged consumption and marginalized fandom, particularly as it has been theorized in the work of Henry Jenkins (1992) and others.

Fittingly, Claire's moments of viewing differ generationally from other, similar moments in the series, such as when David and Keith watch the HBO original series *Oz* together. Claire does not simply watch fellow redhead Danny Partridge and his antics. The two are intertwined and revelatory of each other. On TV, the Partridge kids are trying to convince their mother to let them work—the "family that plays together stays together." In Claire's living room, her older brother Nate is expressing concern for her mental state—and Claire sarcastically tells him about her pimp threatening to "beat" her and "take away [her] smack" because she "can't turn enough tricks"("Familia"). As the scene cuts to a close-up while Danny Bonaduce whines that his sister Tracy should not have "to wait tables in some sleazy strip joint," we become aware of *Six Feet Under*'s ironic subversion of the family in that 1970s television classic. We can also recognize Claire as the viewer-character who acts as a tool for that revision. In the next episode, "An Open Book," she does not simply giggle at the physical humor of *The Nutty Professor*, but later stands in the darkness of the family room watching her mother, who is framed by the window separating the kitchen from the other room, in an attempt to understand. However, it is not until the sixth episode in the first season, "The Room," that the series offers a fuller impression of Claire's connection to fandom and its relevance to the program as a whole.

Fandom Light and Dark

While the first few episodes depict Claire as an avid viewer of (vintage) television and other forms of popular culture, in "The Room" Claire announces herself as a bona fide fan. Although Nate knows of his girlfriend Brenda Chenowith's childhood history, Claire has no idea that when she picks up her brother's copy of *Charlotte Light and Dark*, she is in the presence of her idol "Charlotte"—the pseudonym given to Brenda when, at six years old, she was studied by psychiatrists and analyzed in the aforementioned book.[3] In contrast to Brenda's resentment of her childhood alter ego, Claire discusses *Charlotte Light and Dark* with unabashed admiration, recapping her favorite parts of the book (such as when Charlotte barks at her doctors) and admitting to "totally" identifying with Charlotte. However, not until Brenda's brother Billy reveals her identity does Claire exhibit true fan traits: she responds with exasperation and disbelief and finally exclaims, "Oh my God, oh my God, it's like meeting Ghandi or Jesus!" To make the connection to television fandom of shows like *Star Trek*, *The X-Files*, or *Buffy the Vampire Slayer* even more explicit, Brenda lampoons Claire's identification with the character. Also, Billy points out the existence of a fan website with fans devoted just to Charlotte, fans Brenda describes as "those lonely little girls desperate for something to emulate because, apparently, they're not original enough to come up with anything on their own."[4] While Claire's fandom avoids a specific television show, it has all the hallmarks of members of fan cultures made notorious by the devotees to *Star Trek*.

In her fan appreciation of Charlotte, Claire reveals an attachment of an extreme or excessive nature and expert knowledge of the beloved text, compares her fan object with a religious figure, and desires to identify as completely as possible with her fan object, a process which can extend to dress, speech, and behavior. Every single one of these actions is included in the account of fan behaviors and activities detailed by Henry Jenkins in his influential study of fan cultures, *Textual Poachers: Television Fans & Participatory Culture* (1992), which uses as one of its models *Star Trek* fans. In an effort to explain the development of the term "fan" and the popular view of fan culture, Jenkins elucidates (and attempts to counter) the common perception of excess in fan behavior:

> If the term "fan" was originally evoked in a somewhat playful fashion and was often used sympathetically by sports writers, it never fully escaped its earlier connotations of religious and political zealotry, false beliefs, orgiastic excess, possession, and madness, connotations that seem to be at the heart of many of the representations of fans in contemporary discourse [12].

Certainly, Claire displays a kind of zealotry and orgiastic excess in the presence of her idol. She holds her hands to her mouth, almost in the gesture of prayer, and gasps out, "Oh my God!" making comparisons to meeting Jesus. She stares open-eyed at Brenda and cannot take her eyes away, even when, clearly, both Brenda and Billy are ridiculing her behavior. Later in the episode, after Billy has insinuated himself into Claire's life, she describes Brenda to him with awe and admiration and speculates that her brother must be in love with her, "How could he not be?!" Her devotion is not unrewarded. Although her budding relationship with Billy does not work out, Claire does earn Brenda's companionship, as the older woman picks her up from school when Billy stands her up. Brenda amusedly tolerates effusive admiration from Claire, who exclaims, "I still cannot get over the fact that you are Charlotte Light and Dark!"—by offering a mock serious response, "Well, you have to because it's very irritating!" Finally, in a moment of seeming fan wish fulfillment, the end of the episode finds Brenda and Claire together on her porch laughing and talking together.

However, there can be a dark side to the excess and zealotry of fandom, in stark contrast to the bliss of fan-object union depicted on the porch of Brenda's house in episode six. The series itself sets up contrasting examples of fandom, which are depicted as dangerously excessive or marked by the choice of the wrong object for devotion.[5] Throughout the first season, David Fisher is hounded by a divorcée named Tracy, who has a neurotic habit of visiting the funerals of strangers—she admits that *Harold and Maude* (1971) is her "favorite movie of all time," having "profoundly affected" her life since junior high ("Knock, Knock"). The DVD episode summary for the season's final episode describes Tracy Montrose Blaire as David's "biggest fan," but unlike the depiction of Claire's fandom, the series represents Tracy's devotion as inappropriate, misguided, and, simply, annoying. As an interesting contrast for Claire, she hounds David in episode six during church charity work and misrecognizes his sexual orientation, forcing awkward moments when the closeted David cannot reveal that he is gay, but then cannot rid himself of Tracy's attentions. In comparison, Tracy has chosen the incorrect object to adore and David's discomfort and growing annoyance with her attentions prejudice the audience against *her* version of fandom, which interestingly evokes early representations of "slash" fans who are often heterosexual women romantically pairing two male stars in fan fiction (Jenkins 2002; Penley 2002). She appears sick and delusional, while Claire, who does recognize David's relationship with Keith, is rewarded with union with the *female* object of her fandom. Yet, Tracy's mistaken devotion plays as comic relief, whereas Billy's attachment to the children's book *Nathaniel and Isabel* ultimately proves the most extreme version of fan zealotry.

Billy and Brenda's sibling relationship contrasts sharply with that of the Fisher siblings in its overly intense closeness and, thereby, unsettling nature. Their parents explain the sibling's relationship to Nate (in "An Open Book") through the concept of literary fandom. Having seen Brenda's tattoo of "Nathaniel" on her lower back, Nate asks the parents about "Nathaniel and Isabel" and is shown the book of the same name by Brenda's mother Margaret Chenowith, who admits, "Brenda adored these books as a little girl." Explaining the basic premise of two sibling orphans having adventures and eluding the malevolent nurse who wants to capture them and return them to the orphanage, Brenda's mother recounts how the older sibling would sit next to her brother's crib and read the stories for hours. The two siblings identified strongly with the orphans, as evidenced by their matching tattoos, but only Billy seems to have taken that identification and fandom too far.

In an almost textbook case of pathological fandom (it is established early in the first season that Billy also suffers from bipolar disorder), Billy represents that "obsessed loner" model of aberrant fandom, characterized by Joli Jenson as slipping into "an intense fantasy relationship with a celebrity figure" (1992, 11). These fans, such as Mark David Chapman or John Hinckley, suggest a "risky, even dangerous, compensatory mechanism" at work in fandom, in which "distinctions between reality and fantasy break down" (18). In the final episode of the first season, Billy confirms this conception of fandom gone horribly wrong. When Brenda separates herself from him, denying him access to his Isabel and sig-nificant other, Billy responds by cutting out his tattoo and breaking into Brenda's home to force her to do the same. Insisting that he cannot be Nathaniel anymore, that "he's somebody else now ... and now we can bury him," Billy has attempted to break his bond of over-identification but has failed terribly in separating fantasy from reality. While he recognizes the hold his fan identification has over his life, Billy cannot escape the pull of the narrative, even though Brenda re-asserts, "It's fiction. Nathaniel and Isabel are not real!" He grabs his sister to cut out her visible attachment to their doubles, and his violent action, though unsuccessful, results in Brenda having him committed. Billy has not only chosen the wrong object, his sister, but his fandom suffers from a descent into delusion, which compares fittingly with Claire's recognition of the actual person behind the text *Charlotte Light and Dark*.

Aside from the function of providing a surrogate or model for fans of the series itself, one might ask what is the relevance of portraying Claire as a fan, and as a preferable or favored version of fandom. The answer to this question, I believe, rests in both her choice of object and the use she makes of her fandom. Claire chooses a female, same-sex object for adoration and identification, and, ultimately, her fan instincts and desires translate into artistic production. I would argue combining these two elements is not a coincidence in *Six Feet Under*, which, in addition to its meditation on death and how to live one's life in the shadow of it, concerns itself centrally with the themes of fluid sexuality and desire and the workings of the creative process and artistic inspiration. A recent collection of essays on the HBO original series explains these central concerns through the concept of "liminality" or spaces in between or on the margins of accepted discourse and societal norms. The writers view *Six Feet Under* as a television program dealing fundamentally with "spaces existing on the cultural periphery that are shaped by ambiguity and paradox" (Akass and McCabe 2005, 10). The series shifts between comedy and drama, deals with the liminal space "between death and burial," and focuses on "cultural taboos" such as homosexuality or mental illness and marginalized groups like older women and adolescents (3). Consequently, essays in *Reading Six Feet Under: TV to Die For* discuss the liminal space of waiting for death, the marginalized position of Ruth Fisher as a post-menopausal woman whose liminal status arises from her place beyond or "post" reproduction (the defining feature of "woman"), and the bold depiction of Claire and Brenda who, as outspokenly un-conventional female subjects, seem always on the margins of or resistant to institutional discourses about women.

One might easily add the space of teenage (girl) fandom and fan activities to this list of liminal territories and identities. Fans, for example, are set off from regular "viewers" of television through their expert, exhaustive knowledge or their excessive emotional attachment and investment in the program. Jenkins asserts that fans are marginalized for their ability to blur the boundaries of cultural hierarchies by preferring low (popular) culture: "The fans' transgression of bourgeois taste and disruption of dominant cultural hierarchies insures that their preferences are seen as abnormal and threatening by those who have a vested interest in the maintenance of these standards" (1992, 17). When those fans are young women, the impact of the transgression can be greatly magnified. For example, critics such as Barbara Ehrenreich et al. (1992) associate the liminality of fandom with a marginal space allowing for rebellious alternatives to gender norms for teenage girls. It is significant that they are "teenaged" because adolescence itself may be one of the most notorious liminal spaces in Western cultures. At least since the publication of Rousseau's *Emile*, the modern concept of the adolescent has presented an individual caught between childhood and adulthood, experiencing the changes of puberty, and struggling with the *sturm und drang* of an identity crisis on the margins of adulthood.[6] Claire's fandom, then, has the potential to serve as triply marginalized—as teenaged, female, and queer. In other words, as a teenage girl with an excessive fan attachment to Charlotte (and, later, fellow artist Edie), Claire is finally located in a liminal or queer space between heteronormativity and homosexuality. Moreover, the series not only approvingly portrays and endorses this marginal position of fandom and queerness, but also ties it to another championed liminality: the pursuit of artistic expression and unique vision. Through her negotiation and play within one space, that of fan appreciation of another woman, Claire embodies *Six Feet Under*'s commitment to a marginal position which reflects back on societal investment in heteronormativity, *and* she shows how that play can lead to artistic production and fulfillment.[7]

All of these threads of fandom, queer desire, and artistic inspiration are brought together in early episodes of Season Two when Claire is introduced to her aunt Sarah. Her "bohemian" aunt recognizes an artistic side to Claire that has, until this point, gone unmentioned in the series ("The Plan"). As the series progresses, Claire attempts to establish an independent identity, and in Season Two, the focus of that identity (or the goal which will eventually send her to New York at the very end of the series) is finally defined: to express herself artistically. Her aunt Sarah, who knows many artists and has attempted some artistic production herself, finds "anger, and yearning, passion, resentment of the status quo, some jealousy of it as well" in Claire's paintings, identifying the work as "authentic" and Claire as an "artist."[8] While Claire may not be ready to view herself as an artist, Sarah recognizes the connection between what Gabe saw in the first season (privileged sight) and Claire's art: "You've got an eye ... you see through the veil." The allusion to the Romantic notion of seeing past everyday reality to the sublime underneath the veil of life pleases Claire, but the actuality of an artist's vocation becomes visible to her only through Brenda, who has begun to write a novel.

While Aunt Sarah has offered the idea of the life of an artist, it is Brenda, the adored idol, who embodies the possibility. At the dinner to announce Brenda and Nate's engagement, Claire is thrilled to hear that Brenda might possibly be writing a novel, and she immediately associates the discovery with *Charlotte Light and Dark*. She gushes to tell her aunt that Brenda is Charlotte, and proudly describes her beloved text: "It's this book about a girl who's being analyzed and she's, like, way smarter than the people analyzing her and so she's constantly fucking with them. It's hilarious!" While Brenda and Claire might be amused by this description, only Aunt Sarah makes explicit the connection between Brenda's experiences and her need to create art *and* ties both to Claire's creative instincts. She maneuvers the discussion from being about Brenda's writing to Claire, whom she announces as the "budding artist in the family." While one cannot claim Brenda as a direct cause of Claire's need for artistic impression, the series, here, is making an associative connection. Claire links Brenda's urge to express herself with her beloved fan object, *Charlotte Light and Dark*, and Sarah connects both with the burgeoning young artist. Certainly, Brenda-Charlotte functions as an inspiration for Claire, but here the inspiration is attached to creativity and an identity as an artist.

Several critics have examined the common transition from fan devotion to creative production. Jenkins notes how the process of obsessive rereading or re-viewing and avid discussions among fan groups eventually leads to the fans' own construction of texts: "It is something that can and must be rewritten to make it more productive of personal meanings and to sustain the intense emotional experience they enjoyed when they viewed it the first time" (1992, 75). In the act of creating fan fiction, fans can act as readers, critics, and, finally, writers or scribblers "in the margins" (152).[9] Claire does not attempt to rewrite or produce a new *Charlotte Light and Dark*, but the series is positing a correlation between her fan desires and identification with Charlotte and her "budding" identity as an artist.

What is more, the creators of *Six Feet Under* explicitly articulate both fandom and the ensuing artistic inspiration within a female-centered sphere. Whether focusing on Claire and Brenda on the porch in Season One, Aunt Sarah and Claire in her room in Season Two, and, at the end of episode six, Claire and her mother Ruth in her room, the series creates exceptional *female* spaces for the exploration of identity, desire, and self-expression. While she could become a fan-author in the model of "slash" fan fiction writers who commonly pair two men together from their adored television shows or films, instead Claire chooses a female object and produces art that explores her own female adolescent identity and concerns.[10] At the end of episode six, Ruth comes into Claire's room with a box containing every art project Claire "ever did" and the two look over the items, stopping on one in particular. Claire holds up a child's drawing of a house with three figures out front and notices that her brother Nate and her father are missing. Her childhood drawing, therefore, contains Claire, Ruth, and David, but neither the patriarch nor his heterosexual namesake. Art, then, becomes the realm of the female or the feminized (as homosexual men commonly are in dominant culture), or, in other words, the realm of the marginalized.

Elvis, Elvis, Let Me Be: Bending the Straight Girl Fan

Seasons later, when Claire attends a performance by fellow artist Edie, this connection between Claire's fandom of another woman and artistic production associated with the female is once again reinforced, as her adoration of (and attempted relationship with) Edie inspires her own creative work ("In Case of Rapture"). However, this depiction of teen girl fandom provides an alternative to many critical accounts of girl fans, in which the female adolescent chooses a male idol or object and, through her excessive devotion to that object, subverts normative gender roles. Even though this male object is feminized or androgynous according to the critics, homosexuality, not to mention the pleasures of slash fan fiction, are not mentioned. Such a critical view of teen girl fans, the most prominent example of which might be Ehrenreich, et al.'s article (1992) on Beatles fans, locates fan resistances within the confines of heteronormativity, with the teenage girl adoring the strangely androgynous male star. Claire's example, however, suggests a female object of devotion *and* the homoerotic and queer pleasures between women offered by and even fueling teen girl fandom and creative production.

Much of the work on teen girl fandom, such as Ehrenreich, et al.'s "Beatlemania: Girls Just Want to Have Fun," recognizes challenges to gender norms in fan activities, but not challenges to sexual norms. Whether suffering from the "disease of isolation" or the "disease of contagion," familiar victims emerge in Jenson's article "Fandom as Pathology"—from teenagers to emotional women—and she recognizes the construction of gender differences (1992). The female fan image "assumes that an uncontrollable erotic energy is sparked by the chance to see or touch a male idol," indicating her passive relation to her igniter (15). For the male fan, "the image is of drunken destructiveness, a rampage of uncontrollable masculine passion that is unleashed in response to a sports victory or defeat," which reinforces a notion of active, male aggression (15).[11]

"Beatlemania" describes a rebellious teen girl fandom—one that defies its dominant (parent) culture through sexuality—but relegates the hint of homosexuality to the realm of the male star. For Ehrenreich et al. the hysteria of female Beatle fans during the peak years of Beatlemania, 1964 and 1965, represents "the first mass outburst of the sixties to feature women" (85). This rebellion, an abandonment of control in the form of screaming, fainting, and forming mobs in the presence of four young men who were clearly objects of sexual desire, symbolizes for the authors a "protest" against the sexually repressive double standard imposed on teenage girls at the time. These girls were supposed to uphold the edict of virginity until marriage, even in the face of an increasingly "sexualized society," and their overt, clearly physical desire for the Beatles smashed through these expectations, creating "the first and most dramatic uprising of *women's* sexual revolution" (ibid, original emphasis). What the parent culture viewed as "an affliction, an 'epidemic,'" infected a population of girls who seemed to have little interest in marrying their idols (87).

The draw of stars like James Dean, Elvis Presley or the Beatles was their freedom from the banality of matrimony and domesticity, their promise that "the romance would never end in the tedium of marriage" (96). Also, significantly, they somehow were not "all boy," but tainted by femininity (100). The white middle-class girls of this period, according to the authors, had to repress or channel the desires society found unacceptable in them but natural for boys. Screaming for Ringo "was a way to express sexual yearnings that would normally be pressed into the service of popularity or simply repressed"; therefore, marrying the star was exactly *not* the point (97). Furthermore, certain characteristics of the lads from Liverpool made them especially suitable for active female desire and unsuitable for marriage. They were not the "ideal boyfriend" who was "all boy" and "realistic" about his "destiny," as husband, father, and breadwinner; they were "moody and sensitive" and far from the "pragmatic ideal" a girl sought in marriage (100).

In explaining the "erotics of the star-fan relationship," Ehrenreich, et al. flirt with the notion of "androgyny" in male stars without examining further why these teenage girls were so attracted to the feminine (or at least the blurring of feminine and masculine). Since Ehrenreich, et al.'s article does not address fan fiction, there is no way of accounting for the ties to later developments in slash fiction about homosexual male pairings. For their purposes, the sexual revolution of Beatlemania entails girls actively seeking androgynous young men who hint at "an enormous change in the sexual possibilities open to women and girls" (105). Nevertheless, this "enormous change" does not include homosexuality in women. None of the discussion of androgyny and femininity seems to suggest, to the authors, a desire for the feminine on the part of these girls. When looking for an alternative to the "tedium of marriage," these girls find it in "sexually suspect" and androgynous young men, but this does not also raise the issue of a "*women's* sexual revolution" which might not involve men at all.

My suggestion above of nascent (or suspected) homosexual or queer desire in teen girl fandom of androgynous or feminized male stars (not to mention desire *between* the girls) remains closeted even in recent accounts responding to Ehrenreich, et al. In "Hysterical Scream or Rebel Yell?" Ilana Nash assesses how reactions to and desires of "teenybopper fandom" changed from the mid-sixties to late seventies, contending that by then teenage girls "had been screaming and screwing for a long time" and, therefore, these acts lost revolutionary status (2003, 134). In this rapid turn of events in which the "sexually free girl had lost a lot of her stigma," the seemingly innocent teen-idol fan becomes the pariah, hiding in a childish world of Shaun Cassidy puppy love far from women's sexual revolution. Nash attempts to dispel this stereotyped dismissal of (her own) teen-idol devotion by insisting on the progressiveness and eroticism of her choice.

Nash summarizes her version of feminism: "My friends and I took the received narratives of teenybopper identity and unconsciously modified them, using what we knew of the sexual revolution and feminism to create what we lacked: a cultural space somewhere between reviled childhood and a style of teenhood that seemed unwelcoming, even threatening" (138). Ultimately, Nash presents teenybopper fandom as a "feminist project," in which the girls, in the face of constant belittling by peers and the popular media, persist in their devotion to the more feminine Cassidy, produce fan texts, and find a safe place for asserting their (hetero)sexuality (138).

Although she adeptly shows how the expectations for teenage girls changed in only one decade, Nash's article does not diverge significantly from earlier accounts of fan culture.[12] When introducing the idea of Shaun Cassidy's reputation as a "pretty" (i.e. feminine) and non-threatening choice of object for immature girls, Nash attacks the perception of teenyboppers consuming their idols "because they aren't 'ready' for real sex, real boys, or real masculinity" (138). However, her defense of this position opens her essay up to the unmanageable presence of lesbianism, admitting that her group of fans included one lesbian (139). Therefore, she has improved on Ehrehreich, et al.'s account by allowing the idea of homosexuality to enter the discussion, but once in the door, the lesbian, predictably, becomes a ghost once again with no more mentions.

Even as Nash insists that her cohort of fans "built a space where we could be sexual on our terms," writing "girl-meets-idol fiction" that turned into "riots of good-spirited filth," she does not address the pleasures for *all* the fans in her group. She forecloses the possibility of either a homoerotic attachment to the feminized male idol or a homosexual attachment within girl fan groups, a liminal space for all sorts of queer desires (145). Based on the innocent stories from fan magazines, each "funny" was a story-gift given to another friend in the group in which the writer created a "highly pornographic" tale about Shaun Cassidy and the recipient-friend (145). Like Beatlemaniacs before them, the writers of these "funnies" had no interest in marrying but "wanted to sleep with Shaun," except presumably for one member of the group. One wonders what pleasure could this activity have given Shaun's lone lesbian devotee.

One of the most significant features of Claire's fan experience, I would argue, is that it subverts this common image of the teen girl fan and confirms the undercurrents of queer desire that lingers at the margins of the two articles above. Claire is not the unquestionably straight teen girl who is oddly attracted to the feminine or androgynous male idol. She is, instead, a queer teen girl fan attracted to clearly female idols. Moreover, the artistic output—not Claire as fan-author, but Claire as fan-artist—is not male-centered fan fiction, but female-centered visual art, a creative way to articulate identity through emulation of *and* desire for a female other. While one might counter these claims with the observation that Claire's devotion to Brenda and *Charlotte Light and Dark* involves identification and not sexual attraction (an account of female fandom offered in Lisa A. Lewis' 1992 study of female pop idols), the youngest Fisher's attraction to Edie in Season Four complicates such a claim. The mixture of desire to identify with and simple attraction to Edie lands Claire in a decidedly queer space. Having previously struggled with male influences at LAC-Arts, such as her professor Olivier and fellow artists-suitor Russell, who shook her belief in her own artistic vision, Claire announces her determination to immerse herself in her art again at the opening of Season Four.[13] Taking at least one piece of Olivier's advice, that she try to "break [her] eye open" by learning to see in a new way or without old associations, Claire takes in Nan Goldin's photographs, even standing on her bed and looking down at them at the end of the episode ("Falling Into Place"). In the very next episode, Claire is truly inspired once again, but by a fellow female art student named Edie.

In this first episode of Season Four, Claire discovers and immediately admires the stimulating work and forceful attitude of attractive fellow artist Edie ("In Case of Rapture"). Edie assumes the stage and immediately declares her unabashed feminist position by asking for a moratorium on "angry poems with the words clitoral or vaginal in them ... unless you have one." In contradistinction to the male performers preceding her, Edie's performance piece is a meditation on mother-daughter relationships and the roles offered to and assumed for (and by) women. She plays with the emotions and preconceived expectations of the audience, by first revealing her mother has cancer and playing the pre-recorded sound of an older woman's plea that she feels "so lost" and then turning the tables by admitting that she lied. Edie confronts the audience with their own expectations for a woman whom she describes as "just a fucking victim who's never taken a chance in her life and has nobody to blame but herself" and who is, in fact, vice president of the Midwest Direct Marketing Association. All throughout this performance, Claire is shown, in reaction shots of the crowd, as completely absorbed in the performance. In a series of medium close-ups, we see Claire staring intently, laughing with the rest of the audience, sitting back to take the information in, and in an extreme close-up at the end of the performance, she audibly breathes out in amazement and smiles.

In Edie, Claire has found yet another example, like Brenda, of a strong, vocal female subject who resists and openly confronts the dominant cultural narratives about and consequent pathologization of women. Moreover, this new, impressive female figure for adoration goes beyond the inspiration offered by Brenda and actively encourages Claire to express herself as an artist. Once Claire has declared her gushing praise for Edie's performance, Edie inquires about her work and insists that Claire must return to her own photography. Receiving such advice from another artist who she clearly admires spurs Claire to pick up her camera and record some of the frequent, bizarre events that occur in the Fisher funeral home. When Claire discovers that Edie is a "hard core lesbian feminist," according to Anita, she appears intrigued and so moved by recent events that she makes a change, which is symbolized by burning her old clothes ("Parallel Play"). The proceeding episodes reveal the extent of Claire's serious interest in transforming herself through her growing boldness in relationships and her struggle to communicate meaning in her art. Particularly, Claire's relationship with Edie seems to produce more passion towards her art, as they attempt to plan a mixed media performance event (possibly in a mall) where she can finally "do something really controversial," and, at the same time, she grows closer to Edie ("Terror Starts at Home").

After a series of flirtatious moments such as rolling around together on the front lawn, which inspire more interest and an artistic product (the alluring photograph of Edie that is the first success for Claire in her photography class), Edie brings the flirtation to a crisis by kissing Claire. Claire's reaction perfectly describes her confusion of feelings; she feels as though Edie inspires her art and she wants more contact with her, but she flees when Edie tries to kiss her again ("The Dare"). Finally, Claire makes the decision that they should consummate the relationship and see what happens, but when Edie reminds her of her previous hesitation, Claire recognizes her decidedly queer position: "Part of me thinks this is what I want and part of me thinks it isn't." Edie's pleased smile in response to this statement shows a confidence in Claire's feelings, but the youngest Fisher appears much more ambivalent, caught between heterosexual norms and homosexual desires. She is clearly attracted to Edie, as evidenced by the rapt attention she gives Edie's picture at the beginning of an episode, almost as if she is mooning over a star's pin-up, but refuses to be labeled Edie's "girlfriend" by Anita in art class. She cannot adequately define her feelings for Edie in one direction or another, but the series *is* explicit in connecting those feelings to her artistic expression, possibly because they are indefinable.

Because Claire's desire for Edie or to be with her places her outside of heteronormativity, though not exactly within gay subjectivity, and because her desire is associated with an artistic counter-discourse, I would argue that her fandom and her need for artistic expression have collapsed into the same queer space. Just as Samuel Chambers contends that Russell's queerness in Season Three "forces both the characters around him and the viewer to experience modern categories of sexuality as somehow alienating and inadequate," Claire's awkward fandom for and relationship with Edie is similarly queer (2005, 179). As Halperin defines it apart from the historically constructed homosexual identity, the queer position—always a "marginal location"—is "an identity without an essence," only gaining meaning through its opposition to "the normal, the legitimate, the dominant" (1995, 62).

The lack of a stable definition (or essence) for Claire's sexuality, as with Russell, disrupts the notion of a fixed heterosexual norm, as well as a fixed homosexual identity constructed as the negative other of the norm. Claire and Edie have sex, but Claire fails to have an orgasm, despite Edie's promises to "make her scream" (like any good fan should), and they both decide that Claire might not want sex with women. However, Claire still has a complex attraction for Edie, who is the "coolest and most beautiful" person she has ever seen and someone she admires and to whom she admits feeling physically drawn ("Coming and Going"). When Edie declares the attraction is "aesthetic," defining the relationship solely through her art, they both must add terms denoting an intellectual *and* physical connection. In the end, Claire finally resigns the attraction to being "not necessarily sexual." Not necessarily committing one way or the other, she remains outside of normal or legitimate definitions of sexuality and yet clearly dedicated to her art, which she has defined as openly oppositional to the normal and the dominant.

As the fourth season concludes, Claire proves unsettled (or undecided) sexually, still harboring feelings for Edie, but more committed than ever to the success of her art. Even after she becomes briefly involved with fellow artist Jimmy ("Grinding the Corn"), Claire attempts to reconnect with Edie in the very next episode, though unsuccessfully ("The Black Forest"). Outside of any normative sexual sphere and apart from the female object, Edie, Claire channels that desire into her art, with the help of ex-boyfriend (and other queer adolescent subject) Russell. The collage photographs that earn Claire her newfound success at the end of Season Four come out of the episode "The Black Forest," when Claire cannot pursue her fan desire for Edie and struggles with her own art. As Russell places a torn photo of Claire's own eyes on her face and she asks him to photograph her (demanding an image of herself), the collage concept that brings her a gallery show is created, and Claire does finally seem to be moving toward clear self-definition.[14]

Moving from the success of her photograph of the adored object Edie to the defining moment of the portrait of an artist, Claire has transformed the queer space of fan desire to the marginalized and possibly fragmenting, but rewarding and empowering, space of the artist. What this move might suggest is that, all along, Claire has been not only a surrogate for the fans, but possibly also a surrogate for the creators of *Six Feet Under*. The fan who becomes a visual artist, especially a queer fan, might very well be a familiar model for the shows creators, who have produced a television program defiant of heteronormativity, reflective about other examples of popular culture, and celebratory of queer or liminal spaces at its core.[15] When Claire rides off towards the east, to New York and the possibility of a future artistic vocation, at the series' close, one wonders if the show has always been driven by the inspirations of a young fan, a fan who grows up negotiating queer spaces and hoping to produce art, even if it someday appears on a major cable network.

One might argue, in fact, that the centrality of Claire's experience and voice has been present since the pilot episode. Nathan Fisher, Sr.'s funeral creates a great disturbance for the other family members, but Claire concludes the ceremony with a profound yet humorous conversation with her father's ghost. They both agree how lucky he was to die in an instant, without suffering, and Claire admits to envying his position where there is "no more bullshit" and "no more waiting to die," statements which Nathan Sr. validates with a knowing laugh. Moreover, the episode ends with a lingering note of Claire's final observation through The Devlins' song "Waiting" that leads into the credits, almost as if

Claire's words have returned from outside the diegesis to encapsulate the series as a whole—the viewers waiting for the next death that opens every episode, Nate waiting for the death which eventually comes, David waiting to live a full life, and Claire waiting to find her calling and be free. While a number of other "quality" subscription network series such as *Big Love, Queer as Folk,* or *The Sopranos* place teen concerns within "multigenerational family contexts," according to Ross and Stein's introduction to this collection, *Six Feet Under* places a teen voice at its core.[16] In light of the description above, Claire both opens and closes the series, beginning with her recognition of the liminal state of all their lives—waiting for something to happen—and concluding with her flight into the unknown future.

Within the context of *Six Feet Under*, moreover, this unusual repositioning, taking the teen from the periphery into the center, perfectly reflects the concerns of the series and, particularly, its commitment to exploring and liberating marginalized identities. For this "quality" series dedicated to investigating, giving voice to, and empowering marginalized identities (whether categorized by race, gender, age, or sexuality), the queer teen girl offers a fitting representative. She is not the voice of the patriarchy, she confuses the choice between heteronormativity and its defining other (homosexuality), and she does not possess the authority of adulthood. The teenage girl, while often a figure eliciting concern and anxiety in the twentieth (or twenty-first) century, is rarely taken as the voice of authority, yet that is the position the HBO series gives her. Furthermore, by making her a fan, *Six Feet Under* authorizes its own significance as a popular program, since fans show that popular culture can matter and that the message can be received (though it often undergoes much transformation in the hands of fans). To make her a fan and an artist highlights the place from which the series makes its empowering call—"quality" queer (tele)visual culture—while it also encourages new Claires to drive off into a decentered space of their own inventing.

Notes

1. Andrew O'Hehir (2002) includes himself as one of the "devotees" of the program, while Joshua Gamson, in "Death Becomes Them," *The American Prospect* 12, no.12 (July 2–16 2001): 37, is less approving of the show's "blond network roots."

2. See also, for example, O'Hehir (2002), Robert Tobin (2002), and Janet McCabe (2005).

3. Clearly, the creators of the series are alluding to the title of the enormously popular fictional account of another "troubled" young girl, *Lisa, Bright and Dark: A Novel* (Neufeld 1968), about Lisa Shilling. Selling over two million copies and designated as a "New York Times Outstanding Book of the Year," *Lisa, Bright and Dark* joined a number of books of the period. *Go Ask Alice* (1982) and *I Never Promised You a Rose Garden* (1989) were meant to diagnose (and possibly contain and control through pathologization) a group of young women or teenaged girls with increasingly reported mental

illnesses. Lisa Shilling fluctuates between "light" days when she appears "normal" and "dark" days when she seems depressed and self-destructive. In an odd turn of events where her parents, and especially her mother, actively neglect her, Lisa can only find solace in the talk therapy she performs for her friends, the "doctors" described in the preface to the book as "on a path of aid and comfort that will cause readers to reflect seriously, smile in recognition, and sympathize totally with Lisa and her illness" (7). (John Neufield, *Lisa, Bright and Dark: A Novel*, [New York: S.G. Phillips, 1968]). In some ways, the allusion works better as a point of reference for Claire, who meets with a therapist at school because of her anti-social behavior and "pattern of acting out since her father's death" ("Familia"). In either case, the series seems to seek to subvert once again the exact narratives and popular texts to which it alludes, offering Claire as something other than a victim. As she defends herself to Nate in "Familia," "Why do you have to naturally assume I'm in trouble?"

4. Obviously, Billy's comment about websites and fan clubs could also apply to fans of *Six Feet Under* itself, self-consciously a nod to the fans courted by HBO. For accounts of other fan cultures devoted to television programs, see Jenkins (1992); Penley (1992); Larbalestier (2002); and Scodari and Felder (2002).

5. *Six Feet Under* also offers more examples of "positive" fan devotion, such as the sincere emotion expressed by fans of Viveca St. John, the porn star, at her funeral ("An Open Book"). While these moments remain somewhat comic, the men witnessing at the porn star's funeral do express a love and appreciation in their sincere testimonials to her place in their lives.

6. For a full explanation of the development of the modern concept of "adolescence," see Kett (1977).

7. In the collection *Reading Six Feet Under: TV to Die For* (2005), Samuel Chambers' article "Revisiting the Closet: Reading Sexuality in *Six Feet Under*" argues eloquently for a reading of the program's commitment to challenging sexual norms: "Through Russell's character, the third season of *Six Feet Under* continues the show's unprecedented and still unparalleled tradition of exposing and thereby challenging heteronormativity" (176). He offers the "illegibility of Russell's sexuality" as the central factor in making his character "so very queer" and in forcing both the characters around him and the viewers to "experience modern categories of sexuality as somehow alienating or inadequate" (179). Claire, of course, is one of these frustrated characters (eds. Kim Akass and Janet McCabe, [London: Taurus], 174–88).

8. In "'Like Whatever': Claire, Female Identity and Growing Up Dysfunctional," Janet McCabe suggests that Aunt Sarah's presence offers Claire a "possible alternative" to the fairy tales that "convince women their only happiness can be found in romantic love and caring for a man" through artistic expression (2005, 131). However, she argues that even though Sarah opens up the possibility of "the narrative of a young woman striving to find a unique voice" (132), her own narrative concludes with a return to melodramatic lines relating to her inability to have children. This analysis, though, does not attend to the dual influence of Sarah *and* Brenda during these episodes of Season Two (*Reading Six Feet Under: TV to Die For*, eds. Kim Akass and Janet McCabe, [London: Taurus], 121–34).

9. To explain this notion of fan as author, in "Reception Theory and Audience Research: The Mystery of the Vampire Kiss," Jenkins describes a short story by Susan Douglas called "Music of the Night." This appeared in the fanzine *On the Edge*, as "an appropriation, a creative reworking of textual materials which consciously expands their potential meanings" (167) (in *Reinventing Film Studies*, eds. Christine Gledhill and Linda Williams [London: Arnold, 2000], 165–82). Douglass herself claims her story as an "'alternate-universe version'" of *Thelma and Louise* (ibid). Innumerable articles have been written on the topic of fan fiction and the productive powers of fan cultures. In addition to Jenkins' work, see Baym (2000) and Bacon-Smith (1992).

10. Interestingly, the topic of "slash" or fan fiction that pairs two characters from the same television series or from different television series in, often, homosexual relationships has received much critical attention, beginning with Penley (1992) and Jenkins (1992). However, much of this work focuses on "slash" fiction about two male characters, often written by heterosexual women. The example from the pilot episode wherein Claire

recognizes David and Keith's relationship suggests Claire's affinity with traditional slash fans who paired figures like Kirk and Spock, but ultimately her own fandom-inspired creative work centers around a search for female identity and desire between women.

11. However, the article itself does not introduce complications to heterosexual norms in fan contagion or frenzy. More recently, articles on lesbian slash have redressed this omission: see, for example, Rust (2003). As early as 1992, Henry Jenkins did recognize the beginnings of lesbian slash, citing a few fiction writers who place female members of science fiction programs in relationships; see also Benshoff (1998) and Jenkins (2003).

12. See also Georgeanne Scheiner's *Signifying Female Adolescence: Film Representations and Fans, 1920–1950* (Westport, CT: Praeger, 2000), which praises Deanna Durbin Devotees' exploration of "dimensions of female identity that went beyond parental and mass media definitions of femininity" (126) but does not recognize homosexuality as one of those dimensions. Deanna Durbin Devotees shared club activities that "emphasized alternative conceptions of female behavior and female identity, such as talent, expertise, achievement, creativity and a knowledge of current events" (132). Noticeably, however, none of these alternatives includes lesbianism.

13. Janet McCabe astutely notes that Claire's application to LAC-Arts "coincides with the termination of her therapy" (2005, 132), suggesting that her artistic vocation leads to "her uneasy attempt to intervene and put into discourse another kind of subjectivity" (133). However, this attempt to "move beyond the social roles that confine other female characters" is cut short, according to McCabe, by Claire's pregnancy in Season Three (133). The pregnancy resulting from her broken relationship with Russell threatens to place Claire in a different narrative, that of "dutiful motherhood" (as represented by Ruth), but she decides to have an abortion, which McCabe reads as a turning away from her mother's discourse toward "the one of female resistance" in Brenda (133). While Claire suffers greatly from this decision, the beginning of Season Four shows her still mourning, but also attempting to re-immerse herself in her own art, which is a path certainly modeled on Brenda and not her own mother.

14. I would like to thank Jennifer Gillian for suggesting the importance of this collage series and the defining moment of self-portraiture for Claire.

15. In fact, in *Six Feet Under: Better Living Through Death,* Alan Ball and Alan Poul (the show's creator and director) writes about Claire's wish-fulfillment short story described in therapy with Gary during the first season. This connection suggests that Claire might be more than just the youngest Fisher working through her teen angst and that her invisibility in the beginning and her dramatic entrance at the end might indicate her status as the narrative's core (2005).

16. See "Introduction: Watching Teen TV" in this collection, 19.

References

Akass, Kim, and Janet McCabe. 2005. Introduction: "Why Do People Have to Die?" "To Make Contemporary Television Drama Important, I Guess." In *Reading Six Feet Under: TV to Die For,* eds. Kim Akass and Janet McCabe, 1–15. London: Taurus.
Anonymous. 1982. *Go Ask Alice.* New York: Avon Books.
Bacon-Smith, Camille. 1992. *Enterprising Women: Television Fandom and the Creation of Popular Myth.* Philadelphia: University of Pennsylvania Press.
Ball, Alan, and Alan Poul, eds. 2005. *Six Feet Under: Better Living Through Death.* New York: Pocket.
Baym, Nancy K. 2000. *Tune In, Log On: Soaps, Fandom, and Online Community.* Thousand Oaks: Sage.
Benshoff, Harry. 1998. "Secrets, Closet, and Corridors Through Time: Negotiating Sexuality and Gender Through *Dark Shadows* Fan Culture." In *Theorizing Fandom: Fans, Subculture and Identity,* eds. Cheryl Harris and Alison Alexander, 199–218. Cresskill, NJ: Hampton Press.
Chambers, Samuel. 2005. "Revisiting the Closet: Reading Sexuality in *Six Feet Under.*" In *Reading Six Feet Under: TV to Die For,* eds. Kim Akass and Janet McCabe, 174–88. London: Taurus.

Doherty, Thomas. 2002. *Teenagers and Teenpics: The Juvenilization of American Movies in the 1950s*. Philadelphia: Temple University Press.

Ehrenreich, Barbara, Elizabeth Hess and Gloria Jacobs. 1992. "Beatlemania: Girls Just Want to Have Fun." In *The Adoring Audience*, ed. Lisa Lewis, 84–106. London: Routledge. Gamson, Joshua. 2001. Death Becomes Them." *The American Prospect* 12, no.12 (July 2–16): 37.

Greenberg, Joanne. 1989. *I Never Promised You a Rose Garden*. Reissue ed. New York: Signet.

Halperin, David. 1995. *Saint Foucault: Towards a Gay Hagiography*. Oxford: Oxford University Press.

Hine, Thomas. 2000. *The Rise and Fall of the American Teenager*. New York: Harper.

Jenkins, Henry. 2003. "'Out of the Closet and Into the Universe': Queers and *Star Trek*." In *The Audience Studies Reader*, eds. Will Brooker and Deborah Jermyn, 171–79. London: Routledge.

_____. 2000. "Reception Theory and Audience Research: The Mystery of the Vampire Kiss." In *Reinventing Film Studies*, eds. Christine Gledhill and Linda Williams, 165–82. London: Arnold.

_____. 1992. *Textual Poachers: Television Fans and Participatory Culture*. New York: Routledge.

Jenson, Joli. 1992. "Fandom as Pathology: The Consequences of Characterization." In *The Adoring Audience: Fan Cultures and Popular Media*, ed. Lisa A. Lewis, 9–29. London: Routledge.

Kett, Joseph. 1977. *Rites of Passage: Adolescence in America, 1790 to the Present*. New York: Basic Books.

Larbalestier, Justine. 2002. "*Buffy's* Mary Sue Is Jonathan: *Buffy* Acknowledges the Fans." In *Fighting the Forces: What's at Stake in* Buffy the Vampire Slayer, eds. Rhonda Wilcox and David Lavery, 227–38. Lanham, MD: Rowman Littlefield.

Lewis, Lisa A. 1992. *Gender Politics and MTV: Voicing the Difference*. Philadelphia: Temple University Press.

McCabe, Janet. 2005. "'Like Whatever': Claire, Female Identity and Growing Up Dysfunctional." In *Reading Six Feet Under: TV to Die For*, eds. Kim Akass and Janet McCabe, 121–34. London: Taurus.

Nash, Ilana. 2003. "Hysterical Scream or Rebel Yell? The Politics of Teen-idol Fandom." In *Disco Divas: Women and Popular Culture in the 1970s*, ed. Sherrie A. Inness, 133–50. Philadelphia: University of Pennsylvania Press.

Neufeld, John. 1968. *Lisa, Bright and Dark: A Novel*. New York: S.G. Phillips.

O'Hehir, Andrew. 2002. "The Undertaker's Tale." *Sight and Sound* 12 (May): 6.

Penley, Constance. 1992. "Feminism, Psychoanalysis, and the Study of Popular Culture." In *Cultural Studies*, eds. Lawrence Grossberg, Cary Nelson, and Paula A. Treichler, 479–99. New York: Routledge.

Peyser, Marc. 2002. "Six Feet Under Our Skin." *Newsweek* 139.11 (March 18): 60.

Rust, Linda. 2003. "Welcome to the House of Fun: *Buffy* Fan Fiction as a Hall of Mirrors." *Refractory: A Journal of Entertainment Media* 2 (March) available at http://www.refractory.unimelb.edu.au/journalissues/vol2/lindarust.html accessed March 12, 2006.

Scheiner, Georgeanne. 2000. *Signifying Female Adolescence: Film Representations and Fans, 1920–1950*. Westport, CT: Praeger.

Scodari, Christine, and Jenna Felder. 2002. "Creating a Pocket Universe: 'Shippers,' Fan Fiction, and *The X-Files* On-line." *Communication Studies* 51 (Fall): 238–57.

Tobin, Robert. 2002. "*Six Feet Under* and Post-Patriarchal Society." *Film and History* 32:87–88.

9. "They Stole Me":
The O.C., Masculinity, and
the Strategies of Teen TV

Sue Turnbull

It was a family ritual. On Tuesday nights during the first two seasons of *The O.C.* in Australia, my teenage son and I used to lie on our adjacent couches and watch TV together. If I was not there, he would come looking for me, proving once again the truth of the claim that young people watch TV more often in order to be social than to avoid sociability, even if the only social contact available at the time happens to be your mother.[1] Halfway through the second season of the American Teen TV series *The O.C.*, during a particularly agonizing cliffhanger ad break in which son paced the corridor muttering "The pressure! The pressure!" in a self-reflexive performance of anxious self, he announced, "I am Seth, you know [one of the characters on the show]. They stole me." This claim was a provocation to think, since in the wake of feminist media commentary and analysis, while much attention has been devoted to the portrayal of the feminine on the small screen, less has been devoted to the portrayal of the masculine, or the experience of the male audience.[2]

As my interest in *The O.C.*, its portrayal of masculinity, and its strategies of address began to quicken, I happened to mention this in one of my undergraduate classes concerned with media audience research. The students, both male and female, nodded in recognition of the reported engagement of my son with the show, and his desire for a viewing companion. At least seven of them, in a small tutorial of fifteen, knew of groups of guys in their late teens and early twenties who got together to watch *The O.C.* as part of their own Tuesday night rituals. While I was well aware of *Dynasty* viewing parties in the late eighties, *Melrose Place* nights in bars around the city in the early nineties, and even *Sex and the City* viewing clatches right up until the show's demise, this was the first time I had ever heard of groups of males gathering together to watch a Teen TV melodrama.

What was it about *The O.C.* that could inspire such male audience engagement, I wondered? In this paper, I engage in an exploration of *The O.C.* as a text, focusing on its content and themes, hoping to elucidate what elements might be prompting engagement. I highlight in particular the portrayal of masculinity and its context in the history of Teen TV. What are the textual strategies *The O.C.* employed during its first two seasons in terms of form, style and content, and how do these compare with other teen dramas from the past that have featured male protagonists?[3]

In the first two episodes of *The O.C.*, the character of Ryan, dressed in an iconic white tee shirt and hoodie, is arrested after being involved in a car theft initiated by his older brother. He is subsequently rescued by a benevolent public defender who gives him his card and tells him to call if he needs help. Looking again at these scenes, I was struck by how clearly they referenced and re-worked the events, characters, iconography, and themes, of the fifties teen film, *Rebel Without a Cause* (1955). When I mentioned this to my son, he said simply "I know," since in his satellite world of perpetually recycled TV and film, the media past is as much a part of his cultural reference points as the present. Like Dawson Leery in *Dawson's Creek*, my son has seen all the movies and was already making his second feature film: a noirish pastiche of the recent *Sin City* (2004) with passing reference to the much more elegant *Out of the Past* (1947). As far as his encounters with Teen TV from the past is concerned, in his high school Social Studies class, they regularly showed episodes of the eighties Canadian teen TV series *Degrassi Junior High* (1987–91), which became a cult classic among his group of friends. Not content with intermittent viewings at school, son subsequently bought seasons one and two of *Degrassi*, even affecting the personal style of one of the characters in the show, Joey Jeremiah, who always wore a straw hat on the back of his luxuriant black curls.

Exposure to the ancient history of Teen TV has been fostered not only by school and the recycling of shows on satellite TV, but also the ready availability of TV dramas on DVD at the local electronics megastore. Via the wonders of the boxed set, my son has also become a fan of *21 Jump Street* (1987–91) and Johnny Depp in particular, whose role as officer Tom Hanson in the series probably deserves its own paper.

Hanson regularly flipped from good boy nerdish officer to bad boy under-cover detective with rockabilly style while always looking out for the teen in trouble. My son may be Seth, but he's also been Dawson, Johnny Depp (still and always), Joey Jeremiah and a swag of other identities too, not to mention his earlier incarnations as Thomas the Tank Engine, Batman, Spiderman and Catwoman before the butcher (unfortunately) told him boy heroes can't be girl heroes too (such is the power of hegemonic masculinity).

And yet, on TV as in life, masculinity has always been shot through with contradictions as Miranda Banks (2004) makes clear in her essay on the nineties Teen TV series *Roswell* and *Smallville*. In her fine analysis, Banks (18–20) argues that these two shows constitute a new sub-genre of television, the teen male melodrama, characterized by the re-combination of such already existing elements as the melodramatic blending of music and drama, a self sacrificing young hero, and the portrait of troubled youth borrowed from the teen film. What interests her most, however, is the portrayal of the "new" teen hero so very unlike "the shy, insecure, neurotic or effeminate teen males of the 1950s' cinema melodrama, paralysed by their emotions" (26). The new teen hero is "sweet and gentle," but also "comfortable with his masculinity, making him the ideal mate for a budding young feminist" (26). Already orphaned (which as Banks argues neatly eliminates the Oedipal scenario common to the 50s teen film), these bulked up beautiful boys are inevitably outsiders because of their alien status. Despite their "organic" difference, these new "gender enlightened heroes" are inspired by "enlightened dreams for an equal partner, emotionally fulfilling relationships and a sense of duty" to the community (17).

While certainly convinced by Banks' analysis of the masculinity on display in *Roswell* and *Smallville,* I must confess to being not quite so convinced by the "newness" of this teen hero as a general concept. I think we've seen traces of him before; it's just that we haven't been paying attention. Nor have we been paying attention to whom these images of masculinity are addressed and how. If, as Carol Traynor Williams (1994) suggests, the male hero of the daytime soap opera is an idealized image of what women want in a man, then is it possible that the teen TV male has also morphed into a female ideal given Teen TV's presumed similar address to a female audience? The fact that males then apparently watch these series raises interesting questions about the kinds of emotional education and gender models provided by Teen TV for young men in the making.

Banks suggests that the origins of the teen male melodrama on TV lay within film, and conveniently for my purposes here, points to *Rebel*

Without a Cause as a starting point. Given that *Rebel Without a Cause* features a male protagonist, it's interesting to speculate about just what model of masculinity it offered in the character of Jim Stark as portrayed by James Dean. This is hard to assess, given any reading of Stark is and was inevitably compromised by the real-life ambivalent sexuality and tragic fate of the actor who played him. James Dean was already dead when the film was released in 1955. Looking again at the film, I don't read Jim as effeminate, neurotic or paralysed. Nor is he particularly troubled by his own masculinity. Indeed, I would argue that it is Stark Senior's masculinity that presents a problem to young Jim, signalled by his father's inability to stand up to his wife. Thus, when Stark Senior goes along with his wife's decision to try and cover up Jim Junior's involvement in the death of his high school rival (Buzz), Jim leaves the house in disgust. As a result, he inadvertently creates what amounts to his own surrogate "family" with two other troubled teens, Judy (Natalie Wood) and John (aka Plato, played by Sal Mineo). For all three teenagers, it is manifestly clear that the primary source of their problems past and present is their parents.

Hiding out in a deserted mansion, Jim and Judy play with and then take care of their surrogate child, the deeply troubled Plato. While Judy hums a lullaby, Jim covers Plato with a coat as he falls asleep, recalling the title sequence during which Jim drunkenly covers a toy monkey with a wrapping paper blanket before curling up in a fetal position beside him. Thus, from the first moments of the film, Jim is designated as a caring male. Judy recognizes this, as is evident in their ensuing conversation in the deserted house when she asks him, "What kind of a person do you think a girl wants?" Puzzled by the "person" noun, Jim pushes for clarification, "A man?" To which Judy responds: "Yes, but a man who can be gentle and sweet like you are.... And someone who doesn't run away when you want them ... like being Plato's friend when nobody else liked him. That's being strong."

Judy thus recognizes in Jim the combination of moral strength and gentleness, which she clearly prefers over the more macho and doomed style of her ex-boyfriend, Buzz, whose misplaced bravado got him killed. And Jim realizes that Judy is offering him much more than love—he is offering her companionship. If (in 1955), Judy is a budding young feminist with a vision of a new kind of man, then maybe Jim is a budding new teen hero capable of envisioning a more equal and companionable marriage than the one his parents have modelled.

This representation of masculinity (and indeed femininity) in *Rebel Without a Cause* is far from straightforward, making claims about the "newness" of more recent ambiguous portrayals of masculinity just a little less certain. Furthermore, I'd like to suggest that in the character of Jim Stark we are witnessing the emergence of what I am tempted to call the "emotional androgyne." The emotional androgyne, I would argue, is a character who combines "feminine" sensitivity and tenderness with "masculine" aggression and violence, while acknowledging that this may be a wrongly gendered false dichotomy since most people are capable of the entire range of emotions. The emotional androgyne may therefore be gendered either male or female while their appeal to the audience works in ambivalent, not to mention "queer" ways. As a male student once said somewhat apologetically but insightfully of *Buffy the Vampire Slayer,* whom I take to be a more recent female example of this phenomenon, "I can't work out whether I want to * * * * Buffy or *be* Buffy." The same might well be said about James Dean as Stark without, as Buffy might say, "the dying part." Crude as this student's assertion might be, I think it signals the ambivalent appeal of the teen hero, male or female, with whom the viewer may simultaneously identify and desire.

The emotional androgyne also has a long history on television. Consider the half hour American CBS comedy *The Many Loves of Dobie Gillis,* which ran from 1959 to 1963, which is often described as the first TV series to focus consistently on teenage characters (Osgerby 2004a). Like the film *Rebel Without a Cause,* this TV series deals with middle class youth—a consequence, Osgerby argues, of American Teen TV's general address to the affluent high school and college culture of post second world war America. By way of contrast, Osgerby suggests, the address of British Teen TV was to the consumer culture of working class youth who left school early in order to enter the work force and acquire a disposable income. But what of the gendered address of Teen TV?

While Osgerby briefly discusses the "teen girl" TV shows of the 1950s, he is relatively silent on the issue of masculinity (Osgerby 2004b). However, as Lynne Joyrich (1996) has so cogently argued, the audience for the medium of television has been historically seen as "feminized" in relation to the domestic site of consumption for television, and also in relation to the content and form of specific genres such as the soap opera and the melodrama. The sitcom, on the other hand, would seem to have addressed, at least initially, the idealized family unit it represented on screen as in *The Adventures of Ozzie and Harriet* (1952–66), or *Father Knows Best* (1954–62)—until *The Many Loves of Dobie Gillis,* that is.

Interestingly, while *The Many Loves of Dobie Gillis* screened in Australia, it was never shown in the UK, although it is the British BBC Comedy Guide (www.bbc.co.uk/comedy/guide/articles/m/manylovesofdobie) that offers this useful description: "It was a sitcom that depicted the lives and the thoughts of teenagers at a time when, by and large, America was not yet ready to give them their voice. The characters were boldly *new*, it broke rules and was even surreal in places" (my emphasis). There's that word "new" again, begging the question: In what way were the characters "new" in 1959?

Dobie, the son of a small town grocer, is a hopeless romantic, forever falling in love with intelligent (and not so intelligent) young women who reject him as unsuitable, especially when it comes to his financial situation. As budding feminists, these young women are not so much interested in romance as they are in financial security. Acutely self-reflexive and aware, Linda Sue Faversham admits in the episode aptly titled "Flow Gently Sweet Money," "I have the soul of a cash register" but then "love doesn't butter any parsnips." Given the subsequent second wave feminist attention to (and condemnation of) the seductions of romance for women, it may be that *The Many Loves of Dobie Gillis* had already turned this pattern on its head by suggesting the male teen might be the romantic and/or airhead figure, while the female teen might be the pragmatist with an eye on her financial future.

Every week, Dobie would address the camera (usually accompanied in the frame by a reproduction of the Rodin statue, the Thinker) and introduce the events of the week that had befallen him and his friends, frequently reappearing between scenes to provide additional direct-to-camera commentary. This technique of addressing the audience was hardly new on TV (even though people got very excited about this supposedly postmodern move in the much later John Hughes teen pic *Ferris Bueller's Day Off*, 1986). Such an address can be traced to the origins of TV comedy drama in vaudeville and the early TV shows of both Jack Benny and George Burns and Gracie Allen, which often began with just such a speech to the audience.[4]

What's particularly interesting about this direct address to camera in the case of *Dobie Gillis* is that it positions Dobie as an ironic commentator on his own hopeless love affairs. He may be love's fool, but at least he knows it. Self aware and self-critical, eloquent and expressive, Dobie is always in touch with his emotions even if unable to control them. Could the hapless Dobie be a "new" type of teen TV hero? Is Dobie another example of the emotional androgyne—on the one hand a sensitive soul in touch with his emotions, and on the other a bloke struggling to come to terms with aggressive masculinity as represented by his father?

As the BBC guide notes, one of the most unusual aspects of the show was the relationship between Dobie and his father, Herbert, which was much less idealized than in other contemporary family sitcoms such as

Father Knows Best and *Leave It to Beaver* (1957–63). Dobie and Herbert frequently engage in shouting matches (not all of them funny) as Dobie resists following his father's footsteps into retail business. Like Jim Stark, Dobie is at war with the model of masculinity closest to him. Dobie has other ambitions that subsequently take him into the army and on to college in the (always doomed by the format) pursuit of romantic love and impossible wealth.

While the relationship between Dobie and Herbert might therefore be read as a comic take on the troubled father-son relationship in *Rebel Without a Cause,* since both scenarios are about refusing and re-inventing parental models of masculinity, like *Rebel* the TV series also involved a teen triad. Dobie's best friend, Maynard G. Krebs is a beatnik with a goatee beard and a somewhat surreal take on the world. (He's spaced out well before his time.) Dobie's would-be girlfriend is the loquacious and irrepressible Zelda Gilroy who has already determined that Dobie *will* be hers. As a model of female ingenuity and determination, Zelda is compelling. In the episode "For Whom the Wedding Bell Tolls," Zelda succeeds in getting Dobie to propose to her, but abruptly stops the shipboard ceremony when she realizes that she cannot go through with deceiving him into marriage. (Dobie tells Zelda that he probably *will* marry her in the end—he's just not ready yet.) Pragmatically, the premise of the show insisted that his romantic misadventures should continue as long as the network wanted them.

Having located and bought four episodes of *Dobie Gillis* on e-Bay, I was informed by the other male in our household (an American who was himself a teenager and a regular watcher of *Dobie Gillis* when it was originally on in the States) that for him the most significant character in the show was always Maynard. (He didn't quite say, "I was Maynard" but he did say, "I was a Beat.") As the BBC Comedy Guide suggests, Maynard offered a model of masculinity and style very different from Dobie's "scrubbed, crew-cut, red-blooded, fun-loving, nonsmoking, non-drinking all American boy," however ironically inflected.

With his love of jazz and movie triple bills, his aversion to work, and his lack of materialism, Maynard is, I would argue, not only a precursor of the 1960s teen revolution to come, but also of another type of teen hero who might just be related to Seth in *The O.C.* If, as previously suggested, Dobie (and his troubled relationship with his father) might be read as a comic take on the character of Jim Stark in *Rebel Without a Cause,* then Maynard might be considered as a comic reworking of the disturbed male John/Plato. While Plato meets an inevitable tragic fate within the narrative of the film (he tells a detective early on, "no-one can save me"), the on-going episodic structure of the TV sitcom gave

Maynard many more possibilities for negotiating his continual outsider status.

Of course, there are a lot of years, a lot of genre and format shifts, and a lot of subsequent teen movies and Teen TV series separating the evolving teen triads of *Rebel, Dobie* and *The O.C.* Even so, I would argue that *The O.C.* not only quite consciously echoes and re-inflects many of the more intense and melodramatic elements of Rebel *Without a Cause*, but also (perhaps less consciously) the lighter elements of the Teen TV sitcom which was *The Many Loves of Dobie Gillis*. In its combination of melodrama and comedy, and in its self-reflexive intertextuality, *The O.C.* is typical of many recent Teen TV series which recombine different generic elements in order to produce something new addressed to a teen audience imagined as both male and female. If the melodramatic aspects of the show might be thought to appeal most directly to the female audience, and the sitcom elements to the masculine, then what pulls them together is a combined address to a "teen" viewer who might enjoy both. What differentiates these series are their format and narrative structure and the ways in which this affects the representation of character.

While all three programs feature a clean cut Anglo-American boy as a key protagonist, the different format demands of a long-form drama series such as *The O.C.* requires many more characters and narrative possibilities to secure on-going story lines and interests than a film. Unlike Jim and Dobie, Ryan is by no means the primary focus of *The O.C.*, which shifted over the first two seasons of the show to encompass Ryan's new friends and neighbours (Marissa and Summer, Marissa's parents) and his new family (adopted brother Seth and Seth's parents). *The O.C.* was constructed as a show about the problems of boys, girls, men, women, children and parents and could therefore be assumed to address a broad audience since the perspective was constantly shifting (although the pop music sound track firmly anchored it to the youth market).

What is perhaps more intriguing are the ways in which *The O.C.* initially played around with, reiterated, and changed the sequence of events from *Rebel Without a Cause* in order to broaden its appeal. *Rebel Without a Cause* begins with the arrest of Jim for drunkenness: *The O.C.* begins with the arrest of Ryan for car theft, although it his brother Trey who is the instigator. While Jim talks to the sympathetic detective in juvenile hall, who gives him his card and tells him to call if he needs to talk, Ryan encounters the sympathetic public defender Sandy, who also tells him to call if things don't work out. When Ryan follows up on this after his mother's boyfriend attacks him and he is thrown out of the house, Sandy rescues Ryan and takes him home, where the first person he meets is the troubled teenager from next door, Marissa.

Like Judy, the girl next door to Jim in *Rebel Without a Cause*, Marissa has parent problems, although it would seem that her teen angst is more generalized. "I'm angry," she tells Seth in episode two after she has gotten hopelessly drunk, and been rescued from discovery by Ryan. Like Judy, Marissa has a jealous jock boyfriend, Luke, who runs with the pack, and who immediately recognizes Ryan as a rival. By the end of his first day in Newport Beach, Ryan and Luke are embroiled in a fistfight, which performs the same function as both the knife fight at the observatory and the chicken run on the bluff in *Rebel*. Except Luke does not need to die—this is a long form drama series, not a ninety minute film, and his character will be needed in the simmering rivalry storyline. Luke does, however, get to snarl the immortal line, "Welcome to The O.C., Bitch," as he retreats up the beach. This is a moment of excess that gestures away from the melodramatic intensity of the scene towards the comedic: one can't help but laugh.

After being expelled from Newport the next morning, and then brought back again after Sandy discovers his mother has abandoned him, Ryan spends Sunday with Seth and his family, with the understanding that he will be handed over to child services the next day. That night Seth and Marissa engineer Ryan's escape by hiding him in a half built mansion (one of Seth's mother's residential building projects). Like the abandoned mansion in *Rebel Without a Cause* where Jim, Judy, and John hide out, there is even an empty swimming pool in which Seth cheerfully skateboards, while Ryan and Marissa bond. It's a delightful echo and reversal of the *Rebel* sequence in which Jim, Judy and Plato horse around the pool before Jim and Judy declare their attraction to one another and John is shot.

In *The O.C.* version, the very guarded Ryan and Marissa give only enough away to recognize that they are both somewhat alienated and alone (there are a lot of episodes to go), while Seth blithely oscillates back and forth behind them on his skateboard. It's both a touching and funny moment, melodrama in the foreground and comedy in the background, unlike the similar moment in Rebel *Without a Cause* where the emotional stakes are already ratcheted up given the more compressed narrative form of the ninety-minute film. Unlike the climax to *Rebel Without a Cause* which results in first one of Buzz's gang and then John being shot, the climax in the second episode of *The O.C.* involves a fight between Ryan and Luke during which the mansion is set on fire, Luke returns to rescue the unconscious Ryan, and both hand themselves over to the police. No one dies, but then no resolution is achieved either. Like life, the on-going TV series merely sets itself up for the next complication.

While it is a rewarding exercise to compare the narrative structure of *Rebel Without a Cause* and *The O.C.*, there are also interesting comparisons to be made in terms of the casting and characters. Sixteen-year-old Ryan, like Jim Stark in Rebel, is played by an actor already in his twenties, Benjamin McKenzie. Unlike James Dean, however, who had already acquired media currency via his previous TV and film appearances, McKenzie was a relative unknown. His credibility as Ryan is therefore not overshadowed in the same way that the character of Jim was by the celebrity and sudden death of James Dean.

What is of interest here is that there is more than a hint of Dean about Ben McKenzie in his soulful eyes and hangdog expression occasionally enlivened by a cheeky grin, although physically he is much more muscular, if smaller, than Dean. As a teen hero, the legacy of James Dean has had a long life in popular culture, appearing most significantly for the purposes of this paper in the character of Dylan, the alcoholic rich boy gone bad in the teen series *Beverly Hills, 90210* (1990–2000). Indeed, actor Luke Perry (who once appeared on the cover of *Vanity Fair* in a Dean-like pose) was touted as the new James Dean, and a great deal of the success of the series was attributed to Perry's teen appeal. One wonders to whom this appeal was directed—a heterosexual male, a heterosexual female, or a gay male viewer? I can only gesture in the direction of bedroom walls everywhere, and argue that the male-pinup is as much a feature of the male bedroom as the female, even if we're simply talking rock stars. Men, I would argue, like looking at men, even though that look may have to be justified by a context which more regularly includes sport, music, or the action film as opposed to the teen melodrama.

It is of note that creator Josh Schwartz suggests in DVD commentary that what the Fox network really wanted from *The O.C.* was a new *Beverly Hills, 90210*, but that he and his fellow writers wanted to do "serious stuff" and create a series more like the critically applauded but short lived teen shows *Freaks and Geeks* and *My So-Called Life*. This desire to create a teen series with a serious edge may well have inspired the writers (in a well established narrative convention) to make Ryan a kid from a working class suburb in order to enable them to follow (which they did) story lines which dealt with a clash of class cultures in the United States. The series thus begins in the very down-market world of Chino. The magnitude of Ryan's transition to Newport Beach is underlined in the title sequence of the pilot; although, as Ryan tells Marissa that night at a beach house party fueled by drugs and alcohol, he already recognizes that Chino may be rather less dangerous than Newport. Like Jim Stark, Ryan's troubles are not of his own making, and if he is rebelling against anything, it is against the poverty and hopelessness of his previous lot in life.

Ryan, therefore, arrives as an outsider and an alien in Newport, not just because he feels like one but also because, like the teen heroes about whom Banks writes, he is effectively an alien in strange world. Unlike the heroes of *Smallville* and *Roswell*, however, he is not so much orphaned as abandoned, so that when his mother does reappear, one can feel a familial divorce coming on. Ryan knows he stands a better chance outside of Chino, even though life in the gated community of Newport is anything but idyllic. Like *Dallas* and *Dynasty* in the 1980s, *The O.C.* offers the audience the prospect that rich people can be miserable too, that money can't buy happiness (although it may buy a fabulous house and a designer wardrobe). This, of course, is where Marissa comes in.

While Marissa may be a troubled teen, as revealed by her alcoholic tendencies, she also gets to wear a vast range of stylish outfits before her final exit from the series at the end of Season Three. Indeed, the first night of Ryan's weekend in Newport involves a charity fashion parade, which serves multiple purposes: visual excess, social critique, and an opportunity for Marissa to eyeball Ryan (thus giving Luke the excuse to beat him up later). Like Judy in *Rebel,* Marissa is a daddy's girl and clearly her mother's rival for his affections. Her relationship with her father, however, is not the major source of her problems; her ennui appears to lie much deeper in that she is acutely conscious of the shallowness of the life her family leads.

In the first three seasons of *The O.C.,* the character of Marissa thus performed two simultaneous functions in that while she functioned as a clothes horse for the fashion industry (actress Mischa Barton went on to be a cover girl for almost every magazine on the news stands), she also, within the show at least, was constructed as a critic of the lifestyle the fashion represents. In Season One, her critical assessment was clearly shared by next door neighbour Seth, who also resented having to attend the charity fashion show because "every day's a fashion show" in Newport. In her study of British Teen TV in the late 1980s, Karen Lury (2001) outlines the development of an address that allows the teen audience to position themselves as both cynical and enchanted about what they are viewing on screen. This, I would argue, was a key textual strategy employed by *The O.C.,* most particularly through the character of Marissa. Indeed up until her death at the end of Season Three, Marissa might just have been the rebel *with* a cause in Newport Beach.

But then Seth is initially portrayed as something of a rebel too, except he doesn't get drunk or fight with his parents. Seth's rebellion is far more understated and intellectual: he just refuses, in the first season at least, to join in, preferring his video games, his books, his computer, his boat, and (as we shall discover later) the pursuit of a rich fantasy life involving characters such as Captain Oats (his toy horse) and Marissa's pretty best friend, Summer (who is oblivious to his existence). Seth, although he does not know it yet, is also profoundly cool. As creator Josh Schwartz and executive producer Elizabeth Savage explain on the soundtrack commentary, they spent a great deal of time decorating the set of Seth's room with artifacts from their own collection of posters and books in order to signal Seth's coolness via his allegiance to musicians like Paul Weller, Nirvana, the Ramones, and the Sex Pistols. Taste, especially taste in music, thus becomes an important signifier of character and identity, setting up a number of comic moments in *The O.C.*, including when Seth realizes with incredulity that he and Marissa, to whom he has hardly spoken, actually share a love of punk music and Jack Kerouac's *On the Road*.

The trajectory of the character of Seth in Season One and the treatment of his relationship with Ryan is therefore a key structural difference between the narratives of *The O.C.* and *Rebel Without a Cause*. Instead of one teen male hero, we are given two. *The O.C.* thus moves beyond the male/female romantic pairing dominating *Rebel Without a Cause*, and develops an ongoing male friendship. In this regard, *The O.C.* is more like the comedy series *The Many Loves of Dobie Gillis* in suggesting that the most significant and sustaining relationship a teen male can have is with another teen male. Furthermore, while the character of Ryan remains relatively static in the show (always noble, put upon, and misunderstood), the character of Seth is both comic and dynamic. With Ryan acting as the catalyst for his development as a secure young male, Seth evolves from geekish loner to romantic hero, becoming during that first season the object of not one woman's affections, but two—an inspirational hero indeed.

It has been suggested many times that the generic definition of a teen film, or teen TV series depends simply on the fact that it is addressed to a teen audience. However, while *Rebel Without a Cause*, *The Many Loves of Dobie Gillis*, and *The O.C.* might all be presumed to be addressed to teens because they are about teens, it is also true that all of them are more or less concerned with adults as well. *Rebel Without a Cause* was as much addressed to a middle aged audience worried about teenage delinquency as it was to teens, given that it contained a pedagogic lesson about the dangers of inadequate parenting. Likewise *The Many Loves of Dobie Gillis* regularly featured Dobie's parents and was almost certainly watched by all the family. *The O.C.* is, however, the only one of the three to devote almost as much attention to parental problems and their ensuing story lines as it is to the teens'. Indeed, co-executive producer Elizabeth Savage even suggested on the DVD commentary to the first season that it would be quite possible to take the teens out of *The O.C.* and still have the premise for a viable drama series, a bay side *Dallas* perhaps. *The O.C.* thus also provides its teen viewers with some insight into the emotional lives of adults, inviting them to extend their sympathy not just across genders but across age groups too.

Despite the shared emphasis on the older characters, what drew my son to *The O.C.* in the first two seasons at least (interest waned in Season Three and diminished entirely in Season Four) was the character of Seth, the teen male hero who is neither too beautiful nor too tragic to be true.[5] At least until the end of Season One, Seth is the teenager who feels as if he doesn't belong (adolescence is alienating/the adolescent is an alien), caught somewhere between childhood and adulthood in an intense emotional landscape which we were invited to consider from his point of view. But his was not the only point of view. *The O.C.* is a complicated drama with varied characters who come in and out of focus, and *The O.C.* invited the viewer to consider how this world appeared to those who inhabited it from a number of different perspectives. So while it may have been the images of masculinity that initially attracted teen male viewers to the series, what held them there may have been far more complex. My son may have identified with Seth, but he also identified with Marissa and Ryan—not to mention Seth's parents. The tragic structure of feeling in which Seth is enmeshed invites the viewer to extend his or her capacity for identification with people and worlds well beyond the narrow confines of his or her own gender, age, and class.[6] In other words, identification with the varied dilemmas of a range of characters in a complex dramatic landscape invites us all to be emotionally androgynous.

Much that has been assumed about the representation of masculinity and femininity on screens both cinematic and televisual, and the relationship of the spectator to such images based on fixed gender perspectives, might be usefully challenged.[7] Such a challenge would involve not only thinking through the notion of emotional androgyny in terms of characters but also in terms of audiences' fluid emotional engagement in a fantasy landscape. While the currency of the Teen TV series and the dramatic landscape may change (what's next after *The O.C.*?), I suspect, on the basis of my limited study here, that the ways in which these series draw the teen audience into the text may well be worthy of further consideration. But this time we should look more carefully at the men, both on screen and in the audience.

Notes

1. As Karen Lury (2001) suggests, even watching alone can promote sociability—especially when a teen's social group is watching the same shows. In addition, simultaneous

viewing and communication with friends via telephone and the Internet are increasingly part of the experience of television watching in the home.

2. An essay by Miranda Banks (2004), "A Boy for All Planets: *Roswell, Smallville* and the Teen Male Melodrama," is a rare and welcome exception.

3. As I was finishing this essay in January 2006, it was announced that Fox was cancelling the series at the end of its fourth truncated season (16 episodes). While there was some debate in the popular press about whether or not this could be attributed to the departure of Mischa Barton from the series at the end of Season Three, this was not the primary factor in the my son's loss of interest in the show.

4. While initially George Burns addressed the audience from in front of the curtain or to the side of the proscenium arch, once a studio set began to be used, he turned to other techniques. Like Dobie, George Burns would speak to the camera from another set (his eyrie above the garage) in order to set up and conclude the story for the week (Marc 1984).

5. As a consequence we agreed of a certain repetition in the story lines and the fact that Seth himself no longer seemed to be so awkward and alienated. The death of Marissa was not a significant factor in my son's case.

6. The phrase "tragic structure of feeling" was first used by Raymond Williams (1977) and subsequently employed by Ien Ang (1985) in her influential study of the Dutch audience for *Dallas*.

7. Laura Mulvey's famous 1975 piece on spectatorship and gender is the seminal work here. Mulvey has, of course, modified her position over the years, but the impetus of her seminal article continues to linger, especially in more popular interpretations of representation and spectatorship.

References

Ang, Ien. 1985. *Watching Dallas: Soap Opera and the Melodramatic Imagination.* London: Methuen.

Banks, Miranda. 2004. "A Boy for All Planets: *Roswell, Smallville* and the Teen Male Melodrama." In *Teen TV: Genre, Consumption and Identity,* eds. Glyn Davis and Kay Dickinson, 17–28. London: BFI.

Davis, Glyn and Kay Dickinson, eds. 2004. *Teen TV: Genre, Consumption and Identity.* London: BFI.

Joyrich, Lynne. 1996. *Re-viewing Reception: Television, Gender and Postmodern Culture.* Bloomington: Indiana University Press.

Lury, Karen. 2001. *British Youth Television: Cynicism and Enchantment.* New York: Oxford University Press.

Marc, David. 1984. *Demographic Vistas: Television in American Culture.* Philadelphia: University of Philadelphia Press.

Mulvey, Laura. 1975. "Visual Pleasure and Narrative Cinema." *Screen.* 16, no. 3: 6–18.

Osgerby, Bill. 2004a. *Youth Media.* London: Routledge.

_____. 2004b. "'So Who's Got Time for Adults!' Femininity, Consumption and the Development of Teen TV—From *Gidget* to *Buffy.* In *Teen TV: Genre, Consumption and Identity,* eds. Glyn Davis and Kay Dickinson, 71–86. London: BFI.

Williams, Carol Traynor. 1994. "Soap Opera Men in the Nineties." *Journal of Popular Film and Television.* 22, no. 3 (Fall): 126–35.

Williams, Raymond. 1977. *Marxism and Literature.* Oxford: Oxford University Press.

PART III—CULTURES OF RECEPTION

10. Fashion Sleuths and Aerie Girls: *Veronica Mars'* Fan Forums and Network Strategies of Fan Address

Jennifer Gillan

Televisual Self-fashioning

Knowing Buckle, Lucky, Delia, and Arden B. is the first step to making it into the trendy teen crowd at Neptune High. They all cluster together in the same places so they aren't hard to find. For the most part, they split their time between cyberspace and the mall. If you casually drop their names, others might assume you are one of the in-crowd. Or at least that's what I gathered from something two girls said online in a 2004 TelevisionWithoutPity.com fan forum (TWOP, April 17, 2006). Their insider source at Neptune High is sassy junior Veronica Mars. By following her funky fashion lead, they assume that they are well on their way to becoming trendy teens or least being mistaken for them. They are self-aware about the irony that they are modeling themselves on a TV character, but they continue to do so. Even though they have never met face-to-face, they feel like they can trust each other. No one else they know in the off-line world understands their obsession with Neptune fashion. Eventually, they admit to each other that they aren't really even teens, but twenty-something women with office jobs. Although they are anxious that they might be too old for some of Veronica's outfits, they still wear them and take great pleasure in being mistaken for trendy teenagers.

Online fan forums such as the one at TWOP dedicated to *Veronica Mars* (UPN 2004–6; CW 2006–2007), the TV show about a feisty, teenage sleuth, are fascinating places for learning about the way television shows are transforming broadcast programming into lifestyle experiences by encouraging viewers to follow shows from weekly time-slots to internet sites to shopping malls. Whether visiting mall stores such as Buckle, Delia's, or Arden B, online or on-site, Veronica's faithful followers can find there the clothing worn by TV's latest trendy teen. By following—in a narrative, technological, and consumerist sense—the show's plot and discussion threads and internet links, viewers can feel as if they are participating in the inner lives of the teen characters and sharing in the lifestyle experience on display. Through its analysis of how fans follow *Veronica Mars* (*VM*), this essay contributes to the more general reconsideration undertaken by television theorists (Jenkins 2006; Brooker 2004; Hills 2002; Murray 2000; Gwenllian-Jones 2003) of "what it means to engage with a television program," to "'follow' a specific show" in an era when "the text of the TV show is no longer limited to the television medium" and can be extended through the internet (Brooker 2004, 569).

Building on Williams' (1974) theory of televisual flow and Jenkins' (1992) conceptualization of media convergence, Brooker (2004) explains how this kind of *overflow* "transforms the audience relationship with the text from a limited, largely one-way engagement based around a proscribed time slot and single medium into a far more fluid, flexible affair which crosses media platforms—Internet, mobile phone, stereo systems, shopping mall—in a process of convergence.... A drawing together of media forms" (571). Focusing his analysis on the official *Dawson's Creek* website and its networked links, Brooker identifies how the WB created a lifestyle experience related to the teen TV show, one that was aimed at encouraging "'regular' teenage viewers, not just committed fans" to "seek out the music and clothes favored by the characters and to participate in their lives on a daily basis through online questionnaires and interactive simulations" (Brooker 2003, 324).

UPN might not have had an official *Veronica Mars* cross-promotion deal like the ones the WB had with J. Crew and American Eagle, but it still inspired *VM* viewers to shop at those same mall stores. To confirm this point one only need to visit to the LiveJournal Veronica Mars Fashion Community (LJ-*VM*) and the TelevisionWithoutPity "Veronica Mars: Outta the Closet" (TWOP-VC) fashion forums in which participants exchange information about where they have bought or have sighted clothing from the show. On TWOP-VC one September 2005 contributor explains that she has been keeping the window to the Abercrombie and Fitch online store open on her desktop ever since several of the fan forum participants identified it as a source for Veronica-ware. By switching between the store window and the TWOP-VC, she can either be the first to detect if one of Veronica's separates is from AF or the first to buy it. Her posts reveal that a primary source of pleasure for *VM*'s young female fans comes from proving they are like Veronica, both trendy teens and plucky mystery solvers. Like her, they are capable of following clues and solving a mystery—not just of the Season One mystery of the identity of the murderer of Veronica's best friend Lilly Kane, but also of the names of the stores that are the sources for Veronica's trendy outfits.

In contrast to the WB, which, according to Brooker (2004), specialized in drawing a detailed map to its network of *Dawson's Creek* lifestyle links, UPN, likely for budgetary rather than ideological reasons, left the process of identifying and then locating Veronica's style to its mystery-loving viewers. An analysis of TWOP's "Veronica Mars: Outta the Closet" fan forum dedicated to *Veronica Mars'* style suggests that part of the pleasure of fan interaction with *VM* is the feeling of active participation that the original UPN version of the show encouraged (TWOP April 17, 2006). In contrast, the hostile reactions of *VM* fans posting to the Fall 2006 CW Lounge fan forums (http://www.lounge.cwtv.com, February 20, 2007) indicate that the more overt marketing and cross-promotional strategies employed by the CW when it inherited *VM* in its third season ran counter to the pleasurable investment loyal fans had already made in the idea of themselves as active participants and of *VM* as an alternative teen product, an underdog show on an underdog network.

The formalization of the fashion links on the Season Three CW website suggests that network executives are aware of the fan activity on TWOP and other sites. The American Eagle and *Veronica Mars* Aerie Tuesdays cross-promotion, however, indicates that they had little understanding of the complexities of fan investment in the game of investigating the fashion clues that Veronica left for viewers. This essay explores the complexity of that fan activity and considers its implications for the 21st century TV industry.

Veronica's Closet and Her Fashion Sleuths

VM viewers understand that they can follow the clues within the mise-en-scène—especially costuming and room décor—to get hints about the kinds of accessories required for others to recognize their desired affiliation with a trendy teen identity. Summing up the attitude of many of her fellow participants on TWOP-VC, one fan remarks, "One of my friends said that her shopping motto is now 'What would Veronica wear?' And I have taken that to heart, as well." Others concur that the TV character has become their de facto stylist. A 19 year old who says she looks 14 agrees: "I always find myself saying that this looks like something Veronica would wear" (TWOP April 17, 2006).

These fans look at her fashion in the same way they look at the show's other mysteries: as a series of clues that they need to follow. The mystery these fashion sleuths investigate is how to acquire and pull off the trendy teen identity the show puts on display. The intimacy the show establishes between viewers and Veronica enables her to function as a trusted spokesperson for the trendy teen lifestyle. Unlike the teens on *Dawson's Creek* and *The O.C.*, who spend their days confiding in each other and dissecting all the minor details of their lives, Veronica is a loner who doesn't confide in anyone but the viewers. They understand from her voiceovers and flashbacks that Veronica learned not to trust people both because of her line of work and because of her personal history of betrayal by people she loved and trusted. This backstory combined with the direct address allows *Veronica Mars* to establish a deeper level of intimacy between fans and the character.

The comments posted on TWOP-VC demonstrate how closely fans follow Veronica's fashion clues in each episode. Because the murky noir lighting and the red and green filters make her outfits more difficult to see than in the high key lighting environment of the typical teen TV show, it is not surprising that fans on TWOP-VC explain that they tape episodes so they can get a better look. Technology-savvy, the TWOP-VC participants also have little problem surfing the web for information, sometimes finding a production still or scene capture on an official or unofficial *VM* website and cross matching it to the clothes available on the online shopping sites of trendy teen mall stores. Many of the regular participants clearly get pleasure from being the first to match the outfit with the mall store. This response is representative of the way that "recognizing marketplace interventions has become part of the 'game'" (Jenkins 2006, 88) for fans. That they feel savvy when they identify in which brands the characters are outfitted exemplifies the kind of fan pleasure that comes from "exercising their competencies" (2006, 81). The ultimate thrill for these fans, though, occurs when Veronica appears on-screen wearing the Abercrombie Dillon motorcross jacket or its Claudia faux fur down vest, the Banana Republic Scooter Jacket, the American Eagle Chocolate Messenger Bag, or the Lucky Brand t-shirts and jeans that they already own. Their style sense is validated when it is reflected on TV.

The site visitors use the forums primarily to trade information about where to buy the fashions in Veronica's closet. They function in terms of what Walsh (2003) calls a "collective intelligence paradigm" in which it is assumed that all participants have "something to contribute, even if they will only be called upon on an ad hoc basis" (Jenkins 2006, 53). Building on Walsh's theories, Jenkins explains that "the social process of acquiring knowledge—which is dynamic and participatory, continually testing and reaffirming the group's social ties" holds together the collective intelligence paradigm (Jenkins 2006, 54). A September 2005 TWOP-VC thread (April 17, 2006) epitomizes this social process. After someone posts a question about a particular jacket, several others speculate on where it is from until one confirms that it's from Lucky and proudly declares that she just "bought it and, on sale, nonetheless!" In response, another asks, "how did you get the Lucky Brand Pilot Jacket for 30% off, I covet it desperately." The original poster explains that she lives right near the mall and just happened upon a sale day at the Lucky store: "It's like walking in to Veronica's closet (haha). I wanted everything right then and there. But I restrained (ha) and only bought the jacket :) I actually wouldn't have even gone into the store if it weren't for this thread finding out where articles of clothing come from." Here the fan points to the way individuals in online communities "place great weight," according to Kozinets (1998), "on the judgments of their fellow community-of-consumption members. Collective response influences their consumption and tempers their judgment of marketing communications." These consumers have power because they can also collectively critique a product and raise awareness about its limitations.

In addition to the way it registers the power of the message board, the TWOP-VC forum is also interesting because the participants all start sharing tips for being savvy shoppers and talk about eBay auctions, sales, and consignment stores as places to get the clothes featured on the show without going broke. The source of pleasure here comes from the fans' perception that there is a subversive element to sale shopping. They do not address the fact that the prices of the products are inflated in the first place. More often, they convey a sense of pride in their Veronica-like savvy, as is evident in another thread (TWOP-VC, April 17, 2006) in which several participants trade information on a different jacket. One fan supplies its brand name and then admits that during an earlier forum discussion she withheld a brand name because she was trying to win the piece in an eBay auction. She adds, "I'm sure you all understand." The next month, she gleefully shares that she won the auction for the Andover Plaid J. Crew Pea coat that she "coveted" since she first saw Veronica wear it. Many other participants are similarly committed to finding ways to acquire the clothes featured on the show even if they have limited fashion budgets.

The Veronica Mars Fashion Community on LiveJournal (LJ-*VM*) is committed to this cause. As its original September 2005 profile describes, it is a community "dedicated to finding out just where the wardrobe people pick up Veronica's clothes and accessories and if they are available for us ordinary beings to purchase" (LiveJournal.com, February 20, 2007). These fans are invested in the idea of themselves as independently investigating the clues *VM* offers about new styles, collectively working together to discover the identity of the brands with which Veronica is affiliated, and subversively bypassing mainstream culture by buying online or on sale. One of the posts to LJ-*VM*, however, does acknowledge that sale shopping is sometimes less a fulfilling culturally subversive act than a demoralizing economic necessity: "If I had a lot of cash, I could just point at what I like and buy it, rather than searching for deals" (LJ-*VM*, February 20, 2007).

It is easy to read the ways UPN gets *VM* viewers to, as the TWOP participants put it, "covet everything Veronica owns," only in terms of cynical marketing strategies, but as Jenkins (2006), Brooker (2004), Hills (2002), Murray (2000), and Gwenllian-Jones (2003) have noted, audience response is more complex. To some degree, of course, anything viewers do on any website, official or unofficial, connected to *VM* plays into network overflow strategies as the activities keep them engaged after the weekly program ends. Yet, while producers are banking on emotional investment leading to consumer investment, some groups of fans, again exemplifying Walsh's (2003) collective intelligence paradigm, use their mutual participation in consumer culture as a way to create emotional connections with each other. This behavior demonstrates how, as Jenkins explains, "groups of consumers form intense bonds with the product, and, through the product, with fellow consumers" (2006, 79).

Murray (2000) has analyzed this kind of fan investment in relation to *My So-Called Life* (ABC 1995). In the discussion threads and forums related to the teen melodrama, Murray discovered that female fans "consistently and emotionally voiced the importance of the text's proximity to their own lives" (222). What Murray says of fan response to *My So-Called Life* [MSCL]—that it goes beyond the usual function of TV programming as "entertainment, education on social issues, or fantasy fulfillment," and becomes an emotional "investment in an individual and communal understanding" of their identity—can be applied to the response to *Veronica Mars* (222). Reading the posts to various TWOP discussion threads, for example, one is struck by the frequency in which interpersonal interactions override the discussion of the show itself. *VM*'s message boards often become spaces in which female fans could "discuss and explore their subjectivity as female adolescents," to borrow Murray's description of MSCL fan activity (222). Although this essay only looks closely at the TWOP-VC, other *VM*-related forums also function as springboards for discussions among fans about their negotiation of a host of identity issues, often in relation to adolescence, peer pressure, cultural norms, and gender expectations or stereotypes.

The participants in the TWOP-VC threads engage in such off-topic discussions, confiding in each other about their body and identity anxieties as they share with each other the stumbling blocks they encountered in trying to acquire or pull off the *VM* trendy teen look (TWOP, April 17, 2006). For some, it is a matter of financial access; for others, it is an issue of body type; and for a good number, it is the anxiety that they are already too old at 25 or 28 to get away with some of the teen styles. One describes how she went to the mall and tried on Veronica's Lucky jeans, but saw the price tag and thought, "I still don't know how the character would afford them, but I can see why the wardrobe people would choose them over Gap or Old Navy. They are really flattering jeans." The Seven for All Mankind jeans she wears are apparently even more flattering and, hence, even more outrageously expensive. Most find commiseration from others on the site, but one fan pointedly reminds the others that teen fashions are for tiny teens only. Choosing to ignore the pointed comment, the rest of the participants continue the discussion along more supportive lines. The irony is that although most of the respondents take pains to declare that *VM* fashions are democratic (because they are from the mall and not expensive boutiques and so technically available to all), they acknowledge that they can't always contort their bodies or their hair in the ways that would enable them to fit within or bear any resemblance to the straight haired, petite WASP teen ideal established on the show.

There is a liberating aspect to the way the message board allows everyone to try on Veronica's styles. The participants are free of "such visible markers as sex, 'race' and age which, in offline interactions," Slater (2004) explains, "fix identities in bodies" (600). The problem, to borrow from Butler's (1993) famous formulation, is that bodies do matter and become obstacles to some fans' ability to embody fully the *VM* styles. One TWOP thread addresses this issue. When a fan discloses, "I hate that I'm 25, though, and can't pull off some of the stuff she wears," she adds that she can't copy the hairstyles either because of her "super curly, frizzy hair." Another chimes in and laments her own stubbornly curly hair. She recounts how when she wakes up and her hair is a disaster, she gets exasperated and thinks, "no one has suffered as I have suffered." Then she apologizes for going off topic, but as she explains, "I hardly ever hear about someone else with the same hair. And I see *VM*'s hair and I am sad." That inspires another to declare herself "a curl head" too (TWOP, April 17, 2006). These postings reflect the ambivalence of viewers who understand that the ways their bodies are marked by race, ethnicity, and ancestry will frustrate their desire to adopt mainstream identities, leaving them feeling as if they are poor imitations of an ideal TV type.

Age is also a barrier to an easy adoption of the *VM* look, as an earlier TWOP-VC post notes: "I love what they do with her hair on the show. Sadly it inspires me and I'm not a high school student." She wishes she could go to the office with her hair in pigtails like Veronica's. Two other fans cheer her on. They reveal that they are both 28 and inspired by Veronica's hairdo. One reassures her, "Well I'm 28 and I've just started wearing pigtails again for the first time since grade school due in large part to the fact that Veronica looked so dang cute in them. Of course, I'm not as cute as her, but a girl can try!" She admits that she was nervous about adopting the style, but her bosses did not seem to mind. She was secretly pleased that someone told her that she looked about 16 in them. Another shares, "I'm 24, and have been incorporating my Veronica Mars look into my wardrobe as well.... My boss actually told me I looked cute, and wistfully said she wished her hair was long enough for pigtails" (TWOP, April 17, 2006).

These comments demonstrate that *VM* extends the offer of participation in its lifestyle experience to youth-oriented viewers who range in age from the early teens to the late thirties. Like many programs with teenage main characters and adult followings, it addresses viewers who are still working through teen identities. Some use teen identities to reflect on their own concerns in a dramatized way. Others take pleasure in vicariously reliving high school as the sassy teen with the snappy comebacks who can mock mainstream high school hierarchies and sometimes challenge them. It helps that as a petite blonde bedecked in the latest mall fashions, Veronica looks so good fighting and talking back. True to what Douglas (1995) says about the composite appeal of many female TV characters, the fans posting comments on websites related to *Veronica Mars* admire the title character for both her investigative and fashion savvy, especially her ability to inflect mainstream trendy teen fashions with her own sassy style. *VM* courts teens and anyone else who wants to participate in the trendy teen lifestyle that she represents. The analysis of its affiliated TWOP-VC forum demonstrates that while actual teens experience pleasure in seeing their culture represented and acknowledged, twenty-something and even some thirty-something viewers experience pleasure in acquiring the kind of fashion and tech savvy that leads others to miscalculate their ages.

Veronica Mars: Alterna-Teen and Class Warrior?

That so many of these fans say they are in their twenties and some indicate that they might be more ethnic than WASP are intriguing details. Of course, the problem with any analysis of online fan forums is that there is no way to tell who these people really are or any guarantee that those who assert some kind of identity claim are being truthful. Such potential misrepresentation is the negative side to the pleasure of being mistaken for a teenager. Anyone can come to a site and claim s/he is a teenager or misrepresent him/herself in some other way. Choosing to ignore this issue, the participants on the TWOP-VC and CW-L fan forums take each other at face value. As Poster (2004) explains, "Virtual communities derive some of their verisimilitude from being treated as if they were plain communities, allowing members to experience communications in cyberspace as if they were embodied social interactions" (589). *VM* does address the problem of the vagaries of virtual identity within its diegesis, often dealing with plotlines about the challenges of 21st century identity—including the prevalence of identity manipulation and misrepresentation, whether harmless online and off-line role playing or fraudulent identity theft. Many episodes of *VM* pivot on identity, particularly the ways in which people misrepresent themselves both in their in-person and online interactions.

The investigations that Veronica undertakes for her classmates often involve cases of mistaken identity and identity theft and fraud, or at the very least, one person's victimization by another's misrepresentation. The teens Veronica helps are not as savvy as she is. Not all are as foolish as the ones in "The Wrath of Con" episode who answer one of those "phishing" emails and open themselves to the theft of their savings. Still, many do not know what Veronica knows only too well: technology is a double-edged sword as digital photographs can be easily manipulated or doctored, internet passwords hacked, personal information acquired, and identities stolen. Carmen, Veronica's client in "M.A.D.," learns that lesson the hard way. Without her knowledge, her boyfriend takes a salacious video of her with his camera phone. When she tries to break up with him, he threatens to email the file to the whole school. Fearing that the film will become the next Paris Hilton sex tape or the clip of "that Star Wars kid" everyone in America emailed to his/her friends, she hires Veronica to destroy the video. Veronica agrees, but reminds Carmen that because it is practically impossible to destroy a digital video file, she needs a backup plan. Veronica calls on her network of tech-savvy friends and fellow outcasts and creates an incriminating website about the boyfriend, complete with digitally manipulated photos and doctored voice recordings from Carmen's cell phone. Veronica explains to Carmen that the website is just an insurance policy; if there is "mutually assured destruction," her boyfriend won't circulate the video file. In an odd twist, he does anyhow, but Carmen chooses to press delete instead of send on the email with the website hyperlink. Veronica tells the viewer in a voiceover that she would have pressed send. This ending allows the show to have it both ways—modeling both the "revenge is sweet" and the "take the high road" clichés.

This plotline is part of the situating of *VM* as an alterna-teen show and of Veronica as edgier than her teen TV counterparts. This scene exemplifies how Veronica refuses to be the good girl. Creator Rob Thomas wanted to craft characters "'who aren't always doing the right thing' because when he was a writer on *Dawson's Creek* he would get frustrated by the need always to write admirable characters" (Hughes 2006). Many forum posts on TWOP-VC and the CW-L make similar distinctions, relying on a binary that positions quality shows like *VM* in opposition to shallow teen programs like *Dawson's Creek* and *The O.C.* Their comments indicate how invested fans are in the idea of a fixed binary between mainstream and alternative culture, and between "real fans" whose consumer choices represent active interaction with the TV text and passive viewers who are easily influenced by marketers and producers and mindlessly model themselves on TV characters. One respondent on the CW-L explains that she wears the same clothes as Veronica, for example, not because she is a TV character who has influence over gullible viewers. Instead, she claims that she and the character share the same sensibility so it makes sense that they would independently choose the same clothes. This viewer, like many others posting to the forums, does not interrogate why she likes what she does and how those preferences are culled from a commodified set of choices.

Veronica and her style are broadly appealing because she is one in a long line of rebel types who represent an anti-establishment stance at the same time that she does not veer too far from identifiable mainstream identities. While seeming to occupy an anti-establishment position, Veronica is actually a representative of what Frank (1997) calls "hip consumerism," which he defines as "a cultural perpetual motion machine in which disgust with the falseness, shoddiness, and everyday oppressions of consumer society could be enlisted to drive the accelerating wheels of consumption" (31). That some read Veronica's style as an alternative to consumer culture is a testament to the "counterculture as an enduring commercial myth" (32). Frank contends that corporations since the 1960s have embraced an "anti-establishment sensibility being developed by the youthful revolutionaries" (26). Within the hip consumerism paradigm "no longer would Americans buy to fit in or impress the Joneses, but to demonstrate that they were wise to the game, to express their revulsion with the artifice and conformity of consumerism" (Frank 31). Yet, it is consumerism just the same. *VM* fans might pride themselves in following their own routes, but a reading of the TWOP-VC forum demonstrates that they still end up in the same place—the mall. Judging by the number of posts on Season One and Two *VM* web forums about coveting and acquiring the items in Veronica's closet, UPN's overflow strategies might have been underdeveloped, but they still worked.

On the message boards fans sometimes acknowledge this simultaneity of Veronica as alterna-teen who often sports mainstream clothing choices and of independent viewers not easily taken in by promises of consumer belonging who conform to Veronica's style parameters. More often, they work to efface it because they position Veronica in a binary in which she is the champion of the have-nots against the haves. They like the outcast they first met in the Pilot and the way she spoke directly to them: "This is my school. If you go here, your parents are either millionaires or your parents work for millionaires. Neptune, California, a town without a middle class." So many professional and amateur reviewers have adopted the description that no one ever thinks to analyze its applicability to the fictional town or its main character. Most just accept as fact that Veronica is an underdog who stands firm against the town's social elite, represented at Neptune High by the kids who reside in the prestigious "09" zip code.

Although *VM* does critically explore outsider social and economic positions in the United States, the description of Neptune as a "town without a middle class" (and, by implication, of Veronica as lower class) is misleading. After all, Season One is filled with seemingly middle class kids for whom Veronica investigates cases—often ones involving mistaken identity or some form of misrepresentation related to the technology to which all the non–09ers seem to have access. These are the kids described in the rest of that Pilot voiceover: "If you're in the second group, you get a job; fast food, movie theatres, mini-marts." They all need those jobs as an Abercrombie and Fitch t-shirt would set them back $50 and its faux fur vest would gobble up a paycheck or two. If they are indeed lower class, then they are spending most of their money on clothing that they perceive of as helping them pass for middle to upper middle class. That even Neptune's truly rich kids wear the same mall store fashions suggests that *VM*, like most American Teen TV, flattens out class differences so that everyone is or is depicted as middle to upper middle class or aspiring to be.

A TWOP-VC thread about Abercrombie is interesting for the way it registers this class ambivalence at the heart of Veronica Mars, the character, and the series (TWOP, April 17, 2006). In addition to their politically-charged discussions of hair texture and age-appropriate styles, the fan forum also raises the question about what brands are inconsistent with Veronica's supposed anti-establishment stance. She describes herself as one of Neptune's have-nots, but her taste in fashion (not to mention in white, J. Crew–wearing boyfriends) sometimes positions her as more Mall of America Middle Class. After one of the fashion sleuths' investigations in August 2005 uncovers the fact that several of Veronica's jackets are from Abercrombie, one fan changes the direction of the conversation by lamenting, "Somehow I'm vaguely disappointed that Veronica wears Abercrombie" (TWOP, April 17, 2006).

The fact that Veronica still wears clothes from Ambercrombie and Fitch, the current badge of belonging to the Mall of America Middle Class, feels problematic for others as well. As another fan puts it, "Abercrombie represents that elitist high school/college 09er values that I thought Veronica had left behind" (TWOP, April 17, 2006). After all, Veronica has supposedly totally remade herself after Lilly's murder. She cuts her hair and, as one reviewer put it, "chucks her Abercrombie wardrobe" (Cody 2004). Once transformed into Alterna-Teen, her clothing and hair take on such sharp edges that she resembles a DC Comics superhero (Cody). It seems inconsistent for Veronica, who constantly mocks the Abercrombie-clad kids from Neptune's elite zip code, to wear anything from a store sued for only hiring 09er white preppy types (Safer 2004).

Some of the forum participants (TWOP, April 17, 2006) explain away the Abercrombie pieces as a matter of practicality (she doesn't have enough money to buy all new clothes for junior year). "Let's not forget that Veronica was an 09er herself," one post reminds everyone. "I think it is very plausible that as part of that clique, she would wear clothing targeted toward the preppy elite we see so much in high school. I sincerely doubt that Veronica wouldn't wear her old clothing for the sake of rebellion against 09er culture." Another adds, "Especially if she's cash-poor. I think the wardrobe department does a really good job of 'punk'-ing up Veronica's look while still making use of her preppy stuff, such as Abercrombie." A third takes the argument to the opposite extreme, implying that if Veronica didn't wear Abercrombie, it would be like reverse snobbery: "I think it is perfectly fitting that Veronica wears

Abercrombie because she also wears like, a million other types of clothing. I don't think she'd be one to not go to a store because of who it is marketed to." Abercrombie has to be recuperated because many of the participants share with Veronica a combination of desire and disdain for the commodified identities promoted by mainstream middle class mall culture.

On the TWOP discussion board the uncomfortable topic is soon abandoned and the forum returns to a space for celebrating Veronica's fashion sense and its participants' shopping savvy. Several also praise the *VM* wardrobe department for dressing the characters realistically in clothes that are available at the local mall stores (TWOP, April 17, 2006). A few complain that less realistic items, like Seven for All Mankind jeans are starting to creep into Veronica's Season Two wardrobe. A similar critique is made on the LJ-*VM* during Season Three: "I've always found it so funny that even though Veronica and her dad are supposed to be lower middle class, she is always wearing Sevens and Citizens of Humanity Jeans" (LJ, February 20, 2007). All the posts on the TWOP-VC thread about the jeans eventually prompt the outcry: "They should not change Veronica's style at all!! If I wanted to see clothes from The O.C. I would watch The O.C.!" (TWOP, April 17, 2006). The irony is that such starlet wear is not donned by the 09ers who could realistically afford those fashions. Even Logan, the son of a movie star, is outfitted in mid-level mall store clothes, as one thread about his suede jacket indicates (TWOP, April 17, 2006). Given that the fashion sleuths discover that the jacket comes from Wilson's Leather—an ordinary mall store and, thus, an unlikely place for a movie star's son to buy anything, if we can judge by the actions of LA's Robertson Drive celebrity kid shopaholics—something other than realism seems to be at work. Several fans note that the clothes the 09ers wear really don't fit their characterization as the "haves" in Neptune.

With the toning down of 09er style, the show seems to be leveling the playing field. In doing so, it taps into that American fantasy perpetuated by the media that everyone in the United States is essentially from the same class—the Mall-shopping Middle Class. Sure there are some gradations, but such a view promises that there is no real chasm separating the haves and the have-nots. In a credit card culture, everyone can at least look like a "have," the show seems to be saying. That is probably what one fan felt when she bought Logan's jacket for her husband and her tween daughter and then proudly posted a picture of the two of them wearing their matching jackets. That they are sitting astride a motorcycle reminiscent of those ridden by Neptune's mildly rebellious "PCHer" gang suggests that a rebel "have-not" identity is available for purchase as well (TWOP, April 17, 2006). It is ironic that Logan wears the jacket in an episode entitled "Weapons of Class Destruction." The fact that Veronica, in contrast, is wearing super trendy and super pricey John Fluevos "Bond girl" boots makes one remark, "I think lower-middle-class in the fictional town of Neptune is a lot different than lower-middle-class in real life." Even more interesting is Keith Mars' comment after he secures a bounty hunter fee, "Tonight we eat like the lower-middle-class to which we aspire." In this moment, among others in the episode, there is disconnect between the dialogue and fashion cues about class.

These are ambivalent messages coming from a show whose pilot episode proclaims that Neptune is fiercely divided between the haves and the have-nots. It is not surprising that the TWOP-VC participants found class and racial ambivalence inherent in the costuming and character choices on *VM*. While it is hard not to love the sassy teen sleuth, especially her ability to rise above petty high school social politics, the Abercrombie problem is not the only one that raises issues about her status as an outsider. Veronica might not be an 09er, but her ties to that community are more dormant than severed. That becomes clear in Season Two.

Despite the intended irony of "Normal Is the Watchword," the title of the opening episode of Season Two, the opening exchange between Veronica and Kelvin, a potential teen client who failed the Neptune High student-athlete drug test, makes overt the ambivalence about class and about alternative teen culture that has been creeping into the series ever since the pilot. Despite its reputation for critiques of typical teen conformity, *Veronica Mars* still puts on display the kind of Abercrombie and Fitch Nation teenage normalcy associated with the white, middle class preppy characters in *Dawson's Creek*.

VM's pilot establishes the title character as an outcast, ostracized by her old popular 09er crowd, and therefore deemed an untouchable by the rest of her high school classmates. As Season One unfolds, her interactions with 09ers become increasingly ambivalent, especially given her decreasing hostility and eventual on-again off-again romantic relationship with Logan, the former friend whom the pilot worked hard to establish as Veronica's main adversary. By the first day of senior year and the start of Season Two, Veronica has solved the mystery of Lilly's murder, thereby clearing both Logan and Duncan of suspicion and restoring her father's reputation and hence her own. Through flashbacks we learn that she was dating Logan, but sometime over the summer she severed ties with him and then reunited with ex-boyfriend Duncan Kane. Once Veronica's 09er connections are reactivated, the question of her class position becomes murky again. As Weevil, her former PCHer biker ally says, "Be honest, Veronica—you think you're this big outsider. But push comes to shove? You're still one of them."

While viewers on fan forums speculate on the way Thomas offers details that direct their suspicions toward particular characters, often highlighting a misrepresentation of their identities, they rarely question Veronica's character. So when Season Two opens with this scene in which Kelvin speculates that Veronica had just been playing the part of an outcast until she could revert to her identity, most viewers agreed with Veronica's characterization of him as "an obnoxious jackwad."

When Veronica, standing at the hostess station of the café at which she now works, refuses to take his case and explains, "I don't do that kind of work anymore," Kelvin asks, "So who's supposed to help me out, then?" When he adds, "I guess it's true what they say about you then, huh?" Veronica shrugs and looks mildly taken aback that she is once again the subject of rumors, but still manages a sarcastic retort. Because his final barb is very similar to one from the pilot, viewers are reminded of the first time they were introduced to Veronica the outcast with the ruined reputation. But they also know that Veronica's end of the season romance with Logan, her former 09er adversary, made her position in the Neptune High social hierarchy ambivalent again. Seemingly referring to that relationship, Kelvin continues his allegations: "You're a 09er now. You went and landed yourself some rich boyfriend." He accuses her of just acting like an outsider, but really siding with 09ers. "Figures how none of the rich kids failed their drug test now, huh?" he comments and volleys his parting shot: "You sleep well." The shot counter shot during this sequence suggests that Kelvin has made Veronica uncomfortable even though she dismisses him as a bully. His charge is easy to dismiss too, especially given that in almost every episode some character, sometimes even Veronica herself, is falsely accused and later cleared through Veronica's investigative skills. Kelvin touches a nerve, though, because he does highlight that for Abercrombie-wearing, preppy-dating Veronica, derision for the 09ers has indeed been mixed with desire.

New Networks, Old Alliances

The first episode of Season Three ushered in a 2005–6 season that brought uncertainty for Veronica Mars and the network on which the character and show appear. UPN parent company CBS announced in early 2006 plans for a merger with Warner Brothers that would result in the demise of UPN and the WB, the formation of the CW network, and

a Fall schedule that featured a combination of some of their old programming with new projects. When the new network jettisoned some of
UPN's niche market African American sitcoms and ghettoized the rest
on a single night (Smith 2005), the question Kelvin poses to Veronica in
light of her 09er unions resonated in a different way. If there is no UPN
to "do that kind of work anymore," who will? "The CW's complexion"
definitely seems, as *Denver Post* columnist Edward P. Smith (2005) put
it, "a whole lot lighter than the UPN [network's]." Darnell Hunt, a UCLA
professor of sociology, theorized that the "demise of UPN [would result
in] the loss of more than half of all African-American prime-time characters" with significant screen time. The new network, he added, would
be "going for a mainstream—read 'white'—audience" (quoted in Smith).

Although it might have a bit of a menu approach to its many nonwhite characters, at least *Veronica Mars* has significant nonwhite main
characters. Mixed-race Kelvin might have been right to criticize Veronica as those characters had a bigger role in her life the previous year. During Season Two, the most significant nonwhite characters, Wallace and
Weevil, were sometimes shifted from their roles as Veronica's sleuthing
partners to the sidelines. Center stage was often occupied by Veronica's
09er reunions: Logan-Veronica, the sassy mismatched couple, and Dun-
can-Veronica, the sweet star-crossed lovers.

The merger of former rivals UPN and WB parallels the way Veronica went from rallying viewers against the snotty rich kid 09ers to dating them. In both cases the bitter rivalry between the have-nots and the
haves that defined their oppositional identity claims—UPN was not the
WB, *VM* was not *Dawson's Creek*, and Veronica, the outcast, was not
an 09er—had suddenly turned into alliances. Or perhaps the alliances had
been there all along and the network, the show, and its title character
had just seemed like alternatives to the mainstream when they would
have been better described as subsidiaries.

That their scrappy underdog identity claims depend on those bina-
ries is suggested by this description from *Variety* about the distinction
between UPN and the WB: "UPN has consistently targeted an edgier,
more urban crowd, while the WB has fared better in the suburbs and
with shows set in small towns" (Kissell 2006). The same description
could apply to the difference between UPN's *Veronica Mars* and WB's
Dawson's Creek, both TV shows about high school social networks, with
VM seeming to mock the kind of preppy normalcy the latter took for
granted. Yet, as this essay has shown, the two teen shows are not always
polar opposites, as *VM* is sometimes more of an alterna-inflected iteration of the other.

Further analysis reveals that the idea of a giant gap between the networked haves and the have-nots is also a misleading identification of the complex web of social relations within the television and film industries and within fictional Neptune. *VM* is neither privileged nor underprivileged, and neither is the network on which the show appears. UPN might have been the fifth place network, but its full name, the United Paramount Network, indicates the interlocking webs of power to which the "netlet" had access. In turn, UPN served an important purpose for Paramount, as a space for cross-promotion of its feature films and its courting of the trendy teen lifestyle audience it wants for its films (Caldwell 2006). UPN was really a subsidiary of larger companies (with Viacom, Paramount, and now CBS in the mix), rather than some kind of feisty independent. With the merger even more power has been consolidated. The CW is an offshoot of two of the most "09er" of insiders—CBS and Warner Brothers. That would seem like an unlikely place for *Veronica Mars* if it didn't already feature the grandson of the legendary Hollywood insider, director Frank Capra, playing the part of the Latino leader of the Neptune have-nots.

Despite the way Veronica defines Neptune High in Manichean terms—"If you go here, your parents are either millionaires or your parents work for millionaires"—power in the world of *Veronica Mars* is still insider network power. Within the diegesis, power is based on a web of social and economic networks, exploited with the most financial return by the 09er families, but also often skillfully negotiated by others, especially Veronica. She couldn't solve her mysteries or pull off her sassy maneuvers without the social and technological networked connections she maintains both as the daughter of a former sheriff turned PI and the ex-girlfriend and ex-friend of 09ers. Added to that, she has a Latino motorcycle gang leader on her side as well as an African American best friend with a job in Neptune High's front office and a skilled hacker chick named Mac, among other assorted outcasts, to call on for assistance.

In short, *VM* the character, the show, and the network on which both first appeared seem as if they are outsiders, when, in actuality, their power is based on access to powerful networks. They are less "alternatives to" than "variations on" old school networking and standard teen lifestyle programming. That doesn't change the fact that *Veronica Mars* is, and will likely remain, a fascinating TV text for the way it puts on display a web of issues related to networking—as that term relates to TV studies, to multiple media platform marketing, fandom [network and non-network endorsed], hypertextuality, and social/economic advancements. The new network, with its desire to "strike alternative deals to deliver its content," to its tech-savvy demographic comfortable with the "increasingly time-shifted, multiplatform media world" (Shields 2006), would have seemed to be the right home for a well-written and compelling show already self-reflexive about its target demographic and its thematization of new technologies.

Out of Aerie, Nothing

For its Fall 2006 inaugural season, the CW decided to bundle *VM*, its newly acquired UPN product, with *Gilmore Girls*, its more successful former WB product, and make the latter the Tuesday night lead-in to *VM*, hopefully carrying over some of its audience. Marketing executives struck a deal with American Eagle and came up with Aerie Tuesdays. The commercial segment prior to the opening of both shows featured a commercial for American Eagle's new Aerie "intimates and dormwear" product line and then was followed by the first of several interstitial episodes featuring "real-life" Aerie teen customers commenting on the TV characters and story arcs, focusing especially on the on-again-off-again romances of Luke and Lorelai, and, to a lesser extent, Veronica and Logan. The way the CW structures the on-air and online versions of the Aerie campaign suggests that executives were familiar with the active fan participation of the fashion sleuths even if they did not really understand the fan investment in the forum exchanges and investigations. When *VM* moved to the CW, the network formalized the fashion sleuth link by including on its website a "CW style" section (CWTV.com/thewc/style-veronicamars, February 20, 2007) in which fans could browse—by brand, character, episode, or product—for the clothing that Veronica and the other characters wear in *VM* episodes.

"Die Aerie Tuesdays!" the title of one post on the CW-L (February 20, 2007) and the subsequent pages of posts offering enthusiastic seconds to this proclamation, captures the degree of failure of the CW and American Eagle Aerie Brand joint marketing campaign. In general the postings are hostile to the Aerie Girls, also dubbed "Aerheads," for their inane comments, shallow readings of *VM*, and obsession with love relationships. This response contrasts with the *Dawson's Creek* fans Brooker (2004) studied. He claims that they did not seem to mind that "their participatory culture [was] neatly structured for them, with intertextual spin-offs, and cross-promotions clearly linked up and signposted like stores in a shopping mall." *VM* fans understand these overflow strategies and know, as Jenkins noted, that they are part of the TV game, but they view the network's spoon-feeding approach as insulting. Perhaps the difference in reception can be explained by *VM* mystery-teen hybrid genre position; viewers who choose to watch a mystery already have implicitly expressed a preference for following a chain of evidence to their own conclusions.

By curtailing that process at the outset, the network engages in a sort of spoiling because the fashion links provide the answers and, thereby, "cut off the game that many other group members wanted to play" (Jenkins 2006, 55). When the fashion mysteries are revealed ahead of time, it spoils the fun of unearthing the information and collaboratively disseminating it. Many respondents on CW-L register their annoyance with the CW for underestimating viewers' intelligence. Some call themselves "real fans" who understand the "true" complexity of *VM* and express irritation with the CW's failure to notice how well the fans already play the game on their own. Jenkins would say that these executives do not understand that fans are "drawn toward the collaborative production and evaluation of knowledge" (2006, 57). Instead of allowing fans to find their own ways to the fashions featured on the show, the CW uses obvious (and, by some fan accounts, extremely annoying) on-air and online signposts to lead viewers there by hand. Given this context, it is not surprising that the pleasure the TWOP-VC fashion sleuths derive from their independent investigations contrasts with the annoyance and hostility produced by the patronizing network-sponsored Aerie Tuesday marketing campaign. As Jenkins has pointed out, fans understand that marketing is part of the game, but they want it to participate in the "puzzle solving" (55).

Fans also want to participate more in the decision-making process. Some remark that the comments they post on the CW Forum are likely to be taken seriously by producers and may even influence changes in marketing strategies. If there have to be Aerie girls, fans theorize, then they should have found real fans to talk intelligently about the show. One suggests a radio contest to find better fan commentators. Demonstrating a similar level of awareness about the game, one fan even proclaims that she is just happy that *VM* has a major advertiser. Like the other industry savvy fans on the site, she recognizes the importance of the cross-promotion in convincing the CW that *VM* is a lucrative product: "I'd rather have lame aerie Tuesdays than no Veronica." Others warn CW executives to be aware that their audience is larger than the Aeries girls target demographic: "I certainly hope the suits are reading all of this.... As anyone can tell reading these messages, the audience for Veronica Mars is made up of all ages and both genders." Several agree, with one proposing, "I think we should start a thread saying, 'Suits Listen to the REAL fans' and then we keep it going for a real long time so it does get attention ... we save veronica mars." Clearly, this contributor, like many others on the fan forums, enjoys thinking of herself as able to influence production decisions. Such fans are heartened by the fact that LiveJournal fans credit *VM*'s Season Three renewal to the fact that they hired a plane to fly a "Renew Veronica Mars! CW 2006!" banner over the network's offices in order to influence CW executives' decision about the fate of *VM*. The CW's marketing choices are indicative of the network's fundamental misunderstanding of this kind of fan investment and fan pleasure more generally, especially the kind fans get from participating in their own private investigations into Veronica's closet. They did not anticipate how annoyed fans would get by the network's attempts to structure fan interaction with the text.

Such fan dedication may be inspired, in part, by a perception of a show's underdog or alterna-status, one heightened by constant fears about impending cancellation. Fan buzz that the failure of the Aerie campaign would hasten the cancellation of *VM* was only the latest version of cancellation predictions that had been circulating since the premier of the pilot episode. Cancellation will seal *VM*'s position as iconic alterna-teen TV, allowing it to join *My So-Called Life* as an example of intelligent teen programming that the mainstream failed to appreciate. I count myself among those who are attracted to the alterna-teen feel of *Veronica Mars*. I identify with what Kristin Bell (aka Veronica Mars) terms "the prematurely jaded youth" of Neptune High (Shine 2005) and even find myself coveting Veronica's 250 dollar ultra-trendy John Fluevog boots. In those boots, I too believe that Veronica could "kick Joey Potter's ass," to borrow the comment one post on the TWOP General *Veronica Mars* message board used to explain Veronica's difference from the lead female in *Dawson's Creek* (TWOP, February 20, 2007). There is no question that Veronica Mars and the show on which she appears both have a compelling sense of style. I understand exactly what Stephen King means when he explains his addiction to *Veronica Mars*: "I can't take my eyes off the damn thing" (2006). I am just disappointed that the show did not always live up to its Season One promise, especially when it failed to maintain its scathing class critique about the ever-widening gap between the haves and the have-nots and the role that fashion plays in obscuring it. Like many reviewers, I was impressed by Season One's representation of the grittier side of class warfare in 21st century American high schools; I just wish it could have been sustained.

VM's failures may, however, be less inherent to the show and more a product of the current TV industry environment. All teen shows, even those focused on alterna-teens, are expected to be display cases for sponsor products directed at a highly desirable youth culture demographic. Writers and producers do not always get to make casting, costuming, and setting choices with an eye toward character and storyline consistency;

rather, they are expected to put on display the types of people, styles, and locations that will most easily become spokespersons, samples, and showcases for the consumer products on which the TV industry depends for its financial support. The forum comments indicate that participants are acutely aware of these industry issues. While these fans understand that the CW's "desire to build a community around such programs is part of corporate strategy to ensure viewer engagement with brands and franchises," networks would do well to recognize that fans are most engaged when they are given "spaces to apply their skills and new openings for their speculations" (Jenkins 2006, 56–57).

References

Brooker, Will. 2003. "Conclusion: Overflow." In *Audience Studies Reader*, eds. Will Brooker and Deborah Jermyn, 321–34. New York: Routledge.
_____. 2004. "Living on *Dawson's Creek*: Teen Viewers, Cultural Convergence, and Television Overflow." In *The Television Studies Reader*, eds. Annette Hill and Robert Allen, 569–80. New York: Routledge.
Butler, Judith. *Bodies That Matter: On the Discursive Limits of Sex.* New York: Routledge, 1993.
Caldwell, John Thorton. 2006. "Welcome to the Viral Future of Cinema (Television)." *Cinema Journal* 45, no.1 (Fall): 90–97.
Cody, Diablo. 2004. "Women Are from Venus, Veronica Is from Mars." *City Pages* (Minneapolis/St. Paul), October 13, available at http://citypages.com/databank/25/1245/article12558.asp (accessed April 7, 2007).
Douglas, Susan. *Where the Girls Are: Growing Up Female with the Mass Media.* New York: Random House, 1994.
Frank, Thomas. *The Conquest of Cool: Business Culture, Counterculture, and the Rise of Hip Consumerism.* Chicago: University of Chicago Press, 1997.
Gwenllian-Jones, Sara. 2003. "Histories, Fictions and *Xena: Warrior Princess*." In *Audience Studies Reader*, eds. Will Brooker and Deborah Jermyn, 185–92. New York: Routledge.
Hills, Matt. *Fan Cultures.* New York: Routledge, 2002.
Hughes, Sarah. 2006. "Humphrey Bogart's Back—But This Time Around He's at High School." *The Observer (UK) Online*, March 26, available at http://film.guardian.co.uk/features/featurepages/0.1739601.00.html (accessed April 7, 2007).
Jenkins, Henry. *Convergence Culture: Where Old and New Media Collide.* New York: New York University Press, 2007.
_____. *Textual Poachers: Television, Fans, and Participatory Culture.* New York: Routledge, 1992.
King, Stephen. 2006. "Just Asking." *Entertainment Weekly Online*, January 13, available at http://www.ew.com (accessed April 7, 2007).
Kissell, Rick. 2006. "Nuptials Chill Hot Netlet Race." *Variety Online*, Jan. 30-Feb. 5, available at http://www.variety.com (accessed April 7, 2007).
Kozinets, Robert V. 1998. "How Online Communities Are Growing in Power." *Financial Times.* Nov. 9. Available: Proquest (accessed March 30, 2007).
Murray, Susan. "2000. Saving Our So-Called Lives: Girl Fandom, Adolescent Subjectivity, and *My So-Called Life*." In *Kids Media Culture*, ed. Marsha Kinder, 221–35. Durham: Duke University Press.
Poster, Mark. 2004. "Postmodern Virtualities." In *The Television Studies Reader*, eds. Annette Hill and Robert Allen, 581–95. New York: Routledge.
Safer, Morley. 2004. "The Look of Abercrombie & Fitch." *60 Minutes Online at cbs.com,*

November 24, available at http://cbs.news.com/stories/2003/12/05/60Minutes/main 587099.shtml (accessed April 7, 2007).

Shields, Mike. 2006. "New Net Poised to Make Multiplatform Deals." *MediaWeek*, January 30, available at http://www.mediaweek.com/mw/search/article_display.jsp?vnu_content_id=1001920145 (accessed April 17, 2006).

Shine, T.M. 2005. "Veronica Mars Attacks." *South Florida Sun–Sentinel Online*, January 12, available at http://www.southflorida.com/citylink (accessed April 7, 2007).

Slater, Don. 2004. "Social Relationships and Identity Online and Offline." In *The Television Studies Reader*, eds. Annette Hill and Robert Allen, 596–14. New York: Routledge.

Smith, Edward P. 2005. "TV: Less Diversity Seen at New CW Network." *The Denver Post*, February 15, available at http://www.ocregister.com/ocregister/entertainment (accessed April 17, 2006).

Walsh, Peter. 2003. "The Withered Paradigm: The Web, the Expert and the Information Hegemony." In *Democracy and New Media*, eds. Henry Jenkins and David Thornburn, 365–72. Cambridge, MA: MIT Press.

Williams, Raymond. *Television, Technology and Cultural Forms*. London: Fontana, 1974.

11. The Adventures of a Repressed Farm Boy and the Billionaire Who Loves Him: Queer Spectatorship in *Smallville* Fandom

Melanie E.S. Kohnen

Have you ever wondered if there was something queer between *Smallville*'s Clark Kent and Lex Luthor? Or perhaps between Seth Cohen and Ryan Atwood from *The O.C.*? Or maybe even between Buffy and Spike from *Buffy the Vampire Slayer*? If so, you are not alone. Since TV's earliest days, many dedicated viewers have taken pleasure in watching television through a decidedly queer lens. The following essay will chart the multiple ways in which a diverse audience engages in queer spectatorship, and how that engagement challenges established notions of what constitutes "seeing queerly" and of how viewers engage with Teen TV— a genre that is replete with (heteronormative) romance.

Even though the history of television fandom goes back to a pre-internet era, the emergence of the internet as a mass medium during the 1990s allowed fans of cult films, TV shows, and print media to connect to each other in more efficient ways, resulting in a large jump in participants in fan communities. Scholars have closely studied these online social networks, including websites, message boards, and blogs, paying particular attention to the creation of fan fiction about same-sex romance between nominally straight characters, also known as "slash." Since slash fandoms have been perceived as largely heterosexual female communities, variations of two central questions have guided academic research: one, why do many "straight" women write about sex between men? And two, how are gender and sexuality depicted in these stories? Yet, however interesting these questions might be, the complexity of fan practices far exceeds this framework and thus demands an expansion of earlier inquiries into female fans and slash. Most importantly, especially as a TV studies scholar, one needs to recognize that slash fans of television shows are spectators. As such, their fannish activities are shaped by their engagement with television, and in turn can (re)shape and expand scholarly understanding of what it means to watch TV. I undertake such an expansion by focusing on *Smallville* fandom, specifically the discussions on the website Television Without Pity (TWOP) and on LiveJournal. *Smallville*'s focus on the teenage years of Superman is a particularly productive example. This focus retains the fantastic generic elements that characterize the shows that attracted the first slash fandoms, such as *Star Trek*, but combines these elements with the teen genre, which has traditionally focused on issues connected to finding one's "identity. As such, *Smallville*'s Clark Kent is on a quest that includes fulfilling his superhero destiny and navigating typical teen challenges like first love—both of which are often on a collision course for the young Superman. Slash fans of the show latch onto this volatile mix of themes in new and surprising ways.

Through my analysis of *Smallville* fans' practices of reading and writing online, I not only expand the study of slash, but also introduce a re-conceptualization of televisual spectatorship. Specifically, the spectatorship practices of *Smallville* slash fans show that, while viewer desires may cross gender and sexual divisions (self-identified straight women imagining queer relations between men), a separation between sexual and spectatorial identification is also imperative. In other words, "seeing queerly" is not necessarily related to identifying as queer in "real life."[1]

Seeing Queerly 101

In the context of mainstream television, one needs to divide conceptions of queer spectatorship into two components: one, a way of "seeing queerly," and two, a person or group of persons who can be loosely grouped under the heading "queer spectators." This division is necessary in order to avoid a conflation of ontology and epistemology, i.e., to avoid the conclusion that viewers who identify as "being" queer will automatically read or see televisual texts in a different way from straight-identifying viewers. One certainly has to take into account that many queer viewers regard their relationship to television as different from straight viewers,' and that they explain this difference in relation to their queer identity (see, for example, Michael DeAngelis, 2001). Nevertheless, I want to emphasize that an argument built on a causal relationship between sexual and spectatorial identifications is highly problematic for two reasons: first, it essentializes queer spectators, and second, it lacks the ability to explain certain phenomena regarding viewers' identification with and interpretation of television texts. For example, an argument built on such a direct link cannot, on the one hand, account for the fact that not all queer-identifying spectators see queerly, and on the other, that a number of straight spectators do.[2] Moreover, I do not want to simply argue that straight people can and do see queerly, but rather that, within the context of slash fandom, they understand it as pleasurable, active, and communal way of seeing.

The acknowledgment of straight viewers who see queerly is over-looked in many traditional studies of queer spectatorship, which focus on queer viewing practices by gay and lesbian viewers.[3] In these studies, the queer moments that arise in the complex relationship between audience and text are often implicitly seen as sites of resistance against the ways in which mainstream heteronormative culture finds expression in the media. The idea that straight people might also engage in such practices leads to fears on the part of scholars who regard straight viewers' forays into queer spectatorship as a co-optation of gay and lesbian culture. One notable exception is the work of Alexander Doty, who includes the possibility of taking up a spectatorial position that doesn't align with one's sexual identification when he outlines the multiple meanings of "queer spectatorship" (2001, 5). However, Doty does not pursue this angle of analysis, and rather continues with the traditional route of queer viewers seeing queerly. Thus, even if people like Doty, Brett Farmer (2000), Patricia White (1999), and others make important interventions regarding queer spectatorial practices, they locate these readings with queer spectators, and thereby uphold the binary division of queer versus straight-identified spectators. It is important, however, to question precisely that binary in order to avoid a collapse of ontology and epistemology. Furthermore, such a strict division between queer and straight viewers also keeps queer readings contained as a practice that is limited to a specific subcultural group.[4] This (self-) limitation on the part of queer media scholars ultimately reinforces heteronormative structures. The discourse of heteronormativity insists that heterosexuality and homosexuality are clear-cut categories, and that heterosexuality is the norm and homosexuality the deviation. Consequently, the insistence that seeing queerly is limited to queer spectators implies that a "straight" view is the default view. This argument unwittingly upholds the notion that a division between these two positions is both possible and necessary instead of acknowledging that queer moments can arise anywhere and be seen by anyone.

If queer moments on TV are ubiquitous and accessible to a wide audience, we need to reformulate previous ideas about texts and audiences. Alongside Doty's insistence that every text is potentially queer, we need to recognize that every interpretation is potentially queer as well. Or in other words, just as much as queer visibility cannot be limited to films and TV shows that feature explicitly gay and lesbian characters, queer spectatorship cannot be limited to queer spectators. The recognition that seeing queerly is practiced widely among a diverse audience is crucial at a time in which cultural sexual norms are so hotly contested.[5]

Before moving on to the example of *Smallville* fandom, I briefly want to explain why the term "queer," and not "gay" or "lesbian," best describes this form of spectatorship, and how I understand spectatorship in general. Within the larger framework of queer theory, "queer" signifies an analysis stressing the discursive, non-fixed character of all sexualities, an approach that indicates a move beyond the hetero-homosexual binary. Since my project intends to broaden our understanding of relationships to television that both defy the heteronormative and escape the categories of "gay" and/or "lesbian," the term "queer" is most suitable. Regarding spectatorship, I believe that the meaning and reception of a film or TV program is neither fully determined by formal constraints in the text nor fully initiated by the agency or social position of the audience; rather, we have to speak of a process of ongoing negotiation (Mayne 1993, 9). Moreover, I conceive spectatorship as an activity, experience, and position that goes beyond the narrow time frame of watching a TV program. "Seeing queerly" is thus not a limited activity, but rather a complex and well-articulated position that fans actively seek out (and, as I will show, also defend against other ways of seeing that challenge fans' preferred spectatorial position).

"The Adventures of a Repressed Farm Boy and the Billionaire Who Loves Him"[6]

Since its early days during the first and second seasons of the show, *Smallville* fandom has contributed to a viewing culture that fans describe as "HoYay!" (short for Homoeroticism, Yay!). The phenomenon of HoYay! emerged in November 2001 on the website Television Without Pity.[7] Originally, HoYay! was conceived as a way of describing the strong, or as most fans put it, undeniable, homoerotic aspect of the relationship between Clark Kent and his best friend (or "best friend," depending on your point of view) Lex Luthor, as expressed by a number of longing looks and lasting touches exchanged between them on screen. The friendship between Clark and Lex is one of the most significant ways in which *Smallville* re-imagines the original *Superman* canon, in which Lex Luthor is Superman's arch-rival. Instead of setting up Clark and Lex as enemies right from the start, *Smallville* charts the more explosive route of two young men who become fast friends and who see their friendship torn apart due to the larger circumstances dominating their lives.

Their friendship develops along a number of fault lines that place them in opposition to one another: the farm boy versus the millionaire, the innocent teenager versus the worldly young adult, and so forth. The tension arising out of these oppositions often expresses itself in adolescent crises of identity that lead both Clark and Lex to question their seemingly already established position in *Smallville*'s diegesis. For example, the numerous times that Clark saves Lex from deadly traps lead Lex to question Clark's identity as average American teenager, suspecting he is anything but ordinary; in turn, Lex's fascination with comic books makes him look more like a geeky teen boy than a sophisticated, aloof business man. Fans' interpretative practices add the additional angle of Clark and Lex's growing attraction to each other to this list of crisis-inducing factors. In fact, the attraction between the two characters becomes of such fundamental importance to fans that, from their point of view, it saturates all other differences, infusing them with a homoerotic undercurrent.

The emphatic declaration of "HoYay!" thus quickly evolved from a descriptive term for the longing looks and touches between Clark and Lex into a desired way of seeing, a spectatorial position actively sought out by *Smallville* fans on TWOP. Not coincidentally, this viewing practice follows a motto ending in a celebratory "yay!" Despite its celebratory tone, one shouldn't mistake HoYay! for a naïve or unquestioning spectatorial position. Seeing queerly is a self-reflexive practice, one that questions and challenges numerous choices producers have made regarding the plot on *Smallville*. Via their HoYay!-inspired dissection of looks and touches between Clark and Lex, fans draw attention to the show's queer possibilities and its failure to realize those possibilities. They ask why producers and writers don't award these elements the same kind of recognition in the plot and in official extratextual discussions that they give to similar looks and touches between Clark and Lana Lang (the main female character and Clark's official on-again, off-again love interest). Seen in a larger context, these fan practices draw attention to the preference given to heteronormative narratives on television, even if the elements available in a show's diegesis would support a queer(er) way of telling the same story. In order to get a better sense of what HoYay! is all about, I turn to three examples of how viewers perceive and describe this way of seeing queerly: first, the discussion on Television Without Pity; second, fan art; and third, fan awards.

The HoYay! discussion on TWOP is mostly filled with posts devoted to dissecting various looks, touches, or pieces of dialog that fans declare undeniably queer. The long looks Clark and Lex exchange are special ground for enthusiastic declarations of HoYay! As one fan wrote, "I defy anyone to watch the seven second held gaze in 'Hourglass' without, at the very least, going, 'WTF?' Why are they looking at each other for so long? Why are they kind of smirking at each other while they're doing it? Why? Hmm?" (TWOP, April 23, 2003). Statements like this one are meant to underline the romantic aspect of Clark and Lex's relationship, and defend it against the grasp of heteronormative readings that would insist that they are "just friends." Moreover, in case someone does not see the queerness of the show right away, other fans immediately offer assistance. For example, in response to another fan who explained that he or she did not really see any homoeroticism in *Smallville* and hence his or her "gaydar" must be defunct, another fan replies: "You don't need a working gaydar for this, heck, my cuz's [cousin's] own is as defunct as to be nonexistent and even she believes Clex [Clark and Lex] are making out in the barn" (TWOP, April 23, 2003). In other words, fans consider the homoeroticism so ubiquitous that one does not need any "special" insight (either into *Smallville* or queer culture) to notice it.

Another fan recalls watching the episode "Red" with some uninitiated friends. In regard to this episode, fans mostly concentrate on two scenes. In the first scene, Lex checks out Clark in his new coat (visualized by a slow camera pan up and down Clark's body, shot from Lex's point of view). In the second scene, Lex suggests to Clark that they could move into his penthouse in Metropolis (the capital of Kansas in the *Smallville* universe), in reply to which Clark muses, "Lex Luthor and Clark Kent.... I like the sound of that." The following reaction sums up the overall response that HoYay! fans had to the episode:

Coming in rather late on Red here, but man that was so excellently gay. We watched it together with my sister and her BF [boyfriend], who'd never seen SV [*Smallville*] before, so I had to do lots of explaining.... [At the end, they] turned to me and Mr. laa-laa: "what the hell WAS that? He was checking Lex's a$$ out! They're running away together??" To which I nonchalantly replied, "Oh, they're secret boyfriends." Which, get this, satisfied them. They believed me. Without surprise or question [TWOP, April 23, 2003].

This account is representative of many posts that describe how first-time viewers immediately pick up on the sexual tension between Clark and Lex, and how they readily accept a secret love affair between the two characters as explanation for the drawn-out looks and ambiguous dialog between them. Even the disintegration of Clark and Lex's friendship in later seasons, characterized by numerous hostile confrontations and thus appropriately called "The Rift" by fans, does not put a stop to enthusiastic declarations of HoYay! While still retaining a position of seeing queerly, fans have shifted their interpretation of the relationship between Clark and Lex from one of romantic, first-time love to one that has darker, more sexually aggressive, and thus more "adult" overtones.

In addition to episode discussion, *Smallville* has also inspired a wide range of digital fan art devoted to the exploration Clark and Lex's relationship, for example fanvid(eo)s. Fanvideos are short music videos that are comprised of clips from television shows or movies. In many *Smallville* videos, various looks between Clark and Lex are edited together in such a way that the viewer is encouraged to read them as indication of sexual tension between Clark and Lex. Hence, it is not only the viewers who see queerly here, but Lex and Clark are made to look at each other in a queer way as well.

The creation of these videos allows fans to visualize their queer readings of *Smallville*. Consequently, fanvids are the most active articulation of a specific spectatorial position since they represent a direct intervention in the text: fans literally cut up and rearrange the text according to the vision of the spectator. These vids also show the instability of meaning in the original text. After all, the selected shots come directly from *Smallville* episodes, and it is primarily the editing that foregrounds the divergent possible meanings.[8] Put differently, the editing on the show suggests that Clark and Lex are simply friends, whereas the same visual material, when edited by fans, implies that they are lovers.

There are also a number of websites inspired by the *Smallville* HoYay! discussion, the most interesting of which is devoted to giving out "the weekly *Smallville* GAYLE (GAYest Look of the Episode) awards" (Gayles. tig-tv.com). Besides said gayest look of the week, awards are given to a whole range of looks, lines or plot devices, e.g., the "HoNay!" award for the "usually abysmally unsuccessful scene/person/object exclusively intended to strongly defend and firmly establish the heterosexuality of the present characters." There are two important dynamics in this definition. First, the assessment that the only function of certain plot devices is the (ultimately unsuccessful) defense of heterosexuality indicates that fans contemplate whether the show's producers are possibly trying to curb the display of homoeroticism on *Smallville*.[9] Second, this definition suggests that fans do not consider the nominal heterosexuality of Clark and Lex as something that is self-evident in the show's narrative—rather it needs to be established and repeated. Moreover, it has to be defended. From the fans' point of view, the characters' heterosexuality is precarious, and in Lex's case, definitely questionable.[10]

The "HoNay!" Award also represents an interesting moment in which pop cultural discourse and queer theory echo one another. One of the central arguments of queer theory parallels fans' perception of heterosexuality's precariousness, namely Judith Butler's assertion that "heterosexuality is always in the process of imitating and approximating its own phantasmatic idealization of itself—and *failing*" (21, emphasis in original). Far from being stable or "natural," heterosexuality is ultimately only a continuously failing attempt to realize an ideal. Similarly, *Smallville* fans catalog Lex's numerous short-lived relationships with women or Clark's doomed romance with Lana as failed attempts of establishing their heterosexuality on the part of *Smallville*'s writers and producers. Even in more or less successful moments of heterosexual romance, slash fans feel that queerness lurks just around the corner, as I will discuss in the next section.

"Lexana has been giving me weird Hoyay-ish vibes" (TWOP, accessed September 14, 2006)

The emergence of a romantic relationship between Lex Luthor and Lana Lang (often referred to as "Lexana" by fans) during the fifth season of *Smallville* (2005–6) has caused several interesting shifts in the Ho!Yay discussions on TWOP and in the *Smallville* slash community on the blogging site LiveJournal. While fans on TWOP could write off both Lex's previous relationships with several women and Clark's intermittent dating of Lana as peripheral storyline or naïve teenage romance, respectively, this new development is too central to *Smallville*'s plot to be ignored. Lex, Lana, and Clark have always been put in a triangular relationship to one another (starting with promotional posters for the show's first season), but only the infusion of multivalent and multi-lateral desire into the Lex/Lana/Clark triangle has made this set of relationships ripe for seeing queerly. However, even though some fans on TWOP do raise the possibility of the Lex/Lana/Clark triangle as queer, most prefer to see it as a heterosexualized version of "Clex" (Clark+Lex) with Lana as stand-in for Clark, or as two people commiserating the fact that they can't have the person they really want, namely Clark. Considering fans' previous seemingly blanket endorsement of everything queer, one has to ask why HoYay! fans don't favor the queer Lex/Lana/Clark triangle. This becomes a particularly pressing question if one considers that this constellation, in which everyone wants everyone else, certainly crosses heteronormative boundaries, and that a romantic entanglement of Clark and Lex has become much more difficult to maintain due to the increasingly pronounced rift in their friendship. In other words, the set-up of this triangle invites a queer reading, and it arises at a time when the show offers less potential for "Clex." In order to understand why one community of fans doesn't fully pursue the queer possibilities of the Lex/Lana/Clark triangle, a closer look at the discussions at TWOP is once again necessary.

Aside from continuously cataloging HoYay!-worthy moments between Clark and Lex, or from reminiscing about the "good old days" of incontestable "Clex," many posts during seasons five and six outline theories of how to understand the budding relationship between Lex and Lana. The following excerpt is a typical analysis:

> Lexana has been giving me weird Hoyay-ish vibes. In *Reckoning*, where Lex was yelling at Lana about keeping secrets and asking for favors, I kept thinking that he was talking to the wrong audience. Because, whatever Lana's done pales in comparison to the sheer history of secrets, lies, and favors (on both sides) between Clark and Lex.... The writers should have really given Lexana more of a back story, if they intended to create a Clexana love triangle [TWOP, September 14, 2006].

Despite the fact that this fan recognizes the queer potential of the Lex/Lana/Clark (i.e., "Clexana") triangle, the "Hoyayish vibes" are ultimately attributed to a what-if scenario of Lex arguing with Clark instead of with Lana. Another fan affirms this explanation by saying that "I think the writers *are* trying to build in a little hoyay ambivalence: in 'Mortal' Clark fights Lex, then rushes to have sex with Lana. (And note that Lex's scheme in 'Mortal' puts Lana at risk, *not* a sign of True Love)" (TWOP, September 14, 2006). Once again, the potential for queerness is acknowledged, but only insofar as it relates to Clark or Lex interacting with Lana in a way they would like to interact with each other—or in other words, the heterosexual is seen as a stand-in for the queer. In short, fans do not use HoYay! as a way of characterizing the triangle between Lex, Lana, and Clark as a whole.

Other fans dismiss the possibility that there could be anything queer at all about the Lex/Lana/Clark triangle. In a long post covering all five seasons, one fan describes all the different aspects he or she sees in the "Clex" relationship and comes to the following conclusion:

> Best of all, there's TrueLove!Clex (as seen in [in the episodes] "Shattered," "Prodigal," "Stray," etc.) I miss this side of them in S5 but the consolation is

this: When "Smallville" ends, the characters that go on to have a future
together are Clark, Lex and Lois.... And that's it. Right now, we might be force-
fed a diet of Lana a la Mode but her place in canon is small and incidental (and
SV ain't going to change that.) But the Clex are together forever, baby! [TWOP,
September 14, 2006].

Drawing on established *Superman* canon, this fan argues that, ultimately,
Lana and the relationship between Lex and Lana doesn't matter because
she won't be part of Clark and Lex's future life in Metropolis. Considering how often *Smallville* has already diverged from *Superman* canon
in the course of the past five seasons, including the transformation of
Clark and Lex from instant enemies to friends, this line of reasoning
points to an attitude of wanting to defend and reaffirm the validity of
"Clex." The relationship between Lex and Lana, with Clark as
omnipresent third party, clearly encroaches too far on established "Clex"
territory, and only recourse to the ultimate authority of *Superman* canon
can offer a reprieve (which is somewhat ironic if one considers that
"Clex" is most certainly not, and won't ever be, part of that canon). The
dismissal stems from the long-standing notion regarding Lana's character held by HoYay! fans, namely that Lana is boring, self-involved, and
definitely one of the plot devices the producers like to use to establish
Clark and Lex's heterosexuality. Or in other words, the new developments
on *Smallville* threaten a by then very established way of seeing queerly,
namely the one that privileges the relationship between Clark and Lex
over any other possible romantic entanglement that the show has to offer.
Furthermore, this insight allows the recognition that despite the complex
ways in which fans read the relationship between Clark and Lex, HoYay!
also has its limits.

As I mentioned earlier, seeing queerly is a communal form of spectatorship. In the case of HoYay! it developed in the distinct culture of
the *Smallville* TWOP discussions and over the years has taken on certain self-regulating tendencies.[11] This discourse of HoYay! has been
shaped by the interface on TWOP. For example, the forums on TWOP
only allow a linear sequence of posts, quite similar to a mailing list. This
is a very different set-up from a threaded discussion, in which users have
the ability to respond directly to a post, instead of having to write a different, subsequent post in response. The linear discussion on TWOP thus
moves endlessly forward, allowing divergent viewpoints to be
easily left behind. Additionally, discussions are guided by various pre-
established rules. The general forum dedicated to *Smallville* is divided
into multiple threads with clearly defined topics (like "Homoeroticism,
Yay!"), and "off-topic" discussion isn't tolerated if it moves beyond a
passing reference (for example, a lengthy post extolling the wonders of

Clark and Lana's relationship would be frowned upon in the HoYay! thread).

Finally, all discussion is moderated, meaning that a few people have the authority to edit or delete posts that, in their opinion, don't correspond to TWOP rules. The latter aspect is particularly important to how HoYay! developed into a particular way of seeing queerly as one of the moderators is also the author of lengthy, often sarcastic, episode summaries (called "recaps") that are embraced and celebrated by the community. These recaps set the tone for subsequent episode discussions and often shift attention to aspects privileged by the moderator (such as towards the relationship between Clark and Lex and away from Lana as potential love interest for either or both of them). The combination of all these factors—linear posting, pre-established discussion topics, and moderators—has thus led to a way of seeing queerly that has firmly established parameters, ones that the participants on TWOP are well aware of.

As part of these parameters, fellow fans will embrace "Clex" whereas the idea of Lana as catalyst for a queer triangle between herself, Clark, and Lex encounters disagreement and, in some cases, outright dismissal. Thus, even though the narrative structure of *Smallville* encourages, or at least allows for, a queer reading of the Lex/Lana/Clark triangle, the discursive structure of the HoYay! discussion on TWOP disallows that possibility. This brings me back to what I said at the beginning of this essay, namely that every interpretation is potentially queer. While the potential is there, it doesn't always have to be fulfilled, and the example of fan discussions shows that not all possibilities for queer readings are pursued. The decisive factor is the discursive context within which seeing queerly occurs.

"It's so Clana, it's Clex"[12]

Moving on to a different discursive context, namely the *Smallville* slash fan community on LiveJournal, one can observe quite a different take on the Lex/Lana/Clark triangle. A significant part of this community has embraced the on-screen relationship between Lex and Lana as a possibility to further open up the queer possibilities of *Smallville's* diegetic world. These fans continue to discuss and write stories about a romantic relationship between Clark and Lex, but now have added the Lex/Lana/Clark triangle, and in some cases, also Lex/Lana, as focal points of their creative pursuits. This multi-faceted way of seeing queerly has developed in the interconnected blogs that make up the interface of LiveJournal. In contrast to TWOP, the discussion on LiveJournal takes place in multiple, distributed posts that are not moderated and do not enforce any "off-topic" rules.[13] The lack of the latter in particular allows for the appearance of posts that are not connected to *Smallville* and that instead focus on other television shows, films, current events, or the poster's offline life. Even the *Smallville*-related content is more diverse: it can include "meta" discussion (i.e., questions related to episodes, characterization, narrative arcs, production choices and more), fan fiction or fan art. Despite this more open playing field enabled by LiveJournal's interface, one needs to remember that this *Smallville* slash community also has protocols and rules that shape its discourse of seeing queerly.

Keeping this context in mind, I now turn to a few examples of how fans explore the queer potential of the Lex/Lana/Clark relationship. This exploration mostly happens in the form of fan fiction that realizes the triangular desire between the characters in explicitly described sexual encounters. While one logically might expect many of these encounters to feature Lana, Lex, and Clark engaged in a threesome, most stories actually portray at least two parallel sexual relationships.[14] For example, Lana might be involved with both Lex and Clark, or Lex might sleep with Lana and with Clark, and so forth, with varying degrees of secrecy between the involved partners. These parallel relationships are interesting to fans for three reasons. One, they allow them to uphold the "one true pairing" dynamic between Clark and Lex.[15] Two, the theme of keeping secrets has always figured prominently both in *Smallville*'s diegesis and in *Smallville* slash fiction. Three, the introduction of a heterosexual relationship in stories transgresses the norms of a slash fan community.

Let me explain these three points in more detail. Stories featuring sexual encounters and/or relationships between Lana and Lex and Clark and Lex allow fans to explore the new angle introduced by the *Smallville*'s narrative while also maintaining their long-standing interest in "Clex." New developments on the show are thus integrated into older storytelling patterns, and new narratives emerge that engage with the various possibilities offered by the Lex/Lana/Clark triangle. Many stories introduce at least one of these relationships as an "illicit affair," for example when Lana sleeps with Lex even though she is officially dating Clark and suspects (or perhaps even knows) that Lex desires Clark as much as she does. (See, for example, "When It All Comes Down" [LiveJournal.com, January 13, 2007].)

The varying levels of secrecy surrounding these parallel relationships are very much in tune with *Smallville*'s overall plot. After all, the dynamic resulting from Clark's efforts to protect "his secret" of being an alien with superpowers fuels all relationships he has with the other characters, who frequently seem on the brink of discovering what Clark is hiding.

In fan fiction, this need to both hide and uncover secrets translates easily into sexual desire, and "knowing" Clark takes on a whole other dimension.[16] In fiction written about Clark and Lex during the early seasons, one can often find a scene in which Clark will "come out" to Lex both as gay and as alien within the same conversation. This confession removes the most salient obstacles preventing a romantic relationship between Clark and Lex and allows them to ride off into the metaphorical sunset together. In later seasons, the on-screen relationship between the two characters is so fraught with distrust and deception that, even without the introduction of Lana, fans have a hard time imagining the lighthearted romance of earlier stories. As mentioned before, both the show and its fans now favor an overall darker, more "adult" tone. A resolution via a confession seems impossible now, and the "will to know" Clark's secret now takes on a rather obsessive pursuit that drives both Lex and Lana's desire for Clark (see Foucault 1990, 45).

Finally, the decision to write and publish fiction featuring heterosexual relationships constitutes a transgression within the context of a community invested in slash. Within the discourse of slash communities, same-sex relationships constitute the norm, and heterosexual relationships the exception. Thus, within the context of the *Smallville* slash community, endorsing the Lex/Lana/Clark triangle doesn't only constitute a different way of televisual "seeing queerly," but also a way of queering the way the community looks at itself. Whereas on TWOP, the violation of community rules that declare Clark and Lex as the "one true pairing" leads to a rejection of Lexana, on LiveJournal, this transgression/queering/reworking/expansion of community standards is embraced with much delight.

One thing that is important to remember here is that "heterosexual" does not equal "heteronormative." While some permutations of the Lex/Lana/Clark triangle result in heterosexual encounters and relationships, they don't play out within a heteronormative framework. Both in terms of the sexual practices described in these stories and in terms of the context within which they take place (which is more polyamorous than monogamous), queerness prevails. In other words, I am not arguing that *Smallville* fans suddenly declare all heterosexual relationships that occur on *Smallville* as queer, but rather that they broaden their way of seeing queerly to include specific instances of heterosexuality that are non-normative.

Conclusion

Seeing queerly is a multi-faceted spectatorial position that arises out of the interaction between televisual text, audience interpretation, fan community discourse, and the interface within which this discourse takes place. At the most basic level, this theory of queer spectatorship emphasizes that self-identified straight viewers recognize, embrace, and endorse queer moments on television—an activity that has often only been associated with queer-identified viewers in previous scholarly work. Beyond that, my analysis of the fan communities on TWOP and on LiveJournal reveals that seeing queerly is a self-reflexive practice that often challenges the heteronormative framework that still dominates the diegetic worlds of many mainstream TV shows, including *Smallville*. Instead of accepting the on-screen romances between Clark, Lex, and various female characters, fans invest the friendship between Clark and Lex with a romantic dimension. But I've also shown that factors such as interface design and community structures of online fan sites can limit the full exploration of seeing queerly. Thus, even if every interpretation is potentially queer, this potential doesn't always come to fruition, as the divergent reactions to the introduction of the love triangle between Lex, Lana, and Clark show. While the fans on TWOP dismiss any queer aspects this triangular relationship might have, fans on LiveJournal integrate this new plot development into their discussion and fiction. Or in other words, in one instance, seeing queerly only includes the recognition of romantic relationships between male characters (the previously mentioned "Homoeroticism, Yay!"), whereas in another instance, seeing queerly also includes non-normative heterosexual relationships.

I want to end my analysis of queer spectatorship with a few thoughts on how seeing queerly can also help us to understand a broader conceptualization of queer visibility on television. Consider the "mission statement" which appears on the GAYLE homepage:

> If asked to pick the gayest show on TV, most people would answer *Will and Grace*, or the ubiquitous *Queer as Folk*, or the high-brow *Six Feet Under*, or maybe, if they had the taste of a crack-addicted lemming, *The Ellen Show*. But we on the *Smallville* forum over at Television Without Pity contend that they'd all be dead wrong. We know it's actually the WB's new show about a teenage Superman and his dear friend, rhymes-with-Sex Luthor. That show is *Smallville* [Gayles.tig-tv.com, January 13, 2007].

It is perhaps surprising to see shows that have been hailed as being part of the "explosion of gay visibility" during the 1990s and onwards dismissed in favor of *Smallville*, which doesn't feature any explicitly gay or lesbian characters. This dismissal helps raise questions about the notion of "gay visibility," introduced in heated debates in both the popular and academic press over the past fifteen years (see Walters 2001). Specifically, these debates have almost exclusively focused on shows and films that introduce clearly identifiable gay, lesbian, and queer content, which is then located in opposition to the rest of TV, which is allegedly "straight" in terms of content and characterization.

Smallville has certainly not made the list of frequently analyzed TV shows, and it hasn't received the academic attention it deserves.[17] Yet, fans' engagement demonstrates that at least one (very dedicated) segment of the audience would include *Smallville* in this list (and *Smallville* certainly isn't the only show lacking in gay and lesbian characters but inspiring a large following of fans who read it in a queer way). At the very least, one has to acknowledge that locating queer representations only in shows that include gay/lesbian characters and storylines excludes other forms of queer visibility (for example in the form of themes and metaphors) and limits how queerness can be understood in relationship to TV. Thus, rather than dividing televisual texts that have emerged in the course of the "gay 90s" into "straight" and "gay" with accompanying assumptions about "straight" and "gay" viewers, it is more precise to recognize queer and heteronormative/heterosexual elements across the televisual landscape and a cross the range of available spectatorial positions.

Notes

1. "Real life" is an expression fans use to describe off-line social relations.
2. Of course, not every woman (and the occasional man) participating in fandom identifies as straight. Fans subscribe to multiple sexual and gender identifications. Nevertheless, some women in fandoms focused on male/male pairings do identify as straight.
3. The work of Brett Farmer (2000) and Patricia White (1999) are excellent examples of such studies. Both Farmer and White have expanded the cultural history and the theoretical exploration of gay and lesbian spectatorship in important ways. Nevertheless, I feel they are only discussing one side of the coin, so to speak.
4. One could object here and argue that fandom is also a subcultural group. Slash fans themselves have used this comparison, for example when they talk about the revelation of one's fannish activities as a form of "coming out." Yet, there are distinct differences between both groups, mostly in terms of longstanding discrimination against the LGBTQ community.
5. Regarding the case of *Smallville* fandom specifically, this separation between ontology and epistemology also extends to the question of age, as many fans are older than both the characters and the target audience. Or in other words, the idea that shows featuring teenagers will only attract teenage viewers doesn't hold up when one looks at the self-identified age of *Smallville* fans. See also the essays by Stein and Gillan in this volume.
6. A phrase coined by a fan at TWOP, describing the relationship between Clark Kent and Lex Luthor.
7. TWOP itself is a phenomenon, as it is now recognized as one of the most popular and influential websites for TV fandom discussions. It is not only the primary source of information and exchange for many fans, but is also anxiously watched over by TV producers, who have a particular interest in the immediate reactions fans extol right after episodes air (the count of posts after each new episode of the shows featured on the website goes into the hundreds). See Sella (2002).
8. I say "offered" here because the meanings of vids are by no means univocal. While it is fairly safe to say that most Clark and Lex vids have a dominant homoerotic narrative (just as *Smallville* episodes have dominant heterosexual narratives), this narrative does not preclude other interpretative possibilities.

9. This hypothesis has gathered increasing support among fans throughout the seasons, especially during times when fans perceived a near-absence of HoYay! (for example when Clark and Lex do not share any screen time for a few episodes in a row). Considering the fact that both groups anxiously watch over each other (fans monitor interviews with producers and actors, and TV networks follow online fan discussions), this reasoning is not entirely speculative.

10. The show has shown Lex as someone who disregards many of society's established rules, making it easy for fans to add defiance of sexual norms to the already-existing list of ways in which Lex Luthor transgresses normative behavior. It seems only logical to fans that Lex's sexuality can't be contained within the boundaries of heteronormativity.

11. For more about hierarchies in online communities, see: Zweerink and Gatson (2002) and Lovink (2003).

12. A phrase used by a fan to comment on the intertwining of heterosexual and same-sex sexualities on Smallville, with "Clana" (Clark/Lana) used as shorthand for heterosexual and "Clex" (Clark/Lex) for same-sex desires (LiveJournal.com, September 20, 2006).

13. One exception here is so-called "community" blogs that do have a designated moderator or moderators. Whereas the TWOP HoYay! thread is the only venue in which participants can discuss their queer visions of Smallville, the communities on LiveJournal are one place among many that facilitate such discussions and the moderators don't have the same kind of status they have on TWOP.

14. For an example of a story featuring a threesome, see "Siwi" (Smallvillefanfic.com, January 13, 2007).

15. "One true pairing" is a term fans use to describe that two characters are destined to be romantically involved with each other, and with no one else.

16. The fact that fans shift the focus from a "need to know" desire to a sexual desire should not come as a surprise. As many queer theorists have argued, knowledge is inextricably bound up with sexuality and desire in modern Western societies (Sedgwick 1993, Joyrich 2001).

17. Two notable exceptions to this trend include Louisa Stein's "'They Cavort, You Decide': Fan Discourses of Intentionality, Interpretation, and Queerness in Teen TV" (2005) and Anne Kustritz's "Smallville's Sexual Symbolism: From Queer Repression to Fans' Queered Expressions" (2005).

References

De Angelis, Michael. 2001. Gay Fandom and Crossover Stardom: James Dean, Mel Gibson and Keanu Reeves. Durham: Duke University Press.

Doty, Alexander. 2000. Flaming Classics: Queering the Film Canon. New York: Routledge.

Farmer, Brett. 2000. Spectacular Passions: Cinema, Fantasy and Gay Male Spectatorships. Durham: Duke University Press.

Foucault, Michel. 1990. The History of Sexuality, Vol. I. New York: Vintage Books.

Joyrich, Lynne. 2001. "Epistemology of the Console." Critical Inquiry 27, no. 3 (Spring): 439–68.

Kustritz, Anne. 2005. "Smallville's Sexual Symbolism: From Queer Repression to Fans' Queered Expressions. Refractory 8, available at http://www.refractory.unimelb.edu.au/journalissues/vol8/kustritz.html.

Lovink, Geert. 2003. "Defining Open Publishing: Of Lists and Weblogs." In My First Recession: Critical Internet Culture in Transition, 224–50. Rotterdam: V2 Publishing/NAi Publishers.

Mayne, Judith. 1993. Cinema and Spectatorship. London and New York: Routledge.

Sedgwick, Eve. 1993. "Epistemology of the Closet." In The Gay and Lesbian Studies Reader, eds. Henry Abelove, Michele Aina Barale, and David M. Halperin, 45–62. New York: Routledge.

Sella, Marshall. 2002. "The Remote Controllers." New York Times Magazine, October 20, Magazine Desk. sec.6: 68.

Stein, Louisa. 2005. "'They Cavort, You Decide': Fan Discourses of Intentionality, Interpretation, Queerness in Teen TV." Spectator 25:11–22.

Walters, Suzanna. 2001. *All the Rage: The Story of Gay Visibility in America*. Chicago: University of Chicago Press.

White, Patricia. 1999. *Uninvited: Classical Hollywood Cinema and Lesbian Representability*. Indianapolis: Indiana University Press.

Zweerink, Amanda, and Sarah N. Gatson. 2002. "www.buffy.com: Cliques, Boundaries, and Hierarchies in an Internet Community." In *Fighting the Forces: What's at Stake in Buffy the Vampire Slayer,* eds. Rhonda V. Wilcox and David Lavery, 239–51. Planham, MD: Rowman & Littlefield.

12. Pushing at the Margins: Teenage Angst in Teen TV and Audience Response

Louisa Ellen Stein

Be it in the story of a teenage private eye attempting to come to terms with the murder of her best friend, or of the young Clark Kent facing his alien identity, contemporary Teen TV often dynamically represents adolescents struggling to find sense of self while facing a wide range of constraints, be it from school and peer-pressure, the challenges of dating and romance, the expectations of adults, the dictates of alien rulers, or the forces of supernatural evil. This thematic focus of Teen TV on adolescent limitations makes it a ripe center for fan engagement and creativity. Themes of self definition and discomfort with pre-ordained containment recur across popular media texts favored by fans. Teen TV offers a recurring set of generic themes and contexts which heighten the sense of struggle against outwardly-enforced limitations through the seemingly universal experiences of adolescence. Teen TV's structural focus on constraint makes these programs popular among older as well as teenage fans, especially among those who devote creative energy to authoring new texts based on their favorite teen TV programs.

Theorists such as Roberta Pearson (2003) and Sarah Gwenllian Jones (2002) have argued that qualities of fantasy recur in fan-favored texts, encouraging fan creative engagement. Similarly, themes of adolescent constraint also surface in popular media favored by fans. Indeed, "teen" programs develop active producing fandoms with almost as much regularity as do science fiction and fantasy programs. Themes of constraint also predominate in other genres of media texts popular among fans—from the police procedural or military contexts of cop and science fiction shows (such as *The Sentinel, Enterprise,* and *Stargate Atlantis*) to the disciplinary systems of programs like *Oz* and *Prison Break.* We can think of the incorporation of teen elements as one way of channeling issues of constraint, with constraint functioning as a central theme across almost all texts that spur fan investment.

Sarah Gwenllian Jones and Roberta Pearson both argue that it is the exotic, imaginative dimensions of fantasy that spur fan creativity by opening a wide variety of possibilities for re-imagining the source text. In contrast, Teen TV encourages fan engagement because of its emphasis on limitations rather than options; Teen TV's ongoing focus on defining oneself in the face of external restrictions or expectations seem easily adapted to fannish investment, not only in specific media texts, but in the processes and experiences of fan engagement and authorship. Fan creativity is based on engaging with external media texts and seeking to assert interpretation and authorship, and, in a loose sense, ownership. Themes of (adolescent) constraint spur fan creativity as they resonate metaphorically with the fan position in relation to the mainstream media/source text. Henry Jenkins (1992) posits the fan relationship to mainstream media as one of both perceived powerlessness and eventual limited empowerment; it is this dynamic—this ambivalence—that makes Teen TV texts ripe for fan creativity. Fans engage with a pre-existing "official" media text, and use their creative work, community context, and access to digital technologies to analyze, transform, and fill in that which is offered to them by the program's producers.[1] This puts fans consistently in a liminal, transformative position, a position of negotiation somewhere in between disempowerment and empowerment. Fans are constantly taking that which was not their own creation initially and making it theirs through shared interpretive work and authoring. Such a position is echoed in the experiences of adolescents on the verge of coming into themselves who populate Teen TV. We can take the parallel even further, as these teen characters together form their own communities with their own social codes, much like the fans who carve out community spaces online.

Furthermore, as suggested in the introduction to this volume, Teen TV is itself a contested and heavily weighted liminal category, mired in industrial and popular perceptions of consumerist, poor-quality TV. As such, like adolescents and like fans, Teen TV is itself constantly negotiating its own self-definition, often walking a difficult line between "quality" and "popular." Fan authors and artists inspired by Teen TV become quite invested in these debates, defending their emotional investment in programs which much of the world sees as "trash," as well as their writing of stories for which they cannot claim ownership and which often are accused of being, at best, unoriginal, and at worst, illegal.

Within this essay I will focus on several Teen TV shows and the fan creative works they have spurred, exploring how the programs establish themes of adolescent constraint, and how fan authorship pushes these themes further, at times engaging with social and political issues that the programs only dance around or even eschew. Thus fan authors rehearse their own (pleasure in) limitation and self-expression, both in the act of re-writing their favored programs in their own image, and through their engagement with representations of angstful teenage characters intent on establishing their agency and power.

The Teen TV programs considered here and others like them have been explored fruitfully on an individual basis by scholars such as Will Brooker (2001), Miranda Banks (2004), and in Davis and Dickinson's *Teen TV* (2004), especially for issues of gender and genre. Work on fandoms surrounding individual teen programs is also a promising (although still relatively undeveloped area) from the plethora of work on the highly visible *Buffy the Vampire Slayer* fandom (see Kaveney 2001 and Wilcox and Lavery 2002) to the emerging literature on *Smallville* fandom and slash (see Kelly 2005, Kustritz 2005, Stein 2005, 2006a, 2006b, and Kohnen [this volume]). This essay seeks to trace out larger structures, linking overarching generic discourses and tendencies within Teen TV to the creative dynamics and thematic concerns of the ever-developing world of fan authorship.[2] By beginning to map out this larger picture, we can excavate/unearth connections at the heart of Teen TV's marginalized popularity among diverse sets of fans and of the dynamics of converged fan engagement with contemporary media (Jenkins 2006a.)

My analysis concentrates on programs which explore a range of teen issues and experiences but which share the central theme of the teen struggle against constraint. More specifically, gender is a centrally recurring restraining dynamic across these programs. Both males and females struggle with expectations based on gender and sexuality, seeking to find fulfillment in self and in romance while sifting through and attempting to live up to (or reject) various gender-based rules and cues. *Gilmore Girls* primarily traces the growing pains of a single mother, Lorelai, and her teen daughter, Rory, as they work to find their own paths within and outside of familial and romantic relationships; *Veronica Mars* follows a teen girl turned private eye as she attempts to make sense of her life after the murder of her best friend; and finally *Supernatural* explores two brothers' struggle to define themselves in relation to their father's mission and their own sense of destiny in a familial battle against evil.

Together, these three programs demonstrate both the diversity and continuity of teen TV and its fan reception; all three programs feature coming of age narratives framed to different degrees in social structures including class, gender, and race. All three programs have also fostered dynamic, active fandoms which have produced diverse bodies of fan fiction.

Fannish representations of these teen TV characters and situations in fan fiction and art also explore—and at times take even further—the possibilities of liminal adolescence and self-becoming in the face of constraint. Often these stories deal with the same elements of constraint as those explicitly articulated by the programs themselves. Sometimes fan fiction stories takes the narrative in different directions than those which unfold on the television screen, and at other times stories unpack the nuances of the official narrative; in most cases, be they exploring new possibilities or official "canon," fan fiction engages with the themes of constraint offered by the program itself.

Gilmore Girls

> There are many paths in life. There's the "Hey, you're cute, sure, I'll marry you after graduation and med school"... And then there's my path, where I found myself 16 and pregnant and I realized "I have to get a job, I have to raise a kid and being me, I have to do it all by myself."—*Gilmore Girls*, "Beginnings"

Gilmore Girls explores the difficulties of growing up a young female in the face of societal as well as familial restrictions. The program offers nascent feminism as one possibility (or set of possibilities, as Francesca Gamber argues in this collection) to aid in a young woman's self-definition. Although past her teen years, Lorelai Gilmore was robbed of an innocent coming of age when she found herself pregnant while still in high school, in the back story of the series. While one episode does offer flashbacks of Lorelai as a literal teen, the bulk of the program shows Lorelai as an adult who has not fully let go of a teen recklessness, rebellion, and joy in life. Thus, although she is not a literal teen, we follow her efforts to define herself as an adult with a role and purpose, in much the same way we do her teenage daughter Rory.

Rory is the most overt and central representation of female adolescence on *Gilmore Girls*. The first season opens with her admittance into a prestigious prep school, and later seasons follow her romantic travails, her graduation from high school, her adjustment to college, and her attempts to define herself as an individual and in her relationships with her mother, her grandparents, her friends, and her boyfriends. *Gilmore Girls* envisions Rory facing overlapping sets of limitations—not only those of a "normal" adolescence, but also those specific to growing up with a single mom. Rory straddles two worlds—the world of her grandmother, which her mother rejected, and the world her mother has created for her. Both come with their own sets of (sometimes conflicting, sometimes overlapping) constraints, from her mother's free-spirited and independent attitude towards making one's way in life, to her grandmother's concern with social stratification and etiquette as a framework for life experience.

While Rory is the featured teen in *Gilmore Girls*, we also see adolescent struggle play out compellingly in the narratives of Rory's friends; Lane Kim, indie rock lover and daughter of Korean Seventh Day Adventist, must hide her engagement with youth culture in the floorboards of her room; Rory's competitor turned best friend, Paris, while often used as comic relief, also deals with her share of rallying against the limitations of adolescence, as she constantly sets herself unrealistically high goals of academic achievement in order to secure a successful adulthood.

Furthermore, as is most evident in the case of Lorelai, teen issues are not limited only to teen characters in *Gilmore Girls*. Clearly Lorelai and Rory share adolescent positions, striving to find their way and place in the world, but even Lane's mother, Mrs. Kim, transforms into an adolescent seeking approval in the face of adult expectations upon the visit of Lane's grandmother. A similar dynamic plays out with Lorelai's mother, Emily, when her mother in law visits Emily's home, radiating as much disapproval of Emily's status as an adult as Lorelai has ever felt from Emily herself. This acknowledgement of the power of earlier generations of females casts Emily in the uncertain and rebellious adolescent position rather than in that of the self-certain matriarch.

Gilmore Girls fan fiction similarly focuses on both Rory and Lorelai as adolescent figures, searching for their sense of self and for romantic fulfillment. Lula Bo's "Separation Anxiety" opens with Lorelai mothering Rory, giving Rory caring and wise advice after discovering that Rory has slept with her married ex-boyfriend (in opposition to Lorelai's reaction in the show itself, which is more condemning and less understanding). In this story, it appears at first that Lorelai fully fills the adult role to Rory's confused teen, but even in her advice giving, Lorelai draws parallels between herself and Rory:

> Lorelai kneeled on the bed and put her arms around her daughter. "Oh, honey. Never. What you did, you and Dean? It was wrong; I'm not saying it wasn't.

You cheated, and you can't change that. But Rory, you made a mistake, babe, and there's nothing wrong with that. I've made plenty of them myself—I am the queen of ill-advised actions, you know that. I'm not saying that I'm singing from the rooftops or that I think you should consider it among your greatest achievements, but I am not judging you. Do I wish things had gone differently? Of course I do. But Rory, sweetie, you are my kid and regardless of how you screw up, how badly or what you do, I will never look at you with anything less than absolute acceptance and respect. And that is because I think you are an exceptional person..." [Gilmore-fiction.net, April 6, 2007].

Lorelai's comforting speech to Rory thus portrays her as mother and adolescent at once—she calls upon her own rash, youthful mistakes to connect with Rory's emotional crisis and provide unconditional motherly love.

As "Separation Anxiety" unfolds, it more fully explores Lorelai as adolescent, following both Rory on her trip to Europe and Lorelai coping in Rory's absence at home. Indeed, the very title of the story refers to both/either Rory and Lorelai as holding the childlike position of fearing separation from the other. In Rory's absence, Lorelai turns to love-interest Luke for comfort and companionship. Lorelai teasingly calls Luke "daddy," but any sexual connotations seem overshadowed by her desire for parental nurture; she suggests that he stay the night for comfort rather than sex because she's suddenly an "orphan." Thus, in Rory's absence, the role reversal and casting of Lorelai as an adolescent becomes clear—she is interested in sex but chooses instead for a more virginal comfort, looking to Luke as part lover, part father. This is not an interpretation of Luke and Lorelai's relationship that *Gilmore Girls* itself ever overtly imagines; Luke and Lorelai are shown as adult friends rather than serving as parent figures for one another. However, Lula Bo's envisioning of Luke and Lorelai's relationship as one that is part parental and part virginal/romantic emerges out of *Gilmore Girls'* framing of Lorelai as an adult adolescent, struggling to have adult romantic relationships, despite her age. "Separation Anxiety" thus picks up on *Gilmore Girls'* depiction of adolescence as a shared rite of passage and draws on this theme to explore new dimensions of Lorelai's character and relationships.

Where Lula Bo paints both Rory and Lorelai as adolescent heroines searching for self, Jae's "Three Letters Emily Gilmore Never Sent" turns to the more unlikely figure of Lorelai's mother, Emily, and explores her growth into adulthood (LiveJournal.com [LJ], April 7, 2006). By flashing back to different periods in the life of the matriarch of the *Gilmore Girls*, "Three Letters Emily Gilmore Never Sent" highlights the constraints Emily has faced and the choices she has made in the ongoing process of becoming an adult. This multigenerational approach to coming of age links Emily's quest for self-definition to Lorelai's. Class, gender, and interpersonal relationships all surface here as constraints which Emily negotiates in each of the story's interconnected vignettes.

The story opens with Emily in college, making the crucial choice to spend her summer with Richard (her husband to be) rather than take a prestigious internship with an interior design firm in New York City. Her risk-taking friend encourages her to take the internship, but Emily indicates that her mind is made up; she has found a sense of self in her relationship with Richard. The later vignettes explore her negotiating the distance between herself and her daughter and granddaughter, who have sought careers and professional lives in place of or in tandem with romantic relationships. She envisions herself writing letters to both Lorelai and Rory that share her emotions and explain why she has made the choices that she has in her life.

"Three Letters Emily Gilmore Never Sent" powerfully envisions the defining choices of a young woman turned mother turned grandmother in the face of expectations of class and gender, and more subtly considers the ramifications of those choices on the next generations of women in her family. In many ways, we can also see this multigenerational look at gender, class, and self-definition as the project of the *Gilmore Girls* series as a whole. "Three Letters Emily Gilmore Never Sent" takes even further *Gilmore Girls'* broad thematization of coming of age; this story envisions the matriarch of the Gilmore clan facing adolescent uncertainty and personal growth throughout her life, with the vignettes following her search for self definition from college student to grandmother. Thus, in different ways, both "Separation Anxiety" and "Three Letters Emily Gilmore Never Sent" demonstrate how crucial these themes of universal coming of age are not only to *Gilmore Girls* and Teen TV, but to fan authors who create new texts inspired by these programs.

Veronica Mars

"Tonight we eat like the lower middle class to which we aspire!"—*Veronica Mars*, "Pilot"

Gilmore Girls focuses on the constraints faced by women, with adolescence serving as one of many sets of expectations, limitations, and challenges that women must overcome. The program highlights economic and social factors as crucial to the shaping of gender expectations, but it focuses on limitations emerging from upper class structures; Rory may need to go to a fancy prep school to access a good education, but the narrative does not dwell on this assumption at any length. In contrast, the series goes to much effort to establish that Lorelai's self-starting moxie and rejection of upper class constraints has given her the tools to raise Rory as a freethinker who can flourish in middle and upper class contexts.

Veronica Mars takes further this consideration of gender within social context, positing gendered adolescence within a spectrum of race and class as crucial issues that affect everyone, young and old. However, *Veronica Mars* offers as an identification point one teen girl's pursuit of power and self rather than embracing multiple generations and forms of female adolescence and feminism. Few if any of Veronica's female friends are shown to be self-possessed, driven, and successful; her closest long-lasting friends (with the exception of computer-geek Mac and her murdered, promiscuous best friend Lilly) are in fact male. For the most part, Veronica must find her own way as an empowered female, and her solitary struggle is far from easy; she faces systemic sexism and classism in her everyday experiences, both as a private investigator and as a high school student.

Feminism and female sexuality are both hotly contested ideas in *Veronica Mars.* Unlike Rory, Veronica does not have multiple options or models from which to choose; in fact, with her mother an absent and morally questionable alcoholic, and her best-friend Lilly killed because of her rash flaunting of her sexuality, Veronica has no functional models to choose from. She instead develops her own persona which flies in the face of all social expectations in her town (not to mention broader social and generic expectations, as Andrea Braithwaite explores in her discussion of Veronica as female private eye, or "chick dick," in this volume).

While Veronica's stance is seemingly that of an empowered young female rejecting the constraints of female teen-hood, over its three seasons *Veronica Mars'* outward address of feminism as a viable and desirable possibility for young women has been highly ambivalent. The initial premise certainly sounds feminist enough: a smart young female takes on corruption at all levels, large and small, as she unravels the mystery of her own rape and the murder of her best friend. She is a female private eye, breaking generic codes with both her age and gender. She uses her femininity as part of her disguise, but rails against allowing the men in her life (other than her father) to have control over her. However, Veronica's journey to self-discovery is punctuated by the crucial saving scene at the end of the first season, in which Veronica, locked in a fridge, finds herself at the mercy of a male murderer and finally must be saved by her heroic private eye father. Moments such as this temporarily suggest a return to the gender alignments of traditional noir/private eye narratives and more expected gendered generic roles of female as victim, older male as hero.

The third season continues to offer ambivalent representations of female power and feminism, blatantly playing with the possible vilification of young women who identify overtly as feminists. The twist of the season's first major mystery reveals that the self-proclaimed feminist students on Veronica's campus had faked their own rapes in order to close down an offending fraternity. While Veronica maintains her independence and assertion of her self-possession as a strong-willed female, the series separates her from the militant feminists, who will go to any ends for their political purposes. Thus, *Veronica Mars* seems at times to embrace female power, but distance contemporary, accessible female strength and intelligence from militant, overtly-politicized feminism.

Fans have expressed a range of reactions to *Veronica Mars'* complex representation of female power and feminism, from pleasure at *Veronica Mars'* focus on a powerful and smart, independent young woman to discomfort at the periodic seeming departures from *Veronica Mars'* expected feminist politics. Fan fiction is one forum in which fans explore the possibilities of gender representation offered by *Veronica Mars*, and, in some cases, channel dissatisfaction with *Veronica Mars'* address of gender and feminism. Some fan fiction takes feminism and Veronica's struggle with adolescence and her empowerment further, making issues of gender and power more overt than does the program itself. But even fan fiction that seems predominantly invested in classic romantic narratives between Veronica and her wounded bad-boy boyfriend Logan do not relegate Veronica to the role of devoted and acquiescent girlfriend, instead maintaining her status as alienated yet empowered outsider, emphasizing Veronica's continued role as spunky and independent private eye even as they foreground her romantic travails.

Furthermore, where *Veronica Mars* might not offer multiple visions of either feminism or female adolescence as possible models for its young female protagonists or viewers, it does offer multiple modes of male adolescent strife. In the first and second season of the show, Veronica ricochets back and forth between her wholesome yet mentally unstable first love, Duncan, to her sardonic on again off again boyfriend, Logan. She also depends upon support from her sweet and funny, basketball playing black best friend Wallace, and to the head of the local Latino biker gang, Weevil. The third season introduces alterna-radio geek Piz as yet another sympathetic teen male. Veronica must define herself in relation to all these varyingly troubled young men. *Veronica Mars* fan fiction explores the complex and fraught interactions between Veronica and these young men as they seek to understand themselves in light of each other. In addition, some fan fiction stories feature Veronica's dead best friend, Lilly, quite heavily in flashback, drawing on Lilly as an alternate example of empowered female sexuality. And finally, some stories overtly cast these complex processes of interpersonal gendered relationships within larger frameworks of social constraints.

Sin Addict's "Hollow You Out" serves as a compelling example of how *Veronica Mars* fan fiction authors focus on the already existing series thematics of Veronica's own personal change and growth into a strong young woman after Lilly's death (LJ, April 6, 2007). "Hollow You Out" makes explicit the series' more implicit suggestion that Veronica had not yet fully found herself as an individual before the transformative event of Lilly's murder:

> Veronica before Lilly died was just a shorter way of saying, "Duncan's girl-friend," or "Lilly's best friend," or "the Sheriff's daughter." Veronica before Lilly died was that girl who was always somebody else's something, always defined by the people around her because she had no definition of herself.
> Veronica after Lilly died is a big "fuck you" to the universe.

This story stays within the confines of the emotional, psychological, and social world offered by *Veronica Mars*, but articulates perhaps more explicitly the themes of self, identity, and constraint brought out by the series. The story offers series-based interpretations of all three characters that resonate with the writing and performances in the program itself. This portion about Veronica clearly demonstrates a concern with self-definition in the face of the constraints of social expectations and public opinion akin to the program's central address of this theme.

In addition, this story's allegiance to the basic themes and plot elements of the series itself (what fans call canon) indicate the level of limitation at play in much of fan-based writing, in which fan authors carefully restrict themselves from deviating from the original source text. For many fans, allegiance to canon and "realistic" characterization is of paramount importance. Achieving an "in character" tone of voice for a character or a plot that seems in the spirit of the program itself is a highly valued skill in many fan writing communities. This valuation of canon contributes to the visibility of stories like "Hollow You Out" that seem to build naturally out of the program's official concerns. But, of course, part of the pleasure of fan fiction writing and reading is the fan author's ability to create scenarios that, for various reasons, could not be shown in the series itself. "Hollow You Out" envisions an intimate emotional and physical if not sexual encounter between Veronica, Duncan, and Logan, an encounter which seems resonant with the program's representation of these three characters and their relationships, but which would likely not be included within the official text because it enters into

ideologically taboo areas (especially for network TV), bypassing heteronormative romance to explore an intimate interaction between the three
characters together. Inspired by the characterizations and interrelationships in the source text of *Veronica Mars*, "Hollow You Out" nevertheless pushes past the industrial and generic limits of the television program
itself, and thus imagines an even more complex set of coming of age
questions—including the relationship between friendship, sexuality, and
romance—for Veronica and her friends.

Wisteria's "The View from the Cheap Seats" similarly adheres to central constraints of the tone and voice of the program (LJ, April 6, 2007).
The story includes the voiceovers which are a standard part of *Veronica
Mars'* ongoing homage to noir, thus providing continuity in voice and
theme, highlighting female subjectivity as does the program itself. "The
View from the Cheap Seats" also maintains Veronica and Logan's tense
but (at the time the story was written) platonic relationship. Indeed, the
story establishes that Veronica and Logan's friendship is growing as
Veronica searches for Logan's missing mother (again, all plot elements
directly from canon) through details that seem to be realistic extensions
from the source text, as in the following:

> He calls so often that she gets him his own ringtone—"Baby One More Time."
> Logan would get a kick out of that if they were the kind of people who told
> each other jokes.

Veronica's unknowing choice of ringtone in "View from the Cheap
Seats" references a brief yet significant revelation in Season One in which
we learn that Logan's father beats him. Within the series itself, the actual
beating takes place behind a closed door, with the viewer left to imagine the encounter. "The View from the Cheap Seats" references this abuse
through the tool of Veronica's ring-tone, and through a brief moment of
revelation when we (together with Veronica) actually witness the scars
on Logan's body:

> A couple of months ago, Logan was sitting a few tables away at lunch. He kept
> squirming in his seat, and she overheard him telling a friend that he'd gotten
> bruised playing street hockey. But he leaned forward to grab something, and his
> shirt rode up to show angry welts on his back.
> "Cigarette burns and broken noses," Trina had said. God. She wonders what
> welts and bruises he'll sport on Monday, once his dad finds out. But they're all
> scarred, aren't they? At least hers are on the inside.
> Still, she decides to change his ringtone later.

Thus, while for the most part "View from the Cheap Seats" seems
to extend naturally from the program in itself, this moment pushes just
slightly further than the program would, exposing Logan's body and the
wounds that we simply know must be there from what the program has

shown us. This more explicit invocation of the program's darker and more adult themes reflects fan interest in characters such as Logan who face multiple levels of limitation. Fan fiction often envisions these limitations in the form of abuse, whether the program hints at such a scenario (as in *Veronica Mars*) or not. Two other similar, fan-favored characters, *Smallville*'s Lex Luthor and *Gilmore Girls'* Logan Huntsberger, similarly face the constraints of (at least emotionally) abusive and powerful fathers. Much fan fiction envisions these relationships, in different levels of explicitness, as highly physically abusive, dramatizing the power of adults over children through violence. "View from the Cheap Seats" and other stories like it vividly hyperbolize adolescent struggle against the constraining demands of their parents, literalizing emotional conflict through parental physical as well as psychological abuse.

Where "Hollow You Out" and "View from the Cheap Seats" both (to different degrees) take on the constraint of building realistic characters and interpersonal interactions within the confines of the source text, Mosca's "Nobody Wants to Uncover" overtly discusses themes of social limitation hinted at by the show but rarely, if ever, made central—issues of race and culture as well as class (LJ, April 6, 2007). This story takes the perspective of a character who is often marginalized to subplots rather than given narrative control—Weevil, head of the Latino PCHers biker gang. In the program itself, we most often see Weevil from Veronica's perspective. His appearances are frequently driven by Veronica's needs; we as viewers encounter Weevil when Veronica needs him to facilitate connections to social worlds she would not be able to enter without him.

In contrast, "Nobody Wants to Uncover" maintains Veronica only as a side character, focusing on Weevil as he attempts to write the traditional 500 word college essay, and, in so doing, works through his feelings about his uncertain relationship with Logan. Thus, this story incorporates another level of constraint, this time a formal one: the constraint of the 500 word college application essay. The institutionally-enforced word limitation of this teen rite of passage structures the story, while the content of Weevil's essays (the vehicle through which the story is told) addresses cultural and social realities faced by lower class immigrant adolescents. Whereas the source text of *Veronica Mars* makes class its most overt social constraint, with race as secondary, "Nobody Wants to Uncover" addresses racial divisions and marginalized experience directly. In response to the instruction "Discuss some issue of personal, local, national, or international concern and its importance to you," Weevil recalls his own experience of prejudice stemming from his social interactions with upper class Logan:

There are things that Weevil is against. Police brutality, racial profiling, zero-tolerance drug laws. But all those things seem to be part of something larger. He realized one morning in the shower that what he's really against is double standards. The thing where the only time he has ever been pulled over in Logan's car was the one time he has ever driven it. Logan was too drunk to steer and almost too drunk to explain that he wasn't being carjacked. The cop seemed disappointed that he couldn't even drag Weevil in for DWI.

However, while in instances such as this "Nobody Wants to Uncover" addresses issues of race more overtly than does *Veronica Mars* itself, to some extent it decentralizes these issues to concentrate on questions of sexuality and homophobia. Queerness is another topic which *Veronica Mars* only addresses through marginal characters, but a topic which is a common focus of fan fiction in the thriving subgenre of slash fan fiction, in which fans imagine homoerotic or romantic relationships between a program's nominally-straight characters. "Nobody Wants to Uncover" is a slash story, set against a backdrop of Weevil's relationship with Logan (one of the favored couples among slash *Veronica Mars* fans). Weevil's rumination on the unfairness of double standards as they play out in racial profiling shifts to his frustration at the marginalization of masculine queer sexuality in a range of contexts. Where he initially speaks of feeling out of place in a gay club, he then connects double standards stemming from racial expectations to the double standards that emerge with societal discomfort with masculine queer sexuality specifically:

They were driving home from San Diego, where it had been a whole night of double standards. Girls in halter tops and too much makeup kissing each other to get guys' attention, but if he and Logan ever tried something like that, well, it wouldn't end with them getting laid. Double fucking standards.

Thus, this story thematizes multiple levels of social limitation, some of which are subtly addressed by the source text itself, and others that diverge significantly from *Veronica Mars'* more overt concerns. However, its overall focus on sexuality adheres to slash fan concerns, in which issues of sexuality are central and serve as metaphors for otherness, but in which race is rarely addressed. In fact, it is *Veronica Mars'* own recognition of issues of race that seem to give such questions a place in this story, rather than the ongoing concerns of fan fiction. "Nobody Wants to Uncover" synthesizes *Veronica Mars'* specific vision of a modern day adolescence shaped by the constraints of class and race with slash fan fiction's ongoing evocation of self-discovery through sexuality and the acceptance of queerness.

Veronica Mars introduces questions of class, race, and gender inequality more overtly than do most teen series, and *Veronica Mars* fan fiction at times takes these issues further, focusing on characters that remain marginal in the source text. At other times, *Veronica Mars* fan fiction shifts the concerns of *Veronica Mars* to concerns central to fan culture as a whole, most especially sexuality and intimacy. But throughout this wide range of stories, *Veronica Mars* fan fiction utilizes the figure of the alienated, angst-ridden teen—be it Veronica's particular brand of female empowerment, or Logan and Weevil's restructured, angst-ridden masculinities—to tap into overarching fan concerns about sexuality, liminality, and adolescent self-discovery in the face of constraint.

Supernatural

> "We've been searching for this demon our whole
> lives. It's the only thing we've ever cared about."
> —*Supernatural*, "Salvation"

While teen TV characters like *Veronica Mars*' Logan Echolls, *Gilmore Girls*' Logan Huntzberger, and *Smallville*'s Lex Luthor prompt viewers to imagine a world of masculinity constrained by wealth, expectations, and social etiquette, and the rarer figures such as biker Weevil (and his counterparts in programs such as *The O.C.* and *One Tree Hill*) offer a masculinity limited by poverty and cultural and family ties, there is another breed of tortured males that populate Teen TV: the teen boy who fights the powers and strangeness of his own body, or of forces which have taken hold of his body and his destiny. He is epitomized in Clark Kent (as discussed by Melanie Kohnen in this volume), but also by *Roswell*'s aliens Max and Michael, and by the latest Teen TV program to highlight tortured adolescent masculinity, *Supernatural*.

The first season of *Supernatural* follows brothers Sam and Dean as they search for their father and contend with their familial fate as demon-victims turned demon-hunters. Their mother was killed by a demon in their childhood, and the majority of their life has been shaped by their father's quest to find and vanquish the demon that took his wife. Sam and Dean both must face their own feelings regarding the loss of their mother and their childhood as they decide how much of the mantle of their father's quest they wish to take upon themselves, especially after their father sacrifices himself to the demon for Dean at the end of the first season.

Although at the series outset Sam and Dean are nominally older than the teens featured in *Veronica Mars*, they figuratively fulfill the liminal teen position in multiple ways: because of their supernatural calling, they cannot smoothly or fully make the transition from childhood to adulthood. Sam must abandon his aspirations to go to law school, and Dean does not entertain any aspirations for a life beyond his father's wishes at all. Instead, as young adults they must continually face—at times submitting to and at times railing against—their father's legacy and expectations. Thus they are seemingly located permanently in the position of teen angst held by so many characters in the worlds of Teen TV.

This metaphorical representation of prolonged liminality or adolescence is reflected in fan fiction stories that imagine Sam and Dean at younger points in their lives. Such stories are quite frequent across fandoms, but especially so for characters who faced difficult childhoods with absent or overly-demanding parental figures. These stories often suggest adolescent or childhood causes for later-developed personality characteristics. In *Supernatural* specifically, Sam and Dean's father looms large as the figure who imbued upon them their sense of duty, destiny, and self-sacrifice. These epic-level constraints introduce a gender-oriented set of restrictions—a self-immolating hyper-emphasis on masculinity-as-survival taught to Sam and Dean by their father. In addition to living up to their father's goals for revenge, *Supernatural* conveys the sense that Sam and Dean must perform masculinity in their everyday interactions—with each other, with their father, with the various women they come across on their travels, and with the demons they confront.

However, this sense of hypermasculinity on offensive is complicated by the series' simultaneous focus on emotional interiority, on the psychological wounds and suffering of Sam and Dean as young men who have had to sacrifice normal adolescent rites of passage for larger restrictions of destiny and fate. Whereas *Supernatural* seemed to focus initially on the threat of otherness from the outside, presenting a simplistic morality play, over the first season the series evolved into a study of moral ambiguity and the slippage between self and other. The brothers' ever-defended and highly performative masculinity comes under threat from otherness from within, as Sam recognizes that he himself has become part demon, or part monster. Sam in turn begs Dean to kill him should he transform fully into a monster, leaving Dean to contend with conflicting constraints: his duty as older brother to care for Sam in their father's absence conflicts directly with his internalized familial duty to combat and kill demons. Thus, *Supernatural* offers multiple levels of thematic limitation of just the sort that fans gravitate toward, from the gender constraints of adolescent masculinity and performed machismo, to the restrictions of family duty, to the larger callings of destiny, all embodied in the figures of two angst-ridden, eternally adolescent young men. Given this combination, it is not surprising that *Supernatural* has quickly become a powerhouse in the larger fan community.

For the remainder of this essay, I will consider three short stories written in the world of *Supernatural* fandom. Like *Supernatural* itself, these stories bring together multiple levels of constraint. All three engage with elements of Sam and Dean's past as children or adolescents, positing their later strife as predicated on formative youthful experiences. All three stress Sam and Dean's relationship not only with each other but with their father as crucial to their experiences and self-definition as young adults. Finally, all three also incorporate constraint at the level of form, for all are examples of the fan-specific literary form known as the "drabble." Drabbles are a popular writing form across fandom, in which authors must convey a story or character insight within exactly 100 words. The *Veronica Mars* story I looked at earlier, "Nobody Wants to Uncover," utilized the institutionally enforced 500 word college essay; the drabble as constrained writing form emerges from within the fan community itself, as a structure within which fan creativity can bloom. Just as creativity emerges from fan authors' interplay with the restrictions of the source text or canon, so do fans impose additional levels of restriction in their formation of both literary style and community. These drabbles are an example of how the thematic constraints of adolescence so popular in fandom in general combine with the formal and cultural limitations which shape and spur fan authorship.

Dotfic's drabble, "Offerings," is set in the present day of *Supernatural*, but creates a memory of their youth, akin to memories that the show itself provides in occasional flashbacks (LJ, April 6, 2007). Through the vehicle of this memory, in one hundred words "Offerings" links Sam and Dean's present life on the road with their lost youth with their father:

> Living on the road, they couldn't keep extras, but there was a small duffel bag that held the ribbon Sam won in the second grade spelling bee, his plaque from the third grade science fair, the trophy for best fourth-grade essay. The bag grew heavier with time. Dean was always better at the crossbow, target shooting, and knife-throwing. No ribbons or trophies, but Sam's chest would ache when Dad slapped Dean on the back, smiled a certain way. It took years before Sam finally remembered: It was Dad who bought him the bag and carefully placed that first ribbon inside.

This drabble paints a picture in which their father's expectations have defined Sam and Dean through and through. The remembered detail of the competition award ribbons of their youth, and their father's attempts to encourage Sam as well as Dean, paint an ambivalent picture of the formative force of their father on Sam and Dean's personalities and relationship with each other. This drabble suggests, to the knowledgeable *Supernatural* fan who seeks connections between the words here and the current text of the show itself, that their fostered competitiveness for their father's affection manifests even past his death in their current life on the road, as they find themselves torn between their father's legacy and their own desire for adult lives. Like much of *Supernatural* fan fiction, "Offerings" focuses on the struggles of two boys to become adults while seeking parental if not societal approval.

Maharetr's drabble "Little Accidents" also explores Sam and Dean's past with their father, this time not through a memory but by setting the narrative in their childhood (LJ, April 6, 2007). "Little Accidents" imagines pre-adolescent Sam and Dean, with a preteen Dean taking care of the younger Sam in their father's frequent absence:

> He's four; a big boy now and he can do this on his own, but it's too dark.
> Dean always remembers to leave the light on, the door ajar, but Dean was asleep first tonight and Dad's forgotten. Sammy counts: one, two three ... but it's the actual damp on his thighs that gets him moving, scrambling for the doorknob. The tiles are cold, but it's too little, too late and the tears burn hotter than the warmth down his leg.
> The bathroom light flicks on and Sammy flinches, picturing Dad's frown.
> "Hey," Dean sighs, crouching. "Let's get you cleaned up."

Although this drabble imagines Sam and Dean as children rather than adults, it still looks at the constraints thrust upon them as they must contend prematurely with the transition into adulthood. Akin to "Offerings," this drabble also hints at characteristics born in the young Sam and Dean made manifest in their adult personas: Sam attempting to prove himself and become an adult without his brother, Dean playing the father role in the absence of their father. This short drabble exemplifies fan fiction's ability to explore every step on the path of coming of age by returning to earlier points on the source text's timeline, unpacking transitional adolescent moments that the programs themselves skip over.

Like "Little Accidents," author Maboheme's "Driving Lessons" visits an earlier time in Sam and Dean's life, offering a brief yet telling image of a key moment in Dean's adolescence, when his father teaches him to drive for the first time (LJ, April 6, 2007):

> The car is warm, thick with impalpable history.
> Dean squints, blurring the vision of the steaming highway before him.
> John patiently caresses work-worn hands over the dashboard. He has waited for this first growth spurt, to make sure his boy's legs were long enough to reach the pedal. "Take it slow and easy," he advises. "Treat her with love, and she'll love you back."
> Dean's hands are small, but dexterous. One shaky hand grips the wheel. One turns the key. For the first time the Impala roars to life just for him. And she sings.
> Some things are just destined.

This drabble presents an early rite of passage for Dean, one which is central to who he becomes as a young adult. The car is essential to Dean and Sam's liminal existence: exiled from the normative, forward moving structures of society, their ongoing pursuit of the forces of evil requires that they live between the Impala and dingy roadside hotels. Indeed, the car is one of the essential instruments through which *Supernatural* maintains Sam and Dean's perpetual adolescence. Although Dean imbues the car with love and an almost personified status (he speaks of and treats the car almost as he would a lover), this drabble envisions those very characteristics as being part of the legacy of "impalpable history" that their father left to Sam and Dean, and against which they struggle ambivalently. "Driving Lessons" thus highlights character individuation—a dynamic crucial to both the *Supernatural* source text and to fan engagement. This story then merges its emphasis on individual character development with a larger sense of the forces of destiny and duty—two themes of adolescent constraint central to both *Supernatural* and to fan fiction communities.

Taken together, these three drabbles demonstrate the fan fascination with the development of characters from childhood through adolescence into adulthood, with the various influences that shape the characters fans have come to know and love. In this very character unpacking, we see the dynamic of fan creativity within constraint, as fan authors invent narratives which explain (and interpret) the eventual already-known outcome. The formal limitation of the drabble further demonstrates this dynamic of creativity within constraint. And of course the content of these drabbles—the focus on Sam and Dean's struggles to become individuals and adults in the face of their father's expectations—demonstrates fan investment in the figure of the adolescent as one who negotiates self-expression in the face of constraint.

By exploring all three of these programs and the fan fiction they inspire, we are given the opportunity to consider the broader themes and dynamics at work both in the ever-evolving texts of Teen TV and in the larger world of media fandom. Teen TV's liminal status as both mainstream and narrowcast, derided as popular consumerist trash and lauded as critical innovation, finds a natural resonance with the dynamics of fan authorship, in which fans invest in a source text they didn't create, and work to, within the limitations set not only by that source text but also by their community, create and circulate new texts. Thus the interplay between fan creativity and the Teen TV texts from which many fan authors derive inspiration demonstrates the ongoing dynamic relationship between creativity and constraint.

Notes

1. For work on fan use of technology as both enabling and limiting, see: Baym 2000, Jenkins 2006b, Jones 2006, and Stein, 2006a. For discussion of the significance of

community in fan authorship, see: Jenkins 1992, Baym 2000, Busse 2002, Stein 2002, and Busse 2006.

    2. My approach to generic analysis in this essay has evolved from the work of Jason Mittell (2004) on generic cultural categories to consider genre as discourse weaving through text and metatext. On genre, see also James Naremore's approach to genre (1998) and Stein 2006b. For contemporary work on media fandom see also Hills 2002, Brooker 2003, Hellekson and Busse 2006, and Jenkins 2006b.

References

Banks, Miranda J. 2004. "A Boy for All Planets: *Roswell, Smallville* and the Teen Male Melodrama." In *Teen TV*, eds. Glyn Davis and Kay Dickinson, 17–28. London: BFI.

Baym, Nancy K. 2000. *Tune In, Log On: Soaps, Fandom, and Online Community*. Thousand Oaks, CA: Sage.

Brooker, Will. 2001. "Living on *Dawson's Creek*: Teen Viewers, Cultural Convergence, and Television Overflow." *International Journal of Cultural Studies* 4:456–72.

_____. 2003. *Using the Force: Creativity, Community and "Star Wars" Fans*, rev. ed. New York: Continuum International.

Busse, Kristina. 2005. "'Digital Get Down': Postmodern Boy Band Slash and the Queer Female Space." In *Eroticism in American Culture*, eds. Cheryl Malcolm and Jopi Nyman, 103–25. Gdansk: Gdansk University Press.

_____. 2006. "My Life Is a WIP on My LJ: Slashing the Slasher and the Reality of Celebrity and Internet Performances." In *Fan Fiction and Fan Communities in the Age of the Internet: New Essays*, eds. Karen Hellekson and Kristina Busse, 189–206. Jefferson, NC: McFarland.

Davis, Glyn, and Kay Dickinson, eds. 2004. *Teen TV: Genre, Consumption and Identity*. London: British Film Institute.

Hellekson, Karen, and Kristina Busse, eds. 2006. *Fan Fiction and Fan Communities in the Age of the Internet: New Essays*. Jefferson, NC: McFarland.

Hills, Matt. 2002. *Fan Cultures*. London: Routledge.

Jenkins, Henry. 1992. *Textual Poachers: Television Fans and Participatory Culture*. New York: Routledge.

_____. 2006a. *Convergence Culture*. New York: New York University Press.

_____. 2006b. *Fans, Bloggers, and Gamers*. New York: New York University Press.

Jones, Robert. 2006. "From Shooting Monsters to Shooting Movies: Machinima and the Transformative Play of Video Game Fan Culture." In *Fan Fiction and Fan Communities in the Age of the Internet: New Essays*, eds. Karen Hellekson and Kristina Busse, 261–80. Jefferson, NC: McFarland.

Jones, Sara Gwenllian. 2002. "The Sex Lives of Cult Television Characters." *Screen* 43:79–90.

Kaveny, Roz, ed. 2001. *Reading the Vampire Slayer: The Unofficial Critical Companion to "Buffy" and "Angel."* New York: Tauris Park.

Kelly, Brigid. 2005. "The Transformative Power of 'Hot Gay Sex': Queering Superman, Queering the Fan on the TelevisionWithoutPity '*Smallville*' Boards." *Spectator* 25: 71–82.

Kustritz, Anne. 2005. "*Smallville*'s Sexual Symbolism: From Queer Repression to Fans' Queered Expressions." *Refractory* 18, no.8: available at http://www.refractory.unimelb.edu.au/journalissues/vol8/kustritz.html.

Mittell, Jason. 2004. *Genre and Television: From Cop Shows to Cartoons in American Culture*. New York: Routledge.

Naremore, James. 1998. *More Than Night: Film Noir in Its Contexts*. Berkeley: University of California Press.

Pearson, Roberta E. 2003. "Kings of Infinite Space: Cult Television Characters and Narrative Possibilities." *Scope* (August): originally available at http://www.nottingham.ac.uk/film/journal/articles/kings-of-infinite-space.htm (accessed September 29, 2005). Archive currently unavailable.

Stein, Louisa. 2002. "Subject: 'Off Topic: Oh My god U.S. Terrorism!' *Roswell* Fans Respond to 11 September." *European Journal of Cultural Studies* 5:471–91.

_____. 2005. "'They Cavort, You Decide': Fan Discourses of Intentionality, Interpretation, and Queerness in Teen TV." *Spectator* 25:11–22.

_____. 2006a. "'This Dratted Thing': Fannish Storytelling Through New Media." In *Fan Fiction and Fan Communities in the Age of the Internet: New Essays*, eds. Karen Hellekson and Kristina Busse, 225–44. Jefferson, NC: McFarland.

_____. 2006b. "A Transcending-Genre Kind of Thing: Teen/Fantasy TV and Online Audience Culture." Diss. New York University.

Wilcox, Rhonda V., and David Lavery, eds. 2002. *Fighting the Forces: What's at Stake in Buffy the Vampire Slayer*. Lanham, MD: Rowman Littlefield.

Contributors

Ben Aslinger is a Ph.D. candidate in media and cultural studies at the University of Wisconsin–Madison. He received his M.A. from Miami University of Ohio in mass communication. His dissertation deals with the transmedia travels of popular music.

Caralyn Bolte is a Ph.D. candidate in English at the University of Florida. She received her M.A. in English from North Carolina State University. Her research focuses include British romanticism, women, depictions of travel and tourism, and metaphors of food and consumption.

Andrea Braithwaite is a Ph.D. candidate in communication studies at McGill University in Montreal. She received her M.A. in popular culture from Brock University in Ontario. Her areas of research include: gender and sexuality in popular culture and genre theory (particularly crime/detection/mystery; science/speculative fiction; and the gothic).

Barbara Jane Brickman is an assistant professor of English and film studies at the University of West Georgia, where she is developing a film studies program. She has previously published articles on Southern literature and on the pathologization of the female teen body by medical discourses. Her current project examines representations of adolescent spectatorship, fandom, and fantasy in postwar literature and teen films.

Francesca Gamber is pursuing her Ph.D. in history after receiving her B.A. in Afro-American studies from Harvard University. She has recently published introductory author biographies in *An Anthology of Interracial Literature: Black-White Contacts in the Old World and the New*, ed. Werner Sollors (New York University Press, 2004).

Jennifer Gillan is an associate professor at Bentley College in the English Department. She received a Ph.D. in English from the State University of New York at Stony Brook. She has numerous publications, including: "From Ozzie Nelson to Ozzy Osbourne: The Genesis and Development of the Reality

(Star) Sitcom" (*Understanding Reality Television*, eds. Su Holmes and Deborah Jermyn; Routledge, March 2004); "Focusing on the Wrong Front: Historical Displacement, the Maginot Line, and *The Bluest Eye*" (*African American Review* 36.2, summer 2002); and "'No one knows you're black!' Schepisi's *Six Degrees of Separation* and the Buddy Formula" (*Cinema Journal* 40.3, spring 2001). She is currently working on her manuscript *From Ozzie to Ozzy: Reality Meets the Sitcom.*

Melanie E.S. Kohnen is a doctoral candidate in the Department of American Civilization at Brown University. Her dissertation, "Out of the Closet? The Discourse of Visibility, Sexuality, and Queer Representation in American Film, Television, and New Media, 1969–Present," examines how visibility has become a central category for understanding and discussing queer sexualities and representations in American media. In addition, she researches the history and theory of new media, focusing on conceptualizations of online communities and their relationship to the structure of the physical computer networks within which they exist.

Jeff Martin is pursuing his M.A. in communications at the University of Massachusetts, Amherst after receiving his B.A. in English from the University of Connecticut at Storrs. Jeff is a musician and writer, and also serves as a market research analyst while in school. His research interests include media literacy and performance studies.

Sharon Marie Ross is an assistant professor in the Television Department at Columbia College Chicago, where she teaches in the areas of critical analysis, history, and development. Articles she has published include: "On the Set with *Degrassi: The Next Generation*" and "Teen Choice Awards: Better than the Emmys?" (*FLOW*, an online television studies journal, University of Texas Press, http://idg.communication.utexas.edu/flow/); "Talking *Sex and the City*" (*The Sitcom Reader*, eds. Mary Dalton and Laura Linder; SUNY Press, 2005); "Dangerous Demons" (*femspec*, ed. Batya Weinbaum, vol. 5, issue 2, 2004); "Tough Enough: *Xena, Buffy*, and Knowledgeable Heroism" (*Action Chicks*, ed. Sherrie Inness; Palgrave Macmillan, 2004); and "Dormant Dormitory Friendships: Race and Gender in *Felicity*" (*Teen TV: Genre, Consumption and Identity*, eds. Glyn Davis and Kay Dickinson; BFI, 2004). Dr. Ross is the recipient of faculty fellowships with the Academy of Television Arts and Sciences and the National Association of Television Program Executives; she is currently the associate editor for *Journal of International Digital Media Arts Association*. Dr. Ross recently completed her first book: *Tele-Participation: Understanding TV in the Age of the Internet* (Blackwell Publishing, forthcoming).

Louisa Ellen Stein is an assistant professor of television, film, and new media at San Diego State University. She is the head of the critical studies area and teaches courses that bridge media theory, history, and practice. Her research explores viewer and participant engagement with contemporary media culture, including film, television, the internet and videogames. Her work focuses on unofficial authorship surrounding commercial media texts, including alternative interpretations such as queer readings—the topic of her two most recent essays, "'They Cavort, You Decide': Transgenericism, Queerness, and Fan Interpretation in Teen TV" (*Spectator* 25.2, spring 2005) and "'This Dratted Thing': Fannish Storytelling through New Media" (*Fan Fiction and Fan Communities in the Age of the Internet: New Essays*, eds. Karen Hellekson and Kristina Busse; McFarland, 2006.)

Sue Turnbull is an associate professor in media studies at La Trobe University and a former chair of the Australian Teachers of Media Association (ATOM). She has published broadly in the fields of media education, audience studies, and television with particular attention to comedy and crime. With Vyv Stranieri she is the author of a study guide for the Australian Centre for the Moving Image entitled, *Bite Me: Narrative Structures and Buffy the Vampire Slayer* (2003). Her current research project with Dr. Felicity Collins at La Trobe is concerned with the history of Australian screen comedy and is funded by an Australian Research Council Grant.

Valerie Wee lectures on film and media studies in the Department of English Language and Literature at the National University of Singapore, Singapore. In addition to her research in teen culture and the American culture industries, she has published papers on American horror/slasher films, science fiction films, and on issues of gender and representation in the media.

Index

abuse 65, 144–46
adolescence 6–8, 72
advertising 45, 47, 54–56, 67, 72, 75, 83
alienation 51, 55, 94–97, 101–2, 104, 109–10
American Bandstand 39–40
androgyny 160, 182
authority 97–98, 107, 123, 134, 137, 142–46, 166, 216–17

Beverly Hills 90210 15–16, 49–50, 95, 107, 117, 179
blogging 207, 214, 217
branding 5, 8, 19, 56, 68, 75, 78
Buffy the Vampire Slayer 3, 8–10, 15, 20–21, 44, 48, 50–56, 70, 78, 83–84, 87, 94–95, 99–106, 108–11, 117, 146, 153, 174, 207, 226

class, socioeconomic 6–7, 9, 16, 20, 21, 22, 23, 73, 96–97, 99, 102, 104–8, 116–17, 126, 160, 174, 179, 193, 195–98, 204, 227, 230–31, 235–37
community 7, 66–69, 73, 105–6, 110, 135–38, 150, 172, 186, 189–90, 214, 217–20, 225, 238–39, 241
consumerism 7–8, 11, 18, 22, 36, 40, 43, 152, 174, 186, 189–90, 194–95, 225, 241
CTV network 63, 65
cult TV 9–10
CW network 3, 5, 12, 17–18, 22, 57, 62, 75–76, 114, 118, 187, 193–94, 199–204

Dawson's Creek 10, 15, 44, 48, 50–56, 70, 76, 78–84, 86–87, 95, 117, 171–72, 186, 187, 188, 194, 198, 200, 202, 204
Dean, James 22, 160, 173–74, 179
Degrassi: The Next Generation (DTNG) 16, 21, 62–70, 171

A Different World 14, 71–72
dress *see* fashion
drugs and alcohol 48, 64, 65, 68, 74, 138, 139, 144, 179, 180, 231

education 37, 69, 74, 143, 172, 190, 230; *see also* high school, school

family 4, 5, 11, 12, 14, 15, 17, 34–35, 36, 50–51, 64, 71, 73–74, 97, 111, 116, 119, 121, 127, 128–29, 135, 139, 142, 145, 152, 165–66, 170, 173, 174, 175–76, 177, 180, 181, 230, 237
fandom 9, 21, 22–23, 28, 54, 56, 68–69, 79, 82, 84, 89, 110–12, 150–66, 171, 185–204, 207–21; fan art 23, 213–14, 217–19, 224–41
fantasy 3, 8–9, 48, 55, 85, 93, 106, 110, 155, 180–81, 182, 190, 224–25; *see also* science fiction/sci-fi
fashion 3, 10, 22, 79, 114, 115, 118–19, 122, 124, 125, 180, 185–204
femininity 20, 84–85, 116, 118, 129, 133, 138, 143, 146, 160–61, 182, 231
feminism 20–21, 114–29, 132–47, 161, 227, 231–32
film 4, 7–12, 21, 51–53, 79, 83, 88, 89, 94, 116, 117, 133, 135, 140, 152, 158, 171–73, 176–79, 201, 207, 210, 218, 220
FOX network 12, 14, 15, 16, 19, 21, 45, 47, 49, 55, 81, 83, 179
Freaks and Geeks 83, 179
friendship 48, 50, 51, 73–74, 85, 96, 98, 107, 136–39, 181, 211, 213–15, 220, 234

gender 6, 8, 9, 16, 20–23, 66, 78–80, 84–86, 88–89, 99, 103–4, 116, 118–20, 133–35, 137–38, 140–42, 145–46, 157,

159, 166, 172, 174, 182–83, 191, 203,
  208, 226–27, 230–33, 236, 238
generation 5, 20–22, 46, 54, 70, 72, 117,
  120, 160, 166, 228–31
genre 3–4, 8, 9–12, 14, 20, 21, 31, 35,
  39, 52, 68, 79, 84, 85, 93, 133, 135–
  38, 141, 172, 202, 177, 174, 202, 207–
  8, 225–26, 236
The Gilmore Girls 4, 5, 10, 15, 20, 23,
  70, 88, 114–29, 202, 226–30, 235, 237

HBO 5, 8, 10, 21, 150, 152, 156, 166
heteronormativity 85, 157, 159, 164–66,
  207, 209–10, 212, 219–21
heterosexuality 21, 22, 23, 143, 161, 164,
  209–10, 213–16, 219–21
high school 3, 70, 72, 76, 84, 96–98,
  100–1, 103, 109, 123–25, 136, 138, 141,
  174, 192, 196, 200, 204, 227
homoeroticism 210–17
homosexuality 21, 156, 159–61, 164, 166,
  209

identity 5, 7, 9, 17–20, 47–48, 50–51,
  96, 103–4, 106–8, 116, 143, 157–62,
  164, 181, 187–88, 190–91, 193, 197,
  199, 208–9, 211, 224, 230, 233
individualism 4, 101–2, 116, 125, 133,
  138, 145
Internet 61, 145, 186, 193, 207
intertextuality 52–56, 151, 177, 202

juvenile delinquency 27–30, 34–35

Kellner, Jamie 45–47, 56

language 31, 36, 99–100, 102, 115, 118–
  19, 121, 124–26
liminality 8, 20, 156–57, 238
Livejournal 186, 190, 208, 214, 217–20

The Many Loves of Dobie Gillis 21–22,
  174–77, 181
marginalization 9, 20, 21, 79, 93–112,
  136–37, 152, 156–57, 159, 165–66,
  226, 235–36
marketing 11, 14–16, 19, 46–47, 56, 76,
  82, 187, 189–90, 201, 202–5; network
  branding 5, 8, 19, 56, 68, 75, 78; see
  also promotion
masculinity 20, 84, 85–88, 161, 170–82,
  237–38
melodrama 6, 13, 15–17, 135, 171–72,
  174, 177–79, 190
message boards 191, 195, 207
Millennials 76
morality 67, 238
MTV 6, 12, 14, 15, 19, 48–49, 54, 62,
  76, 80–81
multiculturalism 64, 76

multimedia 10, 111
music (musical, musicians) 3, 9, 10, 12–
  14, 19, 30–31, 34, 37, 39, 40, 78–89,
  110, 124, 150, 152, 172, 177, 179, 181,
  186, 213
My So-Called Life 10, 14, 49–50, 117,
  128, 179, 190, 204

N network (The N) vii, 1, 12, 16, 19, 61–
  77
noir 4, 8, 133, 171, 188, 231, 234

The O.C. 3, 9, 10, 19, 21, 55, 71, 81, 95,
  170–82, 188, 197, 207, 237
overflow 186, 190, 195, 202

Paramount 15, 22, 45, 201
performativity 118–19
postfeminism (postfeminist) 21, 133–38,
  141–46
postmodernism (postmodern) 53, 55,
  151, 175
promotion (cross-promotion, promotional) 17, 53, 55, 67, 72, 80–81, 84,
  186–87, 201–3, 214
public sphere 128, 136–37, 142, 128

quality TV 19, 55, 225
queer spectatorship 23, 207–21
queer theory 6, 23, 210, 214

race 1, 6, 9, 16–18, 22–23, 30, 66, 73,
  105, 107, 109, 166, 191–92, 200, 227,
  231, 235–36
Rebel Without a Cause 21, 171, 173–74,
  176, 177–79, 181
rebellion 160, 180, 196, 227
relationships 20, 48, 50–51, 88, 96–97,
  120, 123, 128, 134–36, 138–39, 140,
  143, 145–46, 150, 163, 172, 202, 210,
  214, 218–20, 226, 228–30, 233–36
romance 8, 55, 73, 86, 108, 133, 143,
  160, 175, 199, 202, 207, 214, 219, 220,
  224, 226, 234
Roswell 4, 8, 10, 21, 44, 48, 50, 54–55,
  146, 172, 180, 237

school 28, 33, 35, 37, 40, 48, 51, 55,
  62–70, 72–74, 76, 78, 84, 95–98, 100–
  1, 103, 105, 106, 108–109, 115, 119, 121,
  123–29, 132, 134–38, 140–43, 145–46,
  154, 171, 173–74, 192, 193, 195–96,
  198, 200, 201, 204, 224, 227, 230–31,
  237
science fiction/sci-fi 8, 17–18, 55, 224–25
self-reflexivity/self reflexive 19, 50, 52,
  54, 55, 75–76, 151, 177, 202, 211, 220
sexuality 3, 4, 9, 20, 21–23, 51, 64, 66,
  70, 79, 85, 87, 89, 117, 85, 87–89, 117,
  128, 141–42, 144–46, 156, 157, 159–61,

164, 166, 173, 208–9, 213–14, 216, 219, 226, 231, 233, 234, 236–37
sitcoms 6, 12–19, 51, 70, 72, 100, 175, 200
Six Feet Under 5, 21, 88, 150–66, 220
Smallville 6, 22–23, 172, 180, 226, 235, 237
soap opera 7, 8, 55, 68, 135, 172, 174
South of Nowhere 73–74
spectatorship 8, 23, 207–21
stereotype 7, 104, 106–8, 110, 161, 191
subculture 9, 84, 86
subjectivity 140, 164, 191, 234
Supernatural 226, 237–41
synergy 78, 81, 83

technology 10, 34, 44, 75, 188, 193, 195, 241
Television Without Pity (TWOP) 22–23, 185–98, 203–4, 208, 210–12, 214–22

transgenericism 8
TV Teen Club 13, 27–40
21 Jump Street 21, 171

UPN 3, 5, 8, 12, 15–18, 22, 45, 55, 57, 62, 75–76, 94, 111, 186–87, 190, 195, 199–200, 201–2

Veronica Mars 4, 5, 9, 19–23, 55, 70, 88, 94, 96, 99, 102, 106, 108, 110, 111, 132, 185–204, 226, 230–37, 239
victimization 101, 193

Warner Brothers (Warner Bros.) 3, 5, 8, 12, 14–19, 22, 43–57, 62, 63, 75, 76, 78–89, 94, 125, 186–87, 199, 200–2, 220
Whedon, Joss 52, 95, 100, 104, 110
Whiteman, Paul 5, 18, 30, 31–34, 37–40